W9-DJM-552

THEY ALL FALL DOWN

RICHARD NICKEL'S STRUGGLE TO SAVE AMERICA'S ARCHITECTURE

Richard Cahan

The Preservation Press

National Trust for Historic Preservation

The Preservation Press
National Trust for Historic Preservation
1785 Massachusetts Avenue, N.W.
Washington, D.C. 20036

The National Trust for Historic Preservation is the
only private, nonprofit organization chartered by
Congress to encourage public participation in the
preservation of sites, buildings, and objects significant in American history and culture. In carrying
out this mission, the National Trust fosters an
appreciation of the diverse character and meaning
of our American cultural heritage and preserves
and revitalizes the livability of our communities
by leading the nation in saving America's historic
environments.

Support for the National Trust is provided by
membership dues, contributions, and a matching
grant from the National Park Service, U.S.
Department of the Interior, under provisions of the
National Historic Preservation Act of 1966. The
opinions expressed here do not necessarily reflect
the views or policies of the Interior Department.

Printed in Singapore
98 97 96 95 94   5 4 3 2 1

All photographs unless otherwise noted are by
Richard Nickel and are used with permission of
the Richard Nickel Committee.

Library of Congress Cataloging-in-Publication Data

Cahan, Richard.

They all fall down : Richard Nickel's struggle to
save America's architecture / Richard Cahan.
        p.   cm.
ISBN 0-89133-215-4
1. Lost architecture—Illinois—Chicago.
2. Buildings—Illinois—Chicago—Salvaging.
3. Nickel, Richard, d. 1972—Criticism and
interpretation.   I. Title.
NA735.C4C25 1993   93-7613
720'.9773'11—dc20

Designed by The Watermark Design Office,
Alexandria, Virginia
Printed by Tien Wah Press, Singapore

For My Family
And to the Memory of My Father

ACKNOWLEDGMENTS

Four people made this book possible: John Vinci, who trusted me; Tim Samuelson, who educated me; Mark Jacob, who edited me; and Catherine Cahan, who lived with me—and with Richard Nickel—for so many years.

Many need to be thanked. Peter Korn, Carol Cahan Nazarian, Robin Daughtridge, Charles Dickinson, and Ginny Holbert read my early drafts. LeRoy Schreiner fixed my computer. Rich Hein and Ward Miller printed and gathered photographs. Janet Peck, Margaret Jung, and Merce Reedy cared for my children so I could work. Patricia Van der Leun, my agent, had confidence in me, and Yong Choi, my mechanic, kept me going.

My father, Aaron S. Cahan, showed me Chicago. My mother, Dorothy Cahan, told me about the value of books. My brother, David, taught me the meaning of art. My "other" parents, Margaret and William H. Griffith, encouraged me from the start. My children—Elie, Claire, and Aaron—kept me young. My friends—Garry Chankin, Mike Ross, Jim Phillips, Paul Motenko, Mike Starkman, Ron Seely, Toby Roberts, Dom Najolia, John Cary, Linda and Bob Badesch, Lynn Sweet, Marc Rosset, Maureen and Bob Eme—were always there.

Publication made possible in part by grants from the Foundation of the Chicago Chapter, American Institute of Architects, and the Graham Foundation for Advanced Studies in the Fine Arts.

Few of Richard Nickel's
photographs are well known.
Some, such as this view of
the Rookery Building
stairway, have become
landmarks themselves.

I FIGURE THAT ANYONE WHO TRIES TO SAVE LANDMARKS IN
CHICAGO IS GOOFY ENOUGH TO PREACH CELIBACY IN A PLAYBOY CLUB
OR NONVIOLENCE TO DICK BUTKUS.

Mike Royko, *Chicago Daily News* columnist.

Chicago's LaSalle Street, like its New York counterpart Wall Street, makes an amazing transformation after the lawyers, bankers, and brokers jam into the last buses and trains at the end of the workday. For the first time, sounds from the Loop—the calls of traffic cops, the cadence of elevated trains, even boat whistles—can be distinguished. Within minutes, LaSalle becomes a world of elderly security guards. Armed only with sign-in sheets and stacks of tomorrow's newspapers, they keep watch over the old giants of buildings.

The 13-story Stock Exchange Building stood right in the middle of the stretch of LaSalle that runs from the big riveted bridge spanning the Chicago River to the imposing Board of Trade Building. By early 1972 only six or seven stories of the Stock Exchange remained upright. Demolition of the building had begun the previous October, and by April the building looked like a surreal architectural joke. Its three-story base stood virtually untouched, just the way it had looked when it was designed by the architects Louis Sullivan and Dankmar Adler. But the remaining stories were beaten and misshapen.

Architect John Vinci had long ago finished his work at the Stock Exchange Building. After spending four months saving architectural ornament from the Exchange's once-opulent Trading Room for the Art Institute of Chicago, he had turned his back and mind away from the building. But when he placed the telephone back on the receiver on the night of Friday, April 14, he knew he had to return.

Vinci had just been told that Richard Nickel, his longtime friend and salvaging partner, was missing.

"Sure, he might have had car trouble," Vinci reassured Nickel's mother, who was on the other end of the line. "Certainly, he is probably on his way home."

Vinci knew better.

He promised to leave right away to see if Richard, having forgotten the hour, might still be scouring the Stock Exchange Building. His mind racing, Vinci telephoned Tim Samuelson, another friend, to see if he knew where Nickel was. Samuelson said he had arranged to meet Nickel Thursday afternoon at the Exchange Building to help him remove several pieces of ornament, but Nickel had not shown up. Vinci and Samuelson agreed right away to meet at the building.

Samuelson caught an elevated train near his North Side apartment and arrived in the Loop just as it was starting to get dark. It was not hard for him to get onto the site, for it was blocked by only two sawhorses and a rope. Once inside the battered building, he found a wooden ladder that provided the only way to the second floor. Although he had been in the Exchange Building many times, Samuelson had never seen it like this. "Pig strings," the kind of lights that hang above used-car lots, were strung throughout the interior. Room partitions were knocked out, leaving jagged spaces where walls had been, and piles of rubble and garbage filled the lower floors. Samuelson imagined himself in an amusement park funhouse where rooms were indistinguishable and doors led to sheer drops. He was moving fast. He planned to pick his way to the third floor, where he thought Nickel might have gone. But the route was blocked, so he decided to check the second-floor Trading Room where he had seen a huge pile of debris.

Access to the Trading Room was not much easier. The entire middle section of the E-shaped building was flattened so that a giant crane could swing what wreckers called the "headache ball." With the middle section razed, travel from one end of the building to the other was hazardous and time consuming.

The two-story Trading Room was the building's gem. Lavished with Sullivan's flowing, geometric stencilwork and colorful skylights, the room was built to woo the newly established Chicago Stock Exchange to LaSalle Street in the early 1890s. Tonight, the demolished space looked eerie. Rubble spilled from the visitors' gallery, plaster hung from the ceiling like stalactites, and water seeped down as if it were

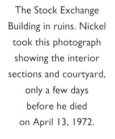

The Stock Exchange Building in ruins. Nickel took this photograph showing the interior sections and courtyard, only a few days before he died on April 13, 1972.

raining inside. A large hole gaped in the center of the room. At least one section of the floor had fallen through to the first floor or the basement.

Until he saw the hole, Samuelson had searched mechanically, not really thinking about who he was looking for or where he was. But now, for the first time, he felt frightened. As he heard Vinci's voice from below, Samuelson noticed a yellow hard-hat—the extra one Nickel said he would bring with him on Thursday—and a rope. Richard had indeed been there.

To Nickel, great buildings were like people. Beautiful when young, they acquired character as they grew older. He could feel buildings. Each had a soul.

To him, genius had rubbed off onto the mortar, stone, and steel of structures built by the lions of architecture. The destruction of their buildings was no less shocking than the ravaging of a museum masterpiece by a madman. It had to be stopped.

Chicago in the impatient 1950s and 1960s would not be concerned with coddling the past. This sturdy city with an eye on tomorrow was in the firm grip of Mayor Richard J. Daley, a Sphinx-faced, malapropism-popping political boss determined to live forever through great public works projects. Daley wanted to clear the terrain of Chicago as neatly as had the Great Chicago Fire in 1871. He wanted to rebuild. Miles of homes, thousands of buildings, even entire neighborhoods were cleared in the name of growth and increased tax dollars.

Nowhere was the city's rebuilding more apparent than downtown, in and around Chicago's 35-square-block Loop. Completion of the 41-story Prudential Building in 1955 marked the start of a downtown building boom, and with it came a wave of destruction unprecedented since the fire. The buildings that were razed— the Pullman Building, Reaper Block, Columbus Memorial, Venetian, Austin, Hartford, and dozens more—had names and personalities. They were demolished without any protest to make way for corporate addresses and parking lots.

Nickel was one of the first to stand up against the demolition of skyscrapers. In the words of *Kansas City Star* architecture critic Donald Hoffmann, Nickel "hit the barricades before anybody knew there was a war." Nickel hoisted the first picket sign in front of the Garrick Theater Building in 1960, prompting attorneys for the theater to drive their limousines up to the building and ask Nickel what the hell he was doing.

"All I could say," Nickel later told a reporter, "was that I didn't want the building wrecked." His feelings went deeper. His unsuccessful year-long fight to save the Garrick gained national attention. Even Daley was forced to take notice. As scaffolding laced the Garrick Theater, marking its execution, a passerby with no architectural background walked up to the grimy structure and sighed: "I don't want to see these old buildings torn down."

It was part of Nickel's quarrel with his time that he could not stop the destruction of fine architecture. He grew to learn that picketing and emotional pleas had little effect. "The forces are so great that there is really almost nothing you can do," he wrote. Economics, the bottom line, demanded the death of these buildings when they stopped bringing a profit.

Sparked by a college assignment during the early 1950s, Nickel embarked on a lifelong search to find and document the work of Louis Sullivan, the fountainhead of modern architecture.

"His passion about building impressed me at first," Nickel recounted years later. "He showed this total devotion to building. Then there were his ideas about functionalism and his devotion to nature, things that I had an affinity toward myself. Now, I wasn't very well read at that point, but I never had encountered a personality like that, one that was so involved with life."

Nickel hunted down dozens of little-known Sullivan buildings and drawings. As his search continued, Nickel went on a rescue mission.

At first, he saved what he found on film—taking intense, quiet, resolute photographs. He was a super-crisp documentarian, using the proper lens and the proper camera to show structures just as he saw them. His work, never well known outside Chicago, was described by photographer Aaron Siskind as "simple and correct and quite beautiful." The photographs became landmarks themselves.

Nickel spoke of himself as "just a photographer who happens to take pictures of buildings." By trade, he was an architectural photographer, but he was no more limited by his subject than Edgar Degas had been bound by ballerinas. Nickel's original purpose was to create a comprehensive photographic record of Sullivan's work. He eventually found that he could use his camera to express himself and confront his audience. Depressed about the imperiled masterpieces he found in his rangefinder, Nickel took photos as a last resort against what he was witnessing.

By returning to wrecking sites, Nickel made a statement that went beyond his effort to document what Sullivan had created. Nickel insisted on being a witness, a recorder of vanishing beauty. More than anything, he wanted to portray death—death before its time.

But the photographs were just part of Nickel's passion. Armed with a wrecking bar, penetrating oil, wrenches, hacksaws, hammers, and screwdrivers, he invaded the hulks of Sullivan's abandoned buildings earmarked for urban renewal and made away with chimney tops, doors, ironwork—any pieces of ornament he could haul home. At six feet and 175 pounds, he had kept his paratrooper's body. He could easily outlift almost anyone on a wrecking site.

By the year of his death, demolition sites were in his blood. Although the wanton destructions often sickened and depressed him, he could not repress his fascination. In a sense, buildings looked best to him during construction or demolition. That was when he could feel the purity of an architect's ideas and their transposition into the physical world. Once completed, buildings were scarred: room dividers set up, pictures and calendars nailed into walls, potted plants placed in corners. A building under siege allowed Nickel to explore fully. As a building gave way to the relentless hammering, Nickel could see things that had remained hidden for decades. Exposed beams and girders disclosed how buildings were put together. Muddy foundation pilings clarified how weight was supported. Trusses and cantilevers hinted at the engineering gymnastics covered up in the finished product.

Watching the wrecker's "clam shell" punch out floors, the headache ball close in on walls, and sledgehammers rip a building naked heightened the experience. As he walked through the wrecks—rummaging through janitors' closets, checking boiler rooms, almost always lugging along a view camera and tripod—he learned secrets nobody could imagine.

"Marvelous being in a work of art under rape," Nickel lamented in a letter to a friend, Robert Kostka, in February 1972. "Tonight, more specifically late afternoon, I was telling the wrecker what the demolition involvement meant to me. How often do you experience the bones, veins, skin of a work of art, even if it be in dissection?"

Yet at the same time, Nickel was responsible for starting the first vigorous, hands-around-a-building preservation campaigns in Chicago that inspired a mass movement throughout the country. His struggle was not the elitist, black-tie, grant-supported cause célèbre of the 1970s and 1980s, but a vociferous one-man crusade determined to put an end to this particular phase of "progress." America's "manifest destiny" gave the nation a license to ravage and destroy the natural world during the 19th century. Eventually, that license encompassed the right to destroy the built world of cities.

Nickel started his fight in ignorance, unaware of the odds against him. But he had the courage to fight on. By 1969, however, Nickel announced that he was withdrawing from his fight to save Chicago's buildings.

"You know," he said, "right now there is no leader in the conservation movement, no one person who has the passion, who is ready to give his life for a building."

"What about Richard Nickel?" a reporter asked.

"I did that once," Nickel replied. "A lot of people see me as the guardian for all these buildings, but I do not spend every moment of my waking life working on that. I have very strong feelings about saving buildings, but I do not lie down in front of wrecking balls."

By this time, the chalky, old-egg odor of water when it mixed with dust at a wrecking site, the cloying smell of rotting wood and shattered plaster, only made Nickel sick.

"I just walk the other way now," he declared.

He was lying, perhaps to the reporter, perhaps to himself. Nickel could not stay away from the Stock Exchange Building.

For almost three years he avoided the bureaucratic battle to save the venerable Exchange Building at 30 North LaSalle Street. Nickel did not want to become a part of the fight, he told those who asked, because he had been involved in too many losing, draining battles. But when the wrecking ball began its slow, measured arc, he was drawn back. To Nickel, the shadows playing off the building's gently bayed facade were as sweet as the sirens' song.

Officially, Nickel returned to help salvage ornament from the Trading Room with Vinci. By late January of 1972, Nickel and Vinci could find nothing more to remove. The small budget for the salvage work was nearly exhausted, and it was getting more dangerous to work in the structurally weakened building.

In February he was hired by the Metropolitan Museum of Art to supervise and photograph the removal and shipment of cast-iron stairs from the Stock Exchange

Scaffolding for demolition is erected at Adler and Sullivan's Chicago Stock Exchange Building in October 1971.

to the museum in New York City. Throughout the wet and chilly spring, he stayed on to purchase architectural ornament from the wreckers for a university collection.

Unofficially, he came back to rummage. He searched the mutilated building to take iron and woodwork, old plat atlas books, picture frames, office stationery, and anything else that was usable. He kept just about anything he could find. He hovered around wrecking sites in Army fatigues and a white T-shirt in warm weather, and coveralls in cold. He compromised in dress as little as he did in other matters. Fashion and appearance, he believed, were no more than the whim of a throwaway society. In his professional life as a photographer, he eschewed the get-ahead formality of button-down oxford shirts, striped neckties, three-button suits, and cordovans for informal Abercrombie and Fitch casuals and Hush Puppies. He wore his hair a bit short well into the 1970s.

Nickel was accustomed to these postmortems, preserving specimens and taking photographs as clinical as autopsies. Even though there was little left to see or take by April, Nickel kept returning to the Exchange Building. He said he felt like he was sitting with a dying friend.

In just two months of serious romance, Carol Ruth Sutter had turned Nickel's life around. Everybody noticed the difference. Nickel's spartan appearance—which made him look like a selfless, misunderstood monk or soldier—faded as he grew his hair longer. Nickel dropped his aloof air. He was carefree, almost giddy. At 43, he was in love.

Since March 1972, Richard enjoyed teasing his mother, Agnes, and father, Stanley, about his new relationship. The first night he did not return to the suburban Park Ridge home he was sharing with his parents, they both asked where he had gone so early. He was delighted by their utter disbelief when he told them he had spent the night with Carol.

In late March, Richard and Carol announced their intention to marry, and on April 14 Richard planned to introduce his 32-year-old fiancée to his only brother, Donald, and Donald's wife, Harriet. Donald and Harriet had driven 250 miles from their farm in central Wisconsin to meet Carol and to take Stanley and Agnes for a few weeks so that Richard could be alone with Carol. The family dinner, the first in a long while, had been called for 5 p.m. Agnes last saw Richard the morning before, when he waved good-bye to her as she hung a load of wash out on the line. Hurrying, carrying a blueberry muffin, Richard told his mother he was going to the Stock Exchange Building and would be home that evening. When he didn't return, Agnes assumed he was at Carol's house. She was surprised to learn that Carol, who arrived alone, had not seen Nickel in several days.

That's when Agnes called Vinci.

After arriving at the Stock Exchange Building that night, Vinci took charge of the search. With Samuelson and Vinci's neighbor, Robert Furhoff, following his lead, Vinci grabbed onto electrical wires for support and shimmied across a small floor stub to pull himself precariously up to the third floor. Nickel's father and brother could hear Vinci calling "Richard, Richard" as they arrived. The yellow circle of lights from LaSalle Street guided the Nickels as they met up with Vinci's search party in the gentle rain. Vinci, holding a flashlight, had hopes of finding Nickel pinned by debris. Within an hour, Vinci realized the only chance of finding Nickel alive would be with the help of the wrecking company and its machinery.

Vinci rushed to the night watchman's office and called Gus Riccio, one of the Three Oaks Wrecking Company partners. Riccio was surprised when his wife came upstairs, woke him around 10 p.m. and told him the watchman was on the phone.

"There's been an accident here," the watchman said. "A fellow by the name of Richard Nickel is supposed to be in the building."

Riccio, groggy with sleep, was confused. He had met Nickel once while the Trading Room was being dismantled, but that project had been completed months ago.

Riccio dismissed it, until Vinci got on the phone.

"Richard Nickel is buried in the building," Vinci told Riccio. "Come down here right away."

"You people must be sick," Riccio roared. "What's going on here? What have you people been drinking?"

Vinci was adamant. "No. We're not lying," he said. "Come down here."

Riccio finally agreed and drove downtown. He spent an hour reluctantly digging by hand through a pile of rubble with Vinci and the others until it started to rain harder and the night's search was called off. When the search began the following morning, Riccio was more cooperative. He was convinced of Vinci's sincerity.

"Here we are," Riccio announced, "and here is the equipment. What do you want us to do?"

Riccio knew that when Nickel's disappearance hit the papers, things would be bad for his company. He had not been in the building for months and did not want to make a move without Vinci's approval. Vinci knew the building well and seemed sure that Nickel was inside.

Vinci insisted the search be continued after Tim Samuelson quietly told him that Nickel had several motives for returning to the Stock Exchange on Thursday afternoon. Nickel had asked Samuelson on Wednesday to help him remove a lintel, an ornamental terra-cotta panel between the second and third floor. Months earlier, the building wrecker had told Nickel he could take half of one lintel panel for the ornament collection he had started at Southern Illinois University at Edwardsville— if he removed it himself. Once dislodged, the four-by-six-foot panel would be manageable, Nickel figured, but he needed Samuelson's help to lower it to the ground. Nickel said he would bring an extra hard-hat on Thursday afternoon and signal from the second-floor Trading Room window if Riccio gave him the okay to let Samuelson enter the building.

Around noon on Thursday, Nickel left a message telling Samuelson to meet him at the Stock Exchange between 1 and 2 p.m. Samuelson arrived around 12:45 p.m. and waited in the alley just south of the Exchange for the signal. Occasionally, he yelled up to the Trading Room windows to try to get Nickel's attention, but he never saw any sign of Richard. As he waited, Samuelson watched the wreckers cut steel uprights off at the sixth-floor level and push them into the back courtyard.

Since the beginning of the demolition, the wreckers had no control of the steel-frame building, he thought, and today was no different. They should have taken the building down in sections. Instead, they pounded away indiscriminately, using the wrecking ball haphazardly after small tractors knocked down columns. Sometimes, the uprights fell the wrong way, ripping through floor slabs and slamming into the lower sections of the building interior. Once, as he waited for Nickel, Samuelson was forced to take cover in the loading dock of the adjacent LaSalle Hotel as a building section gave way, sending a rain of dust out of the Trading Room windows.

"Son of a bitch," cursed one wrecker standing in the alley. Another wrecker, taking refuge with Samuelson, thought the entire building was falling.

For the record, Nickel was there to remove the lintel, but he also wanted to secretly slip out a 10-foot stair stringer, an iron panel from the side of a staircase, for the university along with a section of stainless steel for his darkroom. The stainless steel from the abandoned first-floor restaurant had no value. But Nickel knew he would have to remove the cherished stair stringer without the wreckers noticing.

It wasn't the first time Richard had stolen ornament or mementos from the Stock Exchange. More than once during work on the Trading Room, Nickel and Vinci hid valuables and gimcracks in the truck they were using for their Art Institute work.

By the strict sense of the law, taking anything from the building without permission could be considered stealing. Three Oaks, after stripping the building of some ornament and selling it in a makeshift first-floor shop, was breaking up and discarding tons of ornament. The iron and terra-cotta pieces were left laying in slag heaps that were scooped up and eventually dumped in Lake Calumet on the city's far South Side.

Nickel had justified the thievery long ago. Like Florence's 15th-century chapels, which proclaimed the transition from Medieval to Renaissance building styles, Sullivan's buildings and ornament heralded a new age. To Nickel, Sullivan's ornament was more than historically significant. It was fresh, alive, even sensual. In 1962, Nickel was asked by a newspaper reporter why he saved chunks of buildings. "I don't know what to say except that Sullivan's ornament deals with nature, it's tied in with life. It is in fact a symbol of life."

What Nickel didn't say was that the ornament also symbolized his obsession with Sullivan himself. Here was a towering genius who spilled his guts out in architecture. When his buildings were demolished, his ornament was all that was left.

Most of the search on Saturday was by hand, as Vinci's team of three friends and four wreckers sifted through rubble in the hope that Nickel could still be rescued. They spent much of the day poking through the debris that filled the elevator shafts and courtyards.

The work was exhausting, dangerous, and tedious. Ray Beinlich, a Three Oaks heavy equipment operator, figured the only way to find Nickel was to dig into the large piles of rubble with a bulldozer and dump pieces on the ground for clues. As he drove the machine over the first floor, however, Beinlich could feel the upright portions of the building sag. Three Oaks had sprayed so much water on the building to keep down dust that the building was soaked. Afraid the walls might fall, Beinlich stopped using the tractor and went back to handwork, cutting steel beams with the blow torch so that the others would have better access to the piles.

As the searchers picked their way through the site, they listened to chants and songs from an anti-war rally at the nearby Civic Center Plaza. Two men were arrested there for burning their income tax forms after the crowd was urged not to pay for the illegal Vietnam War.

After hours of work, Vinci rallied his men when he noticed part of a stair stringer sticking out of a pile of debris. Without explaining the stringer's significance, Vinci made the men work furiously. He was certain that Nickel was on the other end.

Time was difficult to figure. It seemed as if the men had been at work clearing the pile for close to an hour when one of them asked if they could quit for the day. Vinci, noticing that morale was starting to flag and that work on the pile was nearly at a standstill, reluctantly agreed. As he made one last pull to free the stringer, the men could hear a whoosh and feel the pile on which they were standing being sucked below. Vinci, Samuelson, and the others could see the pile dropping into the basement and could feel the ceiling above and the floor below give way at the same time.

All eight men jumped from the mountain of rubble as it hurtled down. Seven jumped onto a stationary piece of floor slab. One of the wreckers, standing next to a store-size plate-glass window, jumped through the window and landed a few feet below in LaSalle Street. Nobody—not even the man who crashed through the window—was injured. The outline of his body was shaped in the broken glass. It looked like a scene out of a cartoon.

On Sunday Nickel's 1964 Chevy Chevelle was found by his father and an uncle in a parking lot about a mile north of the Stock Exchange. The pair of trousers in the car indicated that Nickel had slipped into his Army fatigues, as was his habit, before walking downtown to work in the building. According to his parking receipt, he had arrived at the lot around noon on Thursday.

It was not uncommon for Nickel to park a distance from the Loop. He parked and walked to avoid high Loop parking rates. Finding the car dispelled any hope that Nickel might have left the city in search of a Sullivan building. The family's last hope now was that Nickel had amnesia and was wandering around the city, or that he had been mugged and left dazed. Late on Sunday night, Agnes Nickel reported her son missing.

Meanwhile, John Vinci continued the search Sunday with Beinlich and Larry Riccio, Gus's brother, who was called from out of town.

The men started work early, clearing Saturday's debris and checking other rubble piles. The avalanche convinced Vinci it was futile and dangerous to dig by hand. So as not to endanger more people, he discouraged others from searching.

By afternoon, Vinci was dead tired. He looked pallid and talked erratically.

When asked by a friend if he wanted the city to be notified, Vinci did not even nod his head.

News of Nickel's disappearance broke Monday morning. The *Chicago Tribune* described Nickel as an "activist in the preservation movement," while the *Chicago Sun-Times* called him an architectural scavenger. Police and firemen were called out, and TV and newspaper reporters and photographers camped out at the site to get footage of the body.

What they got, instead, were sad photographs of Nickel's parents, standing at the edge of the wrecking site. Agnes Nickel, in a babushka, looked like a round-faced Eastern European peasant. Stanley Nickel, in a brimmed hat, looked like a traveling salesman. They both wore dazed, shocked expressions. Their newly engaged son had for the first time in his life found true happiness. And now look what had happened.

They did not give up hope. They brought Nickel's clothes to the site to assist the police dogs joining the search. Kenneth Griesch, one of the patrolmen assigned to a canine unit, thought the call for dogs was simply for show. The two German shepherds were trained to find narcotics and live people. In Griesch's opinion, the dogs had no chance to find a dead man because the odor from a body is different from the scent of a living person. And the building appeared dangerous, both for himself and the dogs.

However, within 30 minutes one of the dogs found a brown leather briefcase covered by debris. The briefcase contained work gloves, photographs, hacksaw blades, a wire cutter, income tax returns, and a memo that read:

Joe Riccio 1:30 on Thur.
Dr. to bsmt.
Transl. glass on first both windows/stainless steel/stringer.

It was obviously Nickel's.

After the briefcase was found and Larry Riccio ordered his men to start digging into the nearby mounds of rubble, Nickel's parents were taken by police to a room at the LaSalle Hotel to wait for further news. Even with the aid of heavy machinery, it took hours for the men to finish clearing the fallen rubble.

By Tuesday Larry Riccio wanted to kick everybody out and get on with the wrecking. At about noon Riccio refused Vinci's request to search the first-floor restaurant kitchen area. Riccio said he would no longer risk the lives of his men in search of a man he doubted was even in the building. Vinci countered by asking to search at his own risk and offering to sign a paper absolving Three Oaks of liability. Riccio refused, saying the paper would be of no value.

"Why are you so anxious to search the restaurant?" asked Dan Gallagher, Riccio's attorney who had been on the site since Monday.

"Somebody said Nickel said something about the stainless steel sink and other stainless steel things in the kitchen area," Vinci replied.

"That's too vague," Gallagher said.

Vinci finally told Gallagher and Riccio about the meaning of Nickel's memo. It was a list of things to take, and the words "stainless steel" referred to the stainless steel splashback panel behind the kitchen restaurant sink.

Riccio told John Pruitt, the job foreman, to go with Vinci and search the kitchen. They had no trouble reaching it because the debris that had blocked the kitchen for days had been removed on Monday. Later, Gallagher asked Vinci how he supposed Nickel could have entered the kitchen the previous week with the pile so high.

"Richard could always find a way," Vinci told the attorney.

On Tuesday afternoon, Joe Fitzgerald, the city building commissioner, authorized Three Oaks to once again start wrecking—but the demolition was restricted to the outer wall so the search could continue. Fitzgerald and other city authorities were in charge now. Samuelson returned to the building several times a day; he was free to roam the building, and Fitzgerald relied on Samuelson for information about where the search should concentrate. He was in a difficult position. He did not want to talk about Nickel's plan to take items, but knew that the information might help. Nickel liked to work in silence, and Samuelson—ever loyal—did not want to betray a trust. Without giving reasons, Samuelson made it clear he wanted the pile that had collapsed in the Trading Room to be checked again. By midweek, when the area had been fully examined, Samuelson was convinced that Nickel's body must be on the fourth floor, the only floor that had not been searched.

Either there, he thought, or on the east shore of Lake Calumet. Samuelson and his friends checked the Lake Calumet dump regularly because he considered the Riccios unscrupulous enough to trash Nickel's body with the debris. They found no body, but did hit upon a trove of valuable ornament from the Exchange Building and other razed buildings. Samuelson lamented that he had not found the dump years earlier.

Vinci spent almost all his time at the site. Early in the week, he volunteered to check the basement for clues. After all of the sifting of rubble at ground level, Vinci believed that if Nickel's body were in the wreckage, it had dropped to the basement. Although he found no sign of Richard's body, Vinci was tempted to make off with ornamental ventilating grilles he found. He decided against it.

On Wednesday morning, Vinci identified a rope and helmet as Richard's. Found by a wrecker on the second floor, the items provided more evidence that Richard was somewhere in the wreckage, but gave little clue as to where.

None of the found items convinced Thomas Sweeney and Michael Mulcahy, two patrolmen from the missing-persons unit, that Nickel would ever be found in the rubble. Although Vinci pinpointed Nickel's disappearance to just after noon on Thursday, April 13, Vinci's elderly housekeeper and maid told police they were certain Nickel stopped by Vinci's house between 2 and 2:30 p.m. that day in the company of another man driving a cream-colored station wagon. They said the men had come to pick up rope.

The women's stories contradicted statements by Vinci, Samuelson, and several wreckers, and made the two officers suspicious that Vinci was hiding the truth. Sweeney and Mulcahy had three theories. They speculated that Nickel had run off because he was afraid to get married, or that he had faked the whole event to drum up support for the preservation movement, or that he had been killed by Vinci or one of the wreckers.

Richard's brother, Donald, returned to his farm later in the week. Richard's parents never missed a day at the site, watching apprehensively from behind police barricades.

Richard's fiancée, Carol, held out hope that Nickel had gone off brooding as the police suggested. She speculated that Nickel was hiding in the Hotel Windermere, where Louis Sullivan had lived his final years. She asked Vinci to take her there, but he dismissed the idea as absurd.

On Thursday, April 20, Fitzgerald decided to let the wrecking continue in earnest. The building commissioner reasoned that there was still no proof that Nickel was in the building. Even if he were there, he would probably be dead by now. Fitzgerald did not want to risk more lives.

With each passing day, the search was more dangerous. The building's exposed floors were becoming soaked by rain. The mortar was being weakened and portions of the building were collapsing. Already one of the ceilings had dropped on a caged tractor, and Samuelson had torn his hand trying to slide down a buckled floor. Fitzgerald said it was dangerous to leave this hulk up in the middle of the Loop.

Vinci was furious. The Riccios, when given the okay by the city, started using the wrecking ball again on the remaining floors. By the afternoon, the crane was again pounding steel beams down while tractors were pushing them off onto the lower floors.

Eight of Nickel's stark black-and-white photographs of another prominent old edifice, the Rookery Building, were placed on wooden easels in the Chicago City Council chambers later that afternoon. Nickel had taken the photos on assignment for the city earlier in the year. They were now meant to be silent testimony at a public hearing on the proposed designation of the Rookery as a city landmark.

Designed by John Wellborn Root, Sullivan's contemporary, and built from 1885 to 1888, the Rookery looks like a castle, with rough-cut granite at its base and turrets on its corners. The oldest building on LaSalle Street, the Rookery is an early, pure, bold example of the Chicago School of architecture. Although Root designed 250 structures during his 18 years as an architect, most suffered the same fate as Sullivan's buildings. This was Root's only remaining building on LaSalle. It stood about two blocks south of the Stock Exchange.

The Rookery, darkened by grime, tends to look even darker in photographs because little sunlight manages to strike the 11-story structure in the canyon formed by the tall buildings on LaSalle Street. The shadows that obscure the Rookery produce minimal density on a photo negative, and make facade details difficult to render on film. Knowing this, Nickel chose to photograph the building on an overcast day so that he could expose for shadows to show detail.

Nickel had attended most of the public hearings as a spectator. Because he was shy, he seldom spoke up publicly for what he considered were landmarks. Instead, he preferred the role of the soft-spoken missionary, choosing to buttonhole people

Burnham and Root's 1885–88 Rookery Building in Chicago's Loop. This photograph, taken by Nickel several weeks before his death, was used at a public hearing in April 1972 to support the building's landmark status.

at wrecking sites rather than proselytize at City Hall. At meetings of the city landmarks commission, he often positioned himself in the corner and ran a tape recorder.

Only one of the 18 people who testified at City Hall that afternoon mentioned Nickel by name. Wilbert Hasbrouck, executive director of the Chicago chapter of the American Institute of Architects, wanted to use the hearing to make one final statement on the Stock Exchange and on Nickel. Hasbrouck told the audience how he had avoided a real war, but had waged a private war against "greed, destruction, and callousness" in his effort to save landmark buildings.

Hasbrouck paused for a moment, then continued abruptly as if he were startled. "Now I think I remember what is missing from this room as I talk."

I said I missed the military war, but I have not missed the smell of death. Buildings die and sometimes men do too. Always before as we testified, a man we looked to for leadership stood over there and recorded what we were saying. When not doing that, he could always be found somewhere picking up the pieces of some great building which the progress of some seeker had to destroy.

He was at work saving the masterful ornament of Sullivan's Stock Exchange while the work crew, the wrecking had been going on. We have many reasons to believe that Richard Nickel is lying in the rubble which remains at 30 North LaSalle today. I pray to God that I am wrong and that he is only missing still, but I fear the worst. There is no reason for him to have been there. That building could have been saved. Let not the same fate come at the other end of LaSalle Street. The Rookery must remain standing.

By April 21, a week after the search began, Samuelson and Vinci were exhausted. They felt helpless. With resumption of the wrecking, Vinci had no searchers to lead. The wreckers refused to talk to him.

"It's a nightmare," Vinci moaned that evening. "I don't know what to tell people to do any longer."

During the following two weeks, the city assigned building inspectors to make certain that the wreckers were carefully looking for Nickel's body as the demolition continued. All debris that was scooped out of the building was first dropped on the ground and checked, and checked again after it was placed into trucks.

On April 23, Vinci was quoted in *Chicago Today* as ruling out the possibility that Nickel had amnesia, or had left the city. "I can't imagine that. Richard was a totally unique person. He was totally responsible not only to society, but to his family."

On April 24, with the perimeter wall of the building down to the fifth floor, foreman John Pruitt found a section of stainless steel leaning against a corner wall on the first floor. Hidden behind it were pieces of terra cotta, iron stair risers, and a stair stringer.

On April 28, the Landmarks Preservation Council offered a $1,000 reward for information leading to Nickel's discovery.

By April 30, all the steel beams, girders, and columns from the north and east walls of the Stock Exchange had been removed, and by May 5 the wreckers started work on the basement and sub-basement, the last part of the building that might be concealing Nickel's body.

It was a warm, sunny afternoon on May 9 when Ray Beinlich saw what he thought was a shoulder sticking out from deep in the basement rubble. Beinlich, driving a tractor, did not want to touch the body and be blamed if anything went wrong. He called the building inspectors and Larry Riccio, who alerted the police.

Officers Sweeney and Mulcahy arrived a few minutes later and confirmed that Beinlich had indeed seen a body. The corpse was 10 to 15 feet below street level, encased in loose dry cement and plaster beneath sand, bricks, and other debris. It was in an area directly beneath where the dogs had sniffed out the briefcase more than three weeks before. Beinlich realized he had driven his tractor only a few feet above the body when the search had begun. He wondered how many times he had run over the dead man. Today, the teeth of Beinlich's end loader had actually stripped Nickel's shirt off his body. "One more inch and I would have torn him apart," Beinlich said.

Edwin McNulty, a police evidence technician, expected that after 26 days the body would be putrified, but instead he found it had barely started decomposing. The debris, coarse sand, and cold water from the building had wrapped tightly around the body. McNulty had never seen a body so well preserved. There was not even an odor of death.

Richard Nickel died like a statue, McNulty thought to himself. Parts of the dead man were in such good condition that McNulty was able to take perfect fingerprints.

"Don't put no pick in it," McNulty ordered as police and firemen descended. "We are going to dig this man out right."

It took more than two hours for four firemen to extricate the body. It kept getting reburied by rubble as they worked. The corpse was two floors directly beneath the Trading Room in the building's sub-basement. Nickel was crushed and twisted between two I-beams, one of which had fallen across his shoulder blades and a longer one that had fallen lengthwise across the lower part of his body. The death scene had all the earmarks of a crucifixion.

Nickel was pronounced dead three hours later at Cook County Hospital. His body was taken to the Cook County Morgue, where it was examined closely and identified by Richard's aunt, Bernice Bognar. Tim Samuelson, who was at home when the firemen pulled Nickel's body out of the rubble, did not know whether to be relieved or saddened. John Vinci did not learn that the body had been found until the evening, when he watched a TV news report in stunned silence. Harriet Nickel heard about it on the radio. She was planting potatoes in her garden; Donald was planting in a nearby field. Agnes Nickel, who watched firemen lift her son's body onto a stretcher, could not talk.

The day Nickel was buried, May 12, Donald hired a forensic surgeon to perform an autopsy. As expected, the physician found that Nickel had been crushed to death. Not expected was the finding that Richard also suffered from pulmonary emphysema and chronic bronchitis. Although the condition had nothing to do with Nickel's death, the diagnosis stunned Donald. His brother hated the smell of smoke so much that he had once bolted shut the ash tray in his car to discourage others from smoking.

The physician speculated that the emphysema was most likely caused by the dust Richard had inhaled during 20 years in condemned buildings.

Richard Nickel poses in
front of the Institute of
Design, the college that
turned his life around.

CHAPTER TWO

WHAT THE OPERATOR WILL SEE IN HIS CAMERA WILL DEPEND,
THEREFORE, ON HIS GIFTS, AND TRAINING, AND SKILL, AND EVEN MORE ON HIS
GENERAL EDUCATION; ULTIMATELY IT WILL DEPEND ON HIS SCHEME OF
THE UNIVERSE.

Bernard Berenson, *Aesthetics and History*

The year Richard Nickel was born, 1928, was the last full year of what F. Scott Fitzgerald described as the "greatest, gaudiest spree in history." There was little hint of the Depression soon to follow: the Republicans swept Herbert Hoover into office promising "a chicken in every pot, a car in every garage," and the hit songs were "Makin' Whoopee" and "Can't Help Lovin' That Man."

The day Nickel was born, May 31, was an unusually quiet news day. The banner story in Chicago newspapers was President Calvin Coolidge's announcement that he would spend his summer vacation in the woods of northern Wisconsin. The most curious story was a squib quoting Italian leader Benito Mussolini as saying he would never meet a violent end. "No one will ever destroy me with bullets," predicted Il Duce. "I will die a natural death."

Stanley Nickel, a newspaper truck driver, had just finished his collection route when he heard about the birth of his first child. Stanley opened the garage door at the *Polish Daily News* office building right behind the office of his family physician, Dr. Kelly, when somebody shouted, "Tell Nick it's a boy!" Richard Stanley Nickel, born at St. Mary's of Nazareth Hospital on Chicago's West Side, was not named after anyone. He would be called "Rich" by his grammar and high school friends, "Nick" by his Army buddies, and "Dick" by most of his adult acquaintances. But his family and his closest friends—including John Vinci and Tim Samuelson—always referred to him as "Richard." Richard Nickel. The name had a sober quality about it.

Like many immigrants, both Richard's maternal and paternal ancestors put their past lives behind them in an effort to start anew on the promising shores of the United States. The family saved no documents from the Old World and passed down few stories about their lot before emigrating from Poland.

For nearly 100 years the main area in Chicago for Polish immigrants was Stanislawono, a congested, dirty, wedge-shaped neighborhood about two miles northwest of Chicago's Loop. Both sides of Richard Nickel's family settled in Stanislawono. Towering above the district were the twin towers of St. Stanislaus Kostka Church, built for $100,000 in 1893 and billed as the largest Catholic parish in the United States at the time. In its heyday, St. Stanislaus Kostka did 2,000 baptisms, 400 weddings, and 1,000 funerals a year.

Both Stanley and Agnes Nickel were first-generation Americans. Stanley's parents—John Nikiel and Katherine Bross—were born in Posen, but did not meet until their trip to Chicago. John Nikiel left Warsaw during the 1880s because he did not want to serve in "Deutscher Kaiser's" army. According to family lore, he escaped by paying a bribe and came to America by way of the Netherlands. Katherine (changed from Katarzyne) Bross made the journey from Posen alone in 1888, carrying only a "featherstick" and pillow. She had no relatives in Chicago and worked as a chambermaid for a Jewish family on Powell Street. She met John at a Sunday afternoon picnic in Wicker Park around 1892 and they were married soon after at St. Stanislaus Kostka.

John Nikiel, who changed his name to Nickel, was a handsome, short man with blond hair and a blond handlebar mustache. He drove a team of horses, hauling lumber on flat-bed trucks for the Herman H. Hedler Company and later, coal on wagons for the Polonia Coal Company. At night, he drove his wagon downtown to the Dearborn Street train station to pick up Polish immigrants. Stanley recalled the trips: His father identified the immigrants by the tags they wore and wrapped them in feather blankets. Then he transported them to Bucktown, the rough neighborhood just north of Stanislawano where many newer immigrants lived.

Katherine, a tall, quiet, religious woman who wore dresses down to her ankles to cover varicose veins, sent Stanley and her four other children to Catholic grammar schools. They all started public high school, but dropped out quickly because their grammar school background was inadequate.

Agnes's parents, Peter Block and Victoria Gwizdala, took a more circular route to Chicago. Born in Poland, they both moved as children with their families in the early 1870s to Parisville, a farming town about 10 miles west of Lake Huron in Michigan's thumb. Like many Poles, the Block and Gwizdala families were attracted to the area by jobs in the lumber industry. Peter and Victoria Block were married in Parisville around the turn of the century and moved to Chicago with their two children between 1906 and 1909.

Victoria (changed from Wiktorja) baked bread, a cake, and a pie every Saturday. Peter worked for the Burrell Belting Company during the 1910s and later with the Peerless Rubber Company, where he cut and mixed gooey sections of rubber to make tires and Amos 'n' Andy dolls. He often took an extra apple to work so he could share it with his daughters when they met him at the streetcar stop on his trip home. He would peel the apple and dangle the long strip of skin in front of their eyes before they ate.

Agnes Catherine Block, born on September 9, 1902, in Parisville, was working as a seamstress, sewing chenille lettering on shirts for the Wilson Sporting Goods Company, when she met Stanley in the mid-1920s. It was an improbable match. While coquettish Ag frequented dance halls, Stan was shy. He had no girlfriends and didn't know how to dance. Born Stanislaus Nikiel on November 14, 1898, on Chicago's West Side, he had already changed his family name to Nickel and had just taken a job delivering the *Polish Daily News*.

They were married on May 22, 1926, at St. Cyrilla Church on Chicago's West Side. Even on his wedding day, Stanley refused to dance. The couple's first home, where they were living when Richard was born, was the top floor of a two-flat at 4327 West Hadden Avenue on Chicago's West Side. They moved a year or two after Richard's birth less than a block away to 4329 West Crystal Street because their first apartment was too cold in the winter and too hot in the summer.

The Crystal bungalow was in excellent condition. The family who owned it begged the Nickels to move in because they were unable to pay the mortgage without a tenant. The Nickels took over the first floor while the Squeo family moved into the basement. The house was crowded. Along with Stanley, Agnes, Richard, and Richard's brother, Donald, lived John Nickel, Peter Block, and Bernice Block, Agnes's sister.

The neighborhood, a mix of Czechs, Poles, and Italians, was known informally as the "Prairies." It was a friendly place with a rural feeling. Children played ball in the many vacant lots. As with many neighborhoods in Chicago, this one revolved around its church.

Richard attended grammar school at St. Cyril and Methodias and went to mass in the Roman Catholic church for an hour almost every morning. It was here that Richard first became interested in the play of light. He later wrote that he spent much of his time admiring the stained-glass window figures of Saints Ann, Aloysius, Bartholomew, Philip, Thaddeus, Paul, Thomas, Jacob, and Matthew on either side of the church and the Blessed Mother and St. Joseph behind the ornate pulpit.

"That makes an impression on you that you never completely forget," Nickel told a reporter in 1969. "It might be subconscious and, at some point, something triggers it."

Because of his sweet countenance, Richard was called "Angel Face" by the Dominican nuns who ran the strict coeducational grammar school. But young life was more unsettling than what appeared on the surface. As an adult, Nickel recounted on a scrap of paper:

> *peeing in pants in school because afraid to*
> *ask to be excused.*

> *morning mass at St Cyril every a.m., front pews*
> *when young and backing off with age.*

> *spent all those mornings looking at the colored*
> *glass, windows, columns and caps, the paintings on*
> *the wall.*

> *once when nun was gone, flying paper planes back*
> *and forth. She upbraided us and wanted to know who? I*
> *hesitated but hardly anyone raised hands and finally*
> *I was compelled to. She said we would have to stay*
> *after school and make 100 (200?) planes. We started*
> *during the school day and got little help from other*

kids, but it took several hours after school until she
finally excused us. Marvelous penalty.

Going to confession...the mortification.

Richard left St. Cyril in about fifth grade when his family moved three miles north to 2457 North Rockwell Street in the Logan Square area on the city's Northwest Side. He transferred to the nearby grammar school at St. John Berchmans Church, where, Nickel wrote, "nuns pushed education into students rather well."

Years later, Nickel described his new surroundings as "that dumb old Polish neighborhood where I grew up and became happily abnormal." Although predominantly Polish, Logan Square was home to several other white ethnic groups. No one was wealthy; no one was poor. Most of the parents of Richard's friends were first- or second-generation immigrants. Lewis Bugna's father, from Austria, was a policeman. Tom and Jack Cussen's father, from Ireland, worked as a streetcar man. Their family raised chickens during the Depression, so Richard and his buddies frequently had chicken salad sandwiches for lunch. The whole parish had only one doctor and no lawyers.

The Nickels once again took the second floor of a corner two-flat in Logan Square. The three-bedroom apartment boasted a separate garage out back, which for years was the proud home of Stanley's 1940 Oldsmobile. Stanley and Agnes shared one bedroom, Richard and Donald shared another, and Peter Block lived in the third.

Logan Square was a nice place to grow up. On Sunday mornings most of the Nickels' neighbors walked to mass at St. John Berchmans on the south side of broad, tree-lined Logan Boulevard. After church, Stanley often took the family for outings. They rode to Lake Michigan to watch the waves pound ashore, to Palwaukee Airport to watch planes, or to the Museum of Science and Industry. The boys played in Haas Park and Hedler's Field nearby or took motorcoach buses downtown or to museums. From Logan Square, the boys could ride all the way to the lake to fish or north to the large city swimming pool.

Stanley Nickel, who delivered the *Polish Daily News* for 35 years until his retirement in 1962, passed down both a strong work ethic and a sense of style to his sons. Stanley was viewed as a man one step in front of the Logan Square crowd. He saved his money so that he and his family could take out-of-state trips and he told his sons they could have anything except bicycles, which he considered too dangerous. In 1948 Stanley became something of a hero when he took a train to Lansing, Michigan, and returned with one of the first Hydra-Matic Oldsmobiles. More important to Richard was Stanley's interest in photography. Stanley blackened the basement laundry room and set up a darkroom in the Rockwell apartment. He bought a cheap enlarger and made photographic prints, something nobody in the neighborhood had ever done.

Agnes passed down strength and honesty. Besides raising the boys, she worked full time assembling push-button switches, solenoids, and other electric equipment

A family snapshot
shows Richard (left), his
brother, Donald, and
their father, Stanley.

at Oak Manufacturing following World War II. The family was eventually able to buy a home in the suburbs. When Richard brought his college friends to the family's Park Ridge home during the 1950s, she did not dress up, tidy up the house, or change the menu. She supported him and his work. Although she could not tell one of Richard's prized buildings from another, Agnes treasured Richard's photos and even marched with him—placard in hand—to protest the demolition of the Garrick Theater.

Family snapshots show Richard as a slightly built, serious boy who took after his mother's side of the family. Richard posed formally for his father's camera. The boy—or his mother—obviously worked over his long brown hair carefully, making sure it would hang just slightly over his forehead. The photos show Richard wearing knickers, a white shirt, and a white tie beneath a double-breasted suit at his first communion and posing with a face full of chicken pox on the back porch at Crystal Street. Few photos show him smiling. Instead, he chose to wear a wan expression reading a newspaper in the Rockwell Street living room, sitting next to the American Flyer train set that his father took out every Christmas, or examining small bombs on display at a World War II War Bonds rally.

Richard's brother, Donald, and boyhood friends found it easier years later to discuss what Richard did not do as a boy than what he did. Richard was not athletic, did not hum a tune, and was not a practical joker. He was one of the few boys who did not pull and snap his friends' elastic ties. Although tall enough,

Richard took little interest in sports. Stanley liked to hit softballs to his sons, but Richard often just let them roll past.

To adults, Richard was a model youth, neither seen nor heard. But to his friends, Richard was the one with the odd ideas, the one interested in artistic things such as new car designs, and the one who was not afraid to talk about his daydreams. His friend Tom Cussen remembers how Richard wondered aloud "What if I were president," or "What if I was on a deserted island." Cussen's brother, Jack, remembered a more dangerous question: "How do you really know God exists?" Jack tried to make light of the question by repeating the old arguments the boys heard from nuns, but Richard stood his ground and asked how he could be certain. Finally Jack retorted: "Rich, we're going to confession this afternoon. Why don't you come along? We'll get the priest there and you can talk to him." That shut him up.

Richard and Donald were seldom buddies as kids because they had different interests. Donald, the confident golden boy whose blond hair turned white in the summer, loved ice skating, playing the piano, singing, and playing football. Richard, four years older, never assumed the role of big brother. He did not protect or cater to Donald, even after Donald lost vision in one of his eyes. When they fought, Agnes always made the brothers kiss before they started off to school. But as they walked down the stairs out of Agnes's view, Richard often gave Donald a punch and took off. Donald, who grew to be taller and bigger than his brother, could defend himself, but could not catch Richard.

Starting in the early 1940s, Richard spent much of his time building model airplanes. Working with a pungent glue known as "dope," Richard covered the wings with paper or sheet balsawood, then applied coat after coat of filler and sand until the plane's skin looked as shiny as a mirror. Richard's father built him a little desk in the attic on Rockwell, a private place reachable only by way of pull-down stairs. Once in the attic, with the ladder retracted, Richard was alone. It was quiet and hot up there, but he didn't mind. He spent hours working meticulously even on details that would never show.

Richard and his father flew the planes on the football field at Lane Tech High School. He guided the models up and down in 75-foot arcs by two U-control wires connected to the wings. His friends sometimes threw footballs at the planes as they buzzed and circled around in flight. The boys wanted to get Richard's attention and were surprised that their pranks never seemed to bother him. "That's an old one," Richard said if his plane got hit. "I have to build a new one anyway."

For young, tentative Richard, growing up must have been an array of bewildering experiences. In an undated note found among his effects after his death, he wrote:

Donald and Arlene [a cousin] in a closet, quiet, etc., and then a big fuss with both parents bawling them out. I remember feeling so innocent...and perhaps not completely understanding.

Pull knife out of Donald's hand at Island Lake. They made a big fuss and I kind of remember my father grabbing me by the ear and striking me in some way to show his anger. (Somehow Donald was holding the knife by the blade and I pulled it out of his clasped hand!)

As kids, planning to pull up girls' dresses. I remember scheming once with someone of a way we could do it with a wagon handle so as to make it appear accidental. Of course I didn't have the courage to do it, even with the wagon.

As a teen, I remember being left by the Bognars one night with the teenage daughter of some friends of theirs while they went out, and those friends asking openly whether I could be trusted....

Richard and most of his friends attended St. Phillips High School on the Near West Side. About four miles south of Logan Square on the street car, St. Phillips was the first deliberately integrated school in the city. Like most Catholic boys schools, St. Phillips emphasized discipline. The Viatorian and Cervite priests and brothers running the school made the students toe a very strict line.

Richard was a freshman at St. Phillips in 1942, soon after the United States entered World War II. To the Nickels the war meant tin foil balls and gas and shoe rationing. To the boys the war meant that history and geography became real. Growing up suddenly had more of a purpose. The war further stoked Richard's passion for airplanes and it soon went well beyond models. The careful handwriting on the back of family snapshots tells the story of weekends when Stanley took Richard and the family to small airports so they could take short airplane rides for a dollar each. One photograph, taken at Palwaukee Airport, notes: "Mom's first flight, Richard's fifth, May 7, 1944." Another reads: "I flew for a minute."

By his junior year, Richard was designing his own planes, all with U.S. insignia on the side. He photographed them and made technical notes on the back of each print.

Most of the boys in the neighborhood felt that when the time came, they would do their share and enlist. Richard was no different. He took the chemical warfare, manual-of-arms, and military courtesy classes at St. Phillips for juniors and seniors and was neither hesitant nor apprehensive about his future role. Like the others, he assumed that the war would still be going when he graduated. But it ended in 1945, the summer before his senior year.

Richard graduated from high school in June 1946. He was absent only once during his four years and ranked 57th in his class of 202. He distinguished himself by being the first at St. Phillips to bring a ball-point pen to class. It was a Reynolds spun-aluminum pen, which he purchased for $16 in 1943 with money he earned at a 60-cent-per-hour job.

As an adult Richard wrote more about the life lessons than about the class lessons at St. Phillips. He wrote about Brother Tim, who used a "board of education" on those who got out of line, and about his Latin teacher, who frequently came to class drunk. Unsure how to react, Nickel and his classmates talked about Rome while their teacher slept.

He also wrote about the value of an education in a racially mixed surrounding. In 1969 Nickel stopped to help two black women change a tire on the expressway.

> *And when I was done, they were pushing a few dollars on me and I said "No." I wouldn't think of it....And later as they roared by they honked and waved. Very, very nice. That's where the race problems are resolved, by individual men. Not by learned articles, or committees, or Smothers TV shows. I credit it all to my humanistic idealistic Catholic upbringing.*

To celebrate Richard's high school graduation and the end of gas rationing, the Nickels took a grand tour of the West in the summer of 1946. They saw several national parks and stopped at the Victory Tool Company in Fresno, California, to see where Richard's favorite model-plane engine, the Hornet, was made.

Following the trip, Richard and friend Jack Cussen talked about going to college. Noticing the number of newspaper ads for engineers, they decided to apply to engineering schools.

The St. Phillips 1946 yearbook states that Richard was interested in "aircraft" in his senior year and planned to go to DePaul University in Chicago. Instead, he applied to the Illinois Institute of Technology, but was rejected. In September 1946 Richard applied to the Aeronautical Union, a school on Chicago's South Side. Before classes began, however, Cussen convinced Richard to join him in enlisting in the army. The GI Bill of Rights, Cussen argued, offered 30 paid months of college for 18 months of service.

Stanley was surprised but pleased by Richard's decision. He thought his son was too gentle for his own good. The army, he hoped, would force Richard to grow up fast.

Richard kept up his interest in model airplanes right through the summer and early fall of 1946. Just before he left for basic training, he submerged his best engine in a two-gallon bottle of oil so the motor would not rust. It was his last act of childhood.

On October 3, 1946, Richard began his tour of duty at the Army's Fort Sheridan, north of Chicago. A week later he was sent for basic training to the Company C 29th Training Battalion at Camp Polk, Louisiana, where he stayed through mid-November. It did not take long for Richard to regret his decision to enlist. Two days after his arrival in Louisiana, he wrote the Cussen family that he was sleeping in his clothes and under two blankets because of the cold. "I really hated leaving Chicago," he wrote. "We went through the city on the way out and [were] just looking at everything. Makes a person want to jump out the window. I'm just writing a few words to let everyone know I'm alive and that the Army is nothing to brag about."

Most enlistees complained about the heat rather than the cold at Camp Polk.

Richard signed up for the medical corps, but soon realized that the training program was set up to make him a fighting man. He hated the regimen as he learned how to drill and function as a "grunt." He was scared of the snakes that infested the nearby swamps and described Camp Polk as "hell on earth."

In early December, Private First Class Nickel was shipped out to Camp Stoneman, California, to prepare for duty overseas. It was by now clear to Richard that the military had a far greater need for soldiers than corpsmen. The army wanted new recruits to replace the World War II veterans who remained in occupied Japan. At a brief train layover in Kansas City, Nickel met a soldier returning from overseas. The soldier's stories depressed him, but it was too late to turn back. A "sweet 18-19 year old," Nickel described himself years later. After five days at Camp Stoneman, he was shipped to Fort Mason, California, where he boarded the army troop carrier *General A. W. Greely.* He spent Christmas in Guam, and by January 3, 1947, he was in Yokohama, Japan. Like many aboard, he was seasick for much of the journey.

Nickel was one of four million Americans sent to the islands during the official occupation, which lasted from the surrender of Japan in 1945 until the Dulles Treaty of 1952. All of Japan's weapons, fortifications, and industrial factories designed for war purposes were scrapped or destroyed during the second and third years of the occupation when Nickel was on the islands.

As expected, Nickel and the hundreds of other soldiers who signed up to serve as medical corpsmen were told they would be transferred to infantry duty upon their arrival at Yokohama. If they didn't like it, they were told they could fill the ranks up north as paratroopers of the 11th Airborne.

Nickel and two new army buddies—Roland Rogers "Woody" Schumann of Milwaukee, Wisconsin, and Elmer Riddle of Queens, New York—opted to join the paratroops. The airborne paid $50 a month more than the infantry and offered prestige. "We were gung-ho, medal-happy kids, willing to do anything to be noticed including run into machine-gun fire," Schumann said. "We were the type of material any captain would want." The three 18-year-olds must have stood in marked contrast to the rough veterans of the 11th Airborne, which prided itself as the first unit to reach the Japanese home islands during the war. Soon after they joined the 511th Parachute Infantry Regiment, Nickel, Schumann, and Riddle became known as the "cherry boys" of the platoon.

The 11th Airborne Training Center, where Nickel attended a two-week course, was on the abandoned Japanese Takadoti Air Base at Hachinohe, a fishing village in the northern tip of Honshu, Japan's major island.

To Nickel, parachute jumping was as easy as falling out of bed. The key was not losing your nerve. His first lessons were simple vaults from a six-foot platform. Then he made four jumps from a 34-foot tower, plunging while attached to a cable and harness so that he could get the feel of the harness opening. He took his first jump from an airplane above Sendai, about 200 miles south of Hachinohe, in mid-February. On February 27 Nickel won his wings by making his fifth plunge.

From then on he had to make at least one jump every three months to receive his $50 bonus. Jump six was on May 10, 1947. By then Nickel was haunted by the song that the 30 soldiers sang in the C-46 as they readied to jump. It was to the tune

"Beautiful Dreamer," and went like this:

Beautiful streamer, open for me
Blue skies above me but no canopy
Just a malfunction—a cigarette roll
Faster each second, all out of control

The jumps were also becoming physically more difficult. After the first few, the troops were required to drop with a carbine or M1 rifle in a Griswald container slung on front straps. Then the jumpers had to carry down mortars and baseplates. Some jumps were as low as 1,000 feet with full combat pack. While lined up waiting for a jump, Nickel and the rest of the unit watched a soldier hit the ground before his chute had fully opened. The army base paper reported that the soldier died of pneumonia, but the paratroopers knew better. Finally, after his eighth jump, Nickel had had enough. He signed a "quit slip" and was released from the unit on September 9, 1947.

Nickel would later tell his friends there were no atheists in the 11th Airborne. When he would get into dangerous situations, Nickel muttered: "Hell, this is nothing. I used to be a paratrooper."

Richard served the rest of his overseas tour of duty in the IX Corps military police platoon, which kept watch over the city of Sendai and guarded a new army post at Kawauchi Tract. Armed with a .45 caliber automatic pistol, Nickel made roving patrols and helped operate checkpoints. As an MP, Richard saw more of Japan. In April 1947 he sat in a courtroom to watch the Far East International Military Tribunal, which was about to complete its war-crime hearings.

It was during his army years that Nickel first made an effort to document on film what he was seeing. From Camp Polk he sent home playful snapshots of himself in front of the white-frame barracks and in front of a door that said "Commanding Officer." From Takadoti he sent back photos showing him in the cabin of a wrecked Japanese warplane just off the runway at the airbase. He became more serious about photography after becoming a paratrooper, taking along a small Argus camera and an old movie camera to document the jumps. "Note the tail of the plane, static lines, rice paddies, Sendai below," he wrote on the back of one jump photo. On another he wrote: "Here I am in my good old parachute. We just put our chutes on. About 15 minutes after this was taken, my plane taxied up and we shuffled thru the prop blast up into the plane to make jump number 7."

His movies, which later became the rage among his friends back home, were remarkably complete. Richard filmed his fellow paratroopers in the plane preparing to jump, and showed the line in front of him plunging out the open doorway. He tucked his camera away just as he began his descent and took it out once again when he hit the ground.

The relief he felt leaving the war games of the paratroopers is reflected in his photographs. While still in the airborne unit, Richard sent a picture of himself marked: "The ghost of Private R. Nickel— killed in a parachute jump, his main streamer and his reserve had no canopy. Tough." As an MP, Nickel once again began joking with his photos. One of his first was a picture of himself mockingly pointing a handgun to the middle of his chin. He was smiling again.

His tour of duty complete, Richard was sent back to the United States in January 1948. He left Yokohama on January 30 and spent 26 days at sea, sailing past the Philippine Islands, Guam, and Hawaii on the *General Pope.* On March 6, while at Camp Stoneman, Nickel signed up for the inactive reserves. Although he was due to be honorably discharged at any time, he was told that he might be discharged a few weeks early if he signed up. It turned out to be one paper too many: the inactive status made him eligible to be called back. Upon leaving the army on March 9, 1948, Nickel was given the World War II victory medal, $300 mustering-out pay, and $112 travel pay.

His return home was difficult. Nothing seemed right. He did not know what he wanted to do. He got a dead-end job at the Jesse Gorov Store and tried, on a lark, to cross Lake Michigan in an army-surplus life raft with two friends. The Coast Guard made them come back. In late summer Nickel enrolled at the Institute of Design on the Near North Side. He knew nothing of the long tradition he would inherit.

Before the industrial revolution of the mid-1800s, fine artists—painters, sculptors, musicians, and architects—played a leading role in society. Subsidized by patrons, artists were considered vital in the enlightened Western civilization of the Renaissance. Craftsmen were important, too. Until the rise of the machine, most items in the world were made by hand. A craftsman might spend a lifetime making a few thousand shoes or a few hundred pieces of furniture. Suddenly, however, with the advent of mass production during the late 1800s, even unskilled hands were producing objects by the tens of thousands.

The new factory owners had little interest and less need for artists or craftsmen. Many artists, such as Vincent Van Gogh and Paul Gauguin, withdrew. They shunned the new materialism and created bohemian worlds of their own. Because of their alienation, they had little impact on what was mass produced.

A few fought the factory system. One was William Morris, who yearned for the glorious days of the Middle Ages when artisans designed and manufactured products. Born to a comfortable manor life near London in 1834, Morris believed that shoddy machine-made goods degraded the world. During the 1860s his Morris & Company created hand-made furniture and works of art that influenced generations. "The growth of Decorative Art in this country, owing to the efforts of English Architects, has now reached a point at which it seems desirable that Artists of reputation should devote their time to it," he wrote.

Morris was not alone. During the late 1800s and early 1900s, the expressionists, dadaists, constructivists, futurists, cubists, and purists in Europe formed around the principle that artists should lead society back to quality. *L'art pour l'art,* art for art's sake, became a rallying cry.

Another movement, the *Deutscher Werkbund,* sought to combine Morris's love of craftsmanship with the potential of the machine. The *Werkbund* believed that artists and craftsworkers should gain control of the machine to mass-produce fine products. Although the movement was short lived, Walter Gropius, a young German architect, kept its ideas alive when he took control of Germany's Weimar Art Academy and Weimar Arts and Crafts School in 1919.

The merger of both staffs, one of fine artists and one of master craftsmen, gave Gropius the opportunity to unite pure and applied art into the world's first school of design. The new *Staatliches Bauhaus Weimar*, the State School of Building at Weimar, became unofficially known as the "Bauhaus," the house of building.

Gropius opened the Bauhaus with proclamations that sounded like Karl Marx's call to action:

> *Let us create a new guild of craftsman without the class distinctions that raise an arrogant barrier between craftsman and artist. . . .Together, let us conceive and create the new building of the future, which will embrace architecture and sculpture and painting in one unity and which will rise one day toward heaven from the hands of a million workers like a crystal symbol of a new faith.*

The Bauhaus was more of a commune than a school. It was a workshop for masters, trade workers, and apprentices. The old staffs of the Weimar schools worked together until *Bauhausler,* people of the Bauhaus, graduated in the mid-1920s and assumed teaching roles. The graduates, Gropius felt, were true artists, because they understood the "fundamental unity underlying all branches of design."

In its 14 years the Bauhaus became a world center of modern design. Gropius's first staff, which included painters Paul Klee and Wassily Kandinsky along with architects Oskar Schlemmer and Ludwig Mies van der Rohe, attracted students from every continent. The school grew rapidly during the 1920s, producing pupils, products, and publications that influenced the way the world looks. By the early 1930s, however, the progressive nature of the Weimar Republic had waned. The Bauhaus was labeled a "hotbed of cultural Bolshevism" by the up-and-coming Nazis and the paintings produced there were called "degenerate." Gropius, who left the school in 1928, saw his Bauhaus dream shatter when the school was sealed off by police in April 1933.

At age 27 László Moholy-Nagy became the Bauhaus's youngest teacher when Gropius appointed him master of the advanced foundation course and the metal workshop in 1922.

Born in the feudal Hungarian village of Bacsbarshod, Moholy-Nagy (pronounced "Ma-Holy Naj") was a utopian who believed that art, reproduced by machines, could lead mankind to the promised land. Unlike Gropius, who believed that mass production could remake and improve the world, Moholy-Nagy put his faith in mass communication.

"During the war, but more strongly even now, I feel my responsibility toward society," Moholy-Nagy wrote in 1919. "My conscience asks incessantly: Is it right to become a painter in times of social revolution? May I claim for myself the privilege of art, when all men are needed to solve the problems of sheer survival?"

He answered by becoming totally committed to art. The artist, he wrote, could be a visionary, a "refined seismograph of his time" whose power to see and interpret could lead others to a better future.

In 1920 Moholy-Nagy burst upon the progressive art scene in Berlin. The realistic portraits and landscapes he had painted in Budapest and Vienna were replaced by canvases and photographs celebrating symbols of the new age—a T-square, a semaphore, bridges, railway stations, wheels, even transmission belts. He turned to abstraction because it was more intellectually challenging. "From that time on I observed that lines could have a power beyond me," he wrote. Moholy-Nagy rejected the dadaist view of a fractured, upside-down, disorganized, cluttered world because he was a positive person. He wanted to rebuild the world torn apart by the world war. He turned toward the constructivist art movement.

In 1923 Moholy-Nagy began teaching the *Volkurs,* the preliminary course at the Bauhaus. This was the school's most important course, for it was here that new students were taught the building blocks of art: scale, rhythm, light, shade, and color. Although Moholy-Nagy had worked as an artist only a few years and spoke poor German, he quickly established himself as a leading theoretician and teacher. Gropius, who called Moholy-Nagy "the fiery stimulator," later eulogized him by writing, "Much that was accomplished stands to his credit."

Although he won an international reputation as a teacher and as an artist at the Bauhaus, Moholy-Nagy's tenure was short. He resigned with Gropius in 1928 to protest increased governmental censorship and interference. Moholy-Nagy returned to Berlin to work as a stage designer and from there moved to Amsterdam and London. During the 1920s and 1930s he also established himself as a leading photographer, creating abstract designs of light and shadow with his camera. He described himself as a *Lichtner,* a manipulator of light. "One may paint with light as surely as I can paint with oil and pigment," he wrote. "The photograph is a light picture."

In 1937 he was invited to teach in the United States by the Association of Arts and Industries, a group of business leaders founded to establish a Chicago school that would prepare student designers to work with industry. Moholy-Nagy was bewildered when he arrived in Chicago to consider the offer. He wrote that Chicago was a strange town that never got dark or quiet, a town where automobiles honked and police sirens wailed all night long. He wrote about the wide street near Lake Michigan and the dilapidated houses nearby. He concluded by writing that the beautiful lake was "an endless aspect to a very limited civilization."

He was also confused by his hosts. Their Tudor and Georgian homes, their classical furniture, their old-school master paintings indicated they had little appreciation of modern art. When the businessmen proudly took Moholy-Nagy on a tour of the staid, plush North Shore, the modernist designer noted he did not see one decently designed house. "What am I to believe?" he wrote his wife, Sibyl, in London. "Shall I be an optimist and say: Everyone is a potential student; or shall I be a pessimist and say: Forgive them for they know not what they're doing?"

Sibyl was equally dubious, albeit for her own reasons. When she saw the group's letterhead—with the name of Chicago retailer Marshall Field at the top—

she advised her husband to turn down the job. "We in Germany have had enough field marshals," she wrote.

But Moholy-Nagy stayed. There was "something incomplete" about the city, he wrote. He signed a five-year contract.

From the start, Moholy-Nagy made it clear that his "New Bauhaus" was to be more than just another art academy. He wanted to produce "art engineers," he wrote. "If I'm successful, the effort will be history."

László Moholy-Nagy meets with students at the New Bauhaus in 1937. The photo was taken by a *Chicago Daily News* photographer.

The school struggled through its first year in a remodeled mansion on South Prairie Avenue donated by Marshall Field. In the Bauhaus manner, the walls of the 65-year-old house were whitewashed and a modern office wing was constructed. However, the first year was a failure. Only 35 students signed up for the first semester, and only a few more joined the second term. By the end of the school year, the businessmen withdrew their support and the school closed. The tireless Moholy-Nagy did not quit. Using $2,500 of his own money, he renamed the school the "School of Design" and reopened in February 1939, above the Chez Paree Nightclub at 247 East Ontario Street.

For years the school lived a hand-to-mouth existence. Moholy-Nagy, who brought lunch to school every day, paid his instructors low wages and found University of Chicago professors to teach non-art courses on a part-time basis. He contributed his own money earned as a design consultant and solicited money from benefactors. The school was kept alive by Walter Paepcke, who had founded the Container Corporation of America. Paepcke was the only member of the Association of Arts and Industries who kept his faith in Moholy-Nagy.

With a shock of white in his dark slick-backed hair and a riveting stare from sleepy eyes, Moholy-Nagy electrified his students with what one student termed "galactic energy." He was an idealist who believed that all people had the need and the ability to create. But he was also a dogmatic, cocksure tyrant who chided students during the early years not to waste school money by using toilet paper to line toilet seats and who declared to meal companions "the whiter the bread, the faster you're dead."

One either loved Moholy-Nagy or left him.

The years following World War II were golden ones for the school. The GI Bill of Rights helped boost enrollment during the fall 1945 semester. Enrollment rose from a handful of students to hundreds. The school moved to larger quarters and changed its name in 1944 to the "Institute of Design." The following year the school moved again, this time to accommodate 680 students. The students, mostly former GIs, showed exceptional motivation, as had their former Bauhaus counterparts in Germany. Some arrived at 9 in the morning, stayed through the day and evening, and hid beneath tables at midnight so the guards would not send them home.

Moholy-Nagy was at the apex of his career as a painter, photographer, and educator when he died of leukemia in November 1946. His six-paragraph obituary—by its brevity and placement in the *Chicago Daily Tribune* on page 34 next to a Brenda Starr cartoon—proved that he was never well known in the city. But in the art world, Moholy-Nagy was a giant.

The school he founded, like its German predecessor, had become a magnet for artists and a center for modern design. In 1946 Alexander Archipenko, the "father of cubism," came to teach sculpture and drawing. R. Buckminster Fuller worked as an artist in residence from 1948 to 1950. The list of visitors to the school from 1937 to 1948 reads like a directory of the most innovative and productive artists and architects of the day. It includes Alvar Aalto, Berenice Abbott, Siegfried Giedion, S. I. Hayakawa, Henry-Russell Hitchcock, Katherine Kuh, Richard Neutra, Man Ray, Paul Strand, Ray E. Stryker, Jose Luis Sert, and Gropius himself. When artists arrived, classes were dismissed and students congregated in the auditorium to discuss and argue about work. Few students understood the French painter Fernand Léger, who spoke only in his native language, but decades later they still remembered his forcefulness.

By the time Nickel took his first class at the Institute of Design, the school was under the control of Serge Chermayeff, a Russian-born artist whom Gropius had chosen to take over after Moholy-Nagy's death. Unlike Moholy-Nagy, Chermayeff was more interested in the result of what was being produced by students than in the process. Moholy-Nagy would see a smudged drawing, stop and say "Look at the power!" Chermayeff was attracted only to clean final products that could be published or hung on a wall. In his four years at the institute, Chermayeff shifted the school's emphasis from producing students to producing objects. In 1949 he merged the school with the Illinois Institute of Technology, changing the character of the Institute of Design from that of an experimental art school to that of a mainstream accredited college.

Moholy-Nagy's influence was still very much in evidence, however, when Nickel arrived at the school in 1948. Richard had never heard of Moholy-Nagy. Fresh out of the army, Richard had applied to the Institute of Design to study photography because it was in Chicago and because it was free under the GI Bill of Rights. Richard, who had become a "camera bug" during his tour of duty, entertained thoughts of working as a commercial photographer in civilian life.

Richard attended the Institute of Design for three consecutive semesters, starting in the fall of 1948. These semesters constituted a grand foundation course. As at the Bauhaus, students worked with all of the elements that led to creativity. They investigated lines, for example, by drawing to music, changing the weight applied to strokes and quickening the speed of their work. The courses were a mental enema; they flushed you out and let you start with a clean slate.

The first year was directed toward breaking down a student's "sterile hoard of textbook information," Moholy-Nagy wrote. "Man—when faced with all the material and spiritual problems of life—can, if he works from his biological center, take his position with instinctive sureness. Then he is in no danger of intimidation by industry, the haste of an often misunderstood 'machine culture,' or by past philosophies about his creative ways."

Moholy-Nagy taught his students that they must first break apart the components of the visual world—the two-dimensional elements of point, line, texture, value, and color, as well as the three-dimensional element of volume—just as atomic scientists were breaking apart the atom. Moholy-Nagy was searching for *Gestaltung,* the primal significance of elements. His goal was to show students how to put the pieces together again so they would develop an unshakable instinct. He was teaching spontaneity.

At most schools, if a student said, "I'm going to paint an orange cow," the teacher would respond, "but cows aren't orange."

At the Institute of Design, a teacher would say: "Why not?"

Moholy-Nagy's ideas about "a new vision" were heady stuff. Nickel entered college as a naive and unsophisticated middle-class kid. He left years later on a scholarly, artistic pursuit that would define the rest of his life.

Several months after starting at the Institute of Design, Richard met and began dating 16-year-old Adrienne Dembo, described in the lingo of the day as a "shapely, fun-loving, classy gal" who dressed in style. They met in 1949 at the Kraft Bowl on the city's Northwest Side, where Adrienne maintained a 69 average on a team with Nickel's friends. Nickel came to watch. He took up with her fast, and within several months they discussed marriage.

Adrienne was a sheltered only child who loved to dance and go to parties. Her father, a lawyer, saw Richard as a man with little potential. Both her parents thought she was too young to get married. Stanley and Agnes knew little about Adrienne or the relationship, but they objected, too. She was the first woman Richard had ever dated seriously. Above all the objections, Richard and Adrienne were married on June 10, 1950, in Adrienne's parish at St. Wenceslaus Church on the city's Northwest Side.

The reception at the Evanston Hotel was the fanciest ever seen by most of the 75-or-so Nickel friends and relatives who came. Years later they still talked about the ice sculpture and swans. Lewis Bugna, a boyhood friend, remembers standing around a sunken garden in the hotel waiting to see if a drunk would fall into the fish pond. "This is a high-class Polish wedding," Bugna's mother told him. "There won't be any drunks." She was right.

Two weeks after the wedding, on June 25, 1950, North Korean soldiers crossed the 38th parallel into South Korea, forcing the South Korean government to declare war against its neighbor. The United Nations voted immediately to help South Korea repel the aggression, and by the end of the month President Truman had authorized the use of U.S. combat forces in Korea.

When the first GIs landed at Pusan on the South Korean coast in early July, the army had a force of 184,000 active reserves and 416,000 inactive or volunteer reserves in the United States. About 82,000 active reserves were sent to help General Douglas MacArthur during the first months of fighting. On June 30, 1950, Congress gave the president authority to order inactive reservists and national guardsmen into active service for 21 months. The army decided to call the reservists, such as Nickel, into combat first.

Richard was called back into active service as a private a few weeks after the war began. He and Adrienne, upon their return from a Florida honeymoon, were at a party to look at wedding photos with family and friends when Richard was handed his notice. At first he thought the slip was a practical joke. Nickel never considered the possibility of a recall. He had little choice but to report for duty.

To Richard's dismay, Adrienne's father tried to prevent him from being called back. "What an ugly and embarrassing bunch of things we did to keep me out of recall to military service," Nickel wrote. "The army was my salvation at that point."

By the time Richard reentered the army, it seemed that a quick victory was at hand. MacArthur had made his assault on Inchon off the Sea of Japan, retaken

Nickel and his wife,
Adrienne, around 1952.
During those years he
always wore the Rollei
around his neck.

Seoul, and formally handed the country back to the South Korean government. Then, in early October, MacArthur's troops crossed the 38th parallel in an attempt to unify the country. Nobody realized that MacArthur's move would bring China into the war and touch off a battle of superpowers. In late October Chinese troops crossed the Yalu River into Korea, leading to nearly two more years of war.

As he left for the war, Nickel promised Adrienne he would not volunteer for the paratroops. He reported to Fort Riley, Kansas, on October 21, 1950. On his arrival in Korea in early 1951, Nickel was assigned to work as a photographer for the Headquarters and Service Company of the 434th Engineering Construction Battalion because of his college training. The job of the battalion was to reconstruct, improve, and maintain the severely damaged railroad and highway main supply routes supporting U.S. and U.N. units on the front. Nickel's company repaired railroad bridges at Andong, Tanyang, and Wonju; reconstructed the damaged Kyonggyong railroad line for the Eighth Army; built a highway from Ulsan to Wonju as a main supply line for X Corps; and built a road through a mountain to a tungsten mine. In 1952 the battalion was cited for its "meritorious conduct" in support of combat operations.

Korea was a mix of hills, mountains, and valleys. Most of the Korea Nickel saw was filthy and devastated because MacArthur leveled everything in front of him in a desperate effort to win. It was cold, especially for a battalion issued only summer uniforms and sleeping bags. Troops piled dirt around the bottom of their tents to keep in warmth.

As he would do later with buildings, Richard photographed bridges and projects as they were built so that the army would have a record of work done if they had to be destroyed by explosives before falling into enemy hands. "Generally, the work was not dangerous," he wrote. Except for a few industrial accidents, there were few casualties in the battalion, even though the line companies worked only a few miles behind the front line.

But it was strange work. The North Koreans seemed to want the bridges built as much as the South Koreans. Sometimes North Korean army units would pass right by the battalion without firing. Richard told his friends back home that he and the company did not stop working even if they spotted North Korean planes overhead. They would just wave and be mistaken as North Koreans. Only once did Richard fear for his life. A Jeep he was driving broke down in enemy-infested territory 10 miles from camp. "This is it," Nickel thought. "They're going to pick me off. . .I'll never see tomorrow." He hid, waiting until nightfall, and made the trek back to camp without incident.

Nickel did manage to make friends with Lee Sangyun, a South Korean man whom he lived with for two weeks in Andong. "I never forgot your gentlemanship and honourable character which imprinted on my mind," Lee wrote Nickel in 1954. After the war, Nickel sent books, soap, food, and clothes several times to Lee and his young family in Uisong. When the 1955 package arrived, Lee wrote, "Feb. 10 will remain forever in our minds as the happiest day for us." And in 1956 Lee wrote, "We should never forget you and your kindness. We are sure never to forget you while we are on earth."

Nickel as a young military photographer in Korea during the early 1950s.

The pictures Nickel kept on his return show an attempt to record the experience. He photographed training at Fort Riley, boarding the troop train, leaving San Francisco as small gulls followed the boat, a last look at the Golden Gate Bridge, the gulls turning back, and disembarkation at Matsuhima, Japan. In Korea he photographed towns such as Pusan and Uisong, railway bridges and highways, work on the Tungsten Mine Road, rice paddies, and a celebration at the opening of the Naesong Bridge. A photo of a huge girder being put into place on the Tanyang Railroad Bridge was his first published work, appearing in the February 1952 issue of *Civil Engineering News*.

On June 8, 1951, Richard sent a telegram from Yokohama to his wife saying, "Best wishes and love on our first anniversary Adrienne." He was released on September 21 at Camp Carson, Colorado, with the rank of corporal technician. He was greeted there by Adrienne and Donald, who had driven her out in Richard's car. Donald returned by train so that Richard could take Adrienne on a tour of the West before their return to Chicago.

To Adrienne, Richard came back a different person. He was no longer interested in her or in having a family. He woke up frequently in the midst of a recurring nightmare that he was still in Korea. Adrienne's mother called Richard a "casualty of war." Decades later she could not explain exactly how he was different, but an undeniable rift had developed between Richard and Adrienne soon after his return. Richard and Adrienne moved out of Adrienne's parents' home and rented an apartment nearby on the Northwest Side. Richard took two part-time jobs, selling cameras and doing layout work at a printer, and spent long hours in the darkroom after he resumed classes at the Institute of Design.

Unable to decide whether to continue with photography or take up architecture, Richard was moody, quiet, and difficult to live with. All Richard wanted to do was study. Under Moholy-Nagy's spell, Richard muttered about the phoniness of a palm tree in a neighborhood restaurant or about the poor design of a drinking fountain. But mostly he kept to himself. To get a reaction, Adrienne laughed at her husband's kooky complaints; but this only made Richard angrier.

By 1952 their marriage had developed a pattern: she would walk out on him and return to her parents, and he would walk out on her and return to his. They tried to reconcile by talking to a counselor in the archdiocese chancellery office, but found little help. On March 16, 1953, Adrienne received a letter from the archdiocese's Metropolitan Tribunal court stating she could file suit in civil courts for separate maintenance, but not for divorce. "If a divorce is obtained, the guilty party will deprive himself, automatically, of the Sacraments," wrote the Rev. John P. Stankevicius. "This decision is binding in conscience and we expect you to abide by it." Also typed was the warning, "No company-keeping." Nickel was bitter about the archdiocese's ruling. He never attended church regularly again.

A civil divorce hearing was held in June 1953. Richard did not dispute or fight Adrienne's decision to end the marriage. "I was a naive infant, anxious to get out of the mess," he wrote. The divorce decree was signed three days later. It found Richard guilty of "extreme and repeated cruelty" toward Adrienne, who reassumed her maiden name when the marriage was dissolved. Years later, Richard wrote:

> *I'd like not to remember the circumstances but I have to admit there is a small degree of truth in the record. But no basis for the phrase "extreme and repeated cruelty." True, I did sock her once but in circumstances where even today in maturity I might do likewise. It was mainly a case of both of us being immature and petty. But finally after two years (one of these I was in Korea) it was quite hopeless, and although I preferred a separation she wanted the divorce. I was so fed up, I agreed to anything reasonable in order to avoid going to court and arguing about it. I remember questioning "abeyance" and she said it meant "nothing." And I was subsequently induced to pay for the divorce. Had to make a loan to do it.*

Adrienne had little idea why the marriage failed. "Richard was a very private person," she said. "He never talked to me about what was on his mind. I think we just grew apart, had different ideas. I don't think he wanted to be married when he came back."

The divorce cleaned Richard out. He told Adrienne she could keep their joint belongings, then he took out a bank loan to pay the $400 fee for the divorce lawyer. Ashamed, Richard did not tell his parents. When Agnes came to visit him weeks after the divorce, she was horrified to see Adrienne's name no longer on the mailbox. "What are you going to do?" Agnes asked him. He shrugged. Agnes asked Richard to come back and live with Stanley and her in their Park Ridge home. She promised they would keep quiet while he studied.

Richard seldom talked about his marriage. Once in a while he dropped pithy statements to his friends like, "She cared about the poodle more than she cared about me," or, "She ran home to Papa too many times." But he was never willing to go into detail. In fact, many of his friends in later life never knew he had been married. Richard gave off the aura of a saint, and a failed marriage might have tarnished the image.

Richard took the blame for the breakup and felt guilty for "ruining" Adrienne's life. Adrienne went on to pursue a professional career in the airline industry. She saw Richard every several years by happenstance.

The divorce freed Richard. "Yeah, happiness, shmappiness," he wrote in 1967.

> *I get more pure happiness out of a change of weather, the color of a piece of wood, problem solving, freedom, music, etc. When married all I was doing was submitting my will to all kinds of trivia. Life truly began when I got divorced. I've learned to thank God since then. . . .I like to think anyone else but I couldn't bear to live with somebody day after day messing up my work and papers and pussy footing around disturbing the music.*

Richard set up his bedroom upstairs in Stanley and Agnes's one-story home at 1508 Grove Avenue and set up his darkroom in the basement. Finally, there were no more diversions. He was ready to begin his life anew.

Stanley and Agnes Nickel at their house under construction at 1508 Grove in suburban Park Ridge. The photograph was taken during the late 1940s.

Aaron Siskind photographs
Adler and Sullivan's 1882
Max M. Rothschild Flats on
Chicago's South Side
during the early 1950s.
Siskind was surrounded by
neighborhood children and
his students from the
Institute of Design.

CHAPTER THREE

YOU RESEMBLE THE SPIRIT YOU COMPREHEND.

Goethe in *Faust*

The first Louis Sullivan structure Richard Nickel photographed was the Jewelers' Building, a five-story commercial loft that still rises above the "El," or elevated railroad, on South Wabash Avenue in Chicago's Loop. Nickel probably used his new Linhof view camera to shoot the Jewelers' for a class assignment in 1952.

The building, designed in 1881, the first year of Sullivan's association with Dankmar Adler, is different from the other brick lofts that line Wabash Avenue. At first glance the naturalistic ornament on the front of the building seems typical of the period. But it was here that young Sullivan made one of his first breaks with the past, allowing the carved sandstone forms to reach out of their rigid architectural surroundings and move from panel to panel. Here was Sullivan, the design genius of the firm, hinting at a theme that was to consume much of his life. His goal was to take inorganic materials—pressed brick, stone, and cast iron—and bring them to life. He turned the Jewelers' Building into a blossoming flower, culminating in a bursting of detail above the top story.

Richard Nickel didn't notice, at least at first. "My results were miserable," he wrote in recollections typed in 1959.

> *I took some exteriors from atop a building across the street so that the Jewelers' converged the other way. I had no feel about architecture—knew nothing about Sullivan—in short was completely stupid. Part of the original difficulty was lack of equipment and direction. Even though we analyzed the results, it was a slow job getting a grip on the thing.*

Nickel's contact sheets show that he was not unduly modest. Instead of giving any sense of the original building, he focused on the simply picturesque. The art-glass windows, lobby details, and wreath ornament that captured his attention were not even designed by Adler and Sullivan, but were from a later remodeling.

Yet the Jewelers', with its top floors hidden from street view by the El tracks, did teach Nickel a lesson. He learned that there was grace and beauty hiding all about him.

By the time Nickel returned for his second stint at the Institute of Design as a sophomore in the spring of 1952, students there were already interested in the architecture of Adler and Sullivan. The previous semester, photography instructor Aaron Siskind had assigned the class to photograph the firm's majestic Auditorium Building on South Michigan Avenue. The building and its ornament, both inside and out, made for beautiful pictures. The students were so excited they asked to photograph more structures designed by the firm or by Sullivan after his breakup with Adler in 1895.

Siskind brought the student photographs to one of Nickel's first classes and suggested that the new students might want to learn about Sullivan and hunt down other Sullivan structures. Siskind knew that the project would be formidable because Sullivan, who had died in 1924, was something of a forgotten architect who had left few records behind.

Richard took careful notes. "Show voluminous details, structural details, decorative details," he wrote. After Siskind suggested the class consider a "definitive" study of Sullivan, Nickel looked up the definition.

"Adj.," he wrote. "Having the function of deciding or settling determination; conclusive, fixed, and final form."

Beneath the definition, he wrote: "Stock Xchange Building/30 N. LaSalle/Top of?? Wings??"

During his first years back at the Institute of Design, Nickel attended classes in a huge building at 632 North Dearborn Street that resembled a medieval church or fortress. The structure, built as the first home of the Chicago Historical Society, was less effective as a design school. The photography department was crowded and primitive. Students sat on wooden benches. Instead of using timers in the darkroom, students depended on buzzers that rang every minute or so, a haphazard technique that often resulted in ruined negatives.

On the other hand, the mood of the place—shaped by Siskind and head of the photography department Harry Callahan—was stimulating from the start. Siskind was a modernist, pushing the bounds of photography in the same manner that Sullivan had pushed the bounds of architecture. A short, round, outgoing man of informal dress and disheveled hair, Siskind noticed everything. Beneath a black cloth, looking into the ground glass of a view camera, Siskind would peer to the left and then to the right, cough on a cigarette, shift the camera and watched relations emerge and "assert themselves." Sometimes he walked down the street as if in a trance, examining the walls or the trees before setting up his equipment.

For Siskind, growing up poor in New York had been a rich experience. In class he often recounted his life in the streets, sneaking into grocery stores to steal potatoes and roasting them in alleys. He was far more than street smart. Siskind had great knowledge of music and literature. In 1926 at age 23, he began teaching English in the New York City public school system. Four years later he was given his first camera. His first photos were unsophisticated, but he had found a natural way to express himself.

Armed with a $29 fixed-lens camera, Siskind photographed the city, helping produce such projects as "Harlem Document," "Dead End: the Bowery," and "Portrait of a Tenement: St. Joseph's House," as a member of the New York Film and Photo League. He also made a detailed study of the architecture of Pennsylvania's Bucks County.

In the early 1940s, Siskind gave up documentary work. "Subject matter as such ceased to be of primary importance," he wrote. Siskind wanted to interpret rather than mirror what he saw. He mostly photographed the rubble—peeling paint, cracked plaster, broken windows, sidewalk pavement, a work glove—discarded fragments that gave him a chance to create abstract forms. Siskind was not interested in scale or perspective. He wanted to capture form and force on film. "There was in me the desire to see the world clean and fresh and alive as primitive things are clean and fresh and alive," he wrote. Art critic Walter Chappel called the subject of his work "Siskind's hieroglyphics," forgotten markings that tell about life.

Like Franz Kline, Willem de Kooning, and other New York City abstract expressionist painters whom Siskind spent time with during the late 1940s, the photographer was delving into a new vision. "When I make a photograph I want it to be an altogether new object, complete and self-contained, whose basic condition is order," he wrote.

Siskind's first one-man show was held in New York City in 1947. Two years later he quit his public school job to begin work as a freelance photographer and photo instructor. In the summer of 1951, Callahan offered him a job at the Institute of Design.

Callahan, an extreme introvert, saw the camera as a way to break out of his shell and learn about the world. Unlike Siskind, Callahan was not interested in exploring abstract structure. He did not pack hidden ideas into his work, and was amused when critics later read meaning into his photographs. Instead, Callahan took simple pictures—of his wife and young daughter, of nature, of people lost in thought on city streets. Photography was a great adventure that moved him all of his adult life. "It's the subject that counts," he wrote. "I'm interested in revealing the subject in new ways to intensify it." With intuition as his guide, Callahan's lens captured powerful reflections of everyday scenes.

It was photographer Arthur Siegel, Callahan's friend in Detroit, who convinced him to apply for a job at Moholy-Nagy's Institute of Design in the summer of 1946. Callahan was an unlikely candidate. He had never finished high school, and his only professional experience was working as a technician in a General Motors photo lab. Moholy-Nagy told Callahan over the telephone there were no job openings, but he agreed to critique Callahan's work.

"That son of a bitch," Callahan said to himself as he approached Moholy-Nagy's summer home in downstate Illinois. "If he says one thing against my photographs, I'll tell him off."

Callahan never had the chance. Moholy-Nagy said he had seldom been so moved by anyone's work, and he offered Callahan a job on the spot.

Siskind and Callahan complemented each other. Siskind, who got involved with his students, could get all but the most worthless undergraduates to work.

Callahan met with students by appointment and only at school. He let few people get close to him. Siskind, who became Callahan's guardian, promoter, and stabilizer, was an exception.

They were both strong role models. Art came first in their lives. Siskind drove a third-hand Studebaker and gave his photographs away to anyone who helped him. Likewise, Callahan spent little on himself. His sofa was made out of worn cushions placed atop an old door and his end tables were boxes.

Nickel attended the Institute of Design for five straight semesters, earning his bachelor's degree in the spring of 1954. He started the photography sequence by making "photograms," pictures without a camera. This, he learned, was the same way Moholy-Nagy had begun. The shadow images Nickel made by placing objects between light and photo-sensitive paper taught him about exposure, development, fixing, washing, and drying. Then he learned about focus, texture, and tone by photographing crumpled and torn paper. These early assignments, wrote Siskind and Callahan, were intended to demonstrate "the infinite detail the medium can produce, and the effect of light."

During their two years in the photography sequence, Nickel and his classmates studied reflection, distortion, and correction. They learned to compensate for the loss of light due to bellows extension. And they learned the effect of changing viewpoints, shutter speeds, and depth-of-field. "It is intended that these become means for expressive ends, not just so many technical gimmicks," the teachers wrote.

The final year was devoted to a historical study of the masters of art and photography. To earn a degree, students were required to complete a research project constituting "a true testing ground of the young photographer's knowledge and spirit." Nickel later wrote of the experience:

> My own education began late in college under the influence of certain teachers who literally pushed me out into the world with problems to solve: library utilization, architecture and art history projects—all involving observation, research, interviewing, correspondence, travelling, etc. This method produced self-education and self-responsibility. A student who has to ask a teacher what area of study he has to "work on" for a graduate degree, who doesn't know what needs to be done or is not impassioned with something, simply shouldn't bother.

Callahan gave no formal assignments. Perhaps because of his shyness, he worded exercises in a minimal manner. Early in the program, for example, he told the class to photograph "people without people"—that was all. Like Moholy-Nagy, Callahan loved to experiment. He was preparing his students to photograph people, but first wanted them to understand the power of a camera. Students left wondering what Callahan meant, which was exactly what the teacher intended.

In 1953 Callahan assigned "the focus problem" to Nickel and his class. After thinking for two days, Richard photographed moving cars in and out of focus. Soon, however, he realized that this was not what Callahan wanted.

"I came to the conclusion that the most *absolute[ly]* significant thing was people, and so decided on close-ups with background out of focus," Richard wrote. First he spent a Saturday afternoon shooting well-dressed women at the entrance to Marshall Field's, the fashionable department store. He tried to focus on their "masks"—furs, jewelry, makeup, hats—but most of the pictures were slightly out of focus. He pressed on days later, photographing moviegoers leaving the State-Lake Theater after "The Robe." With the marquee lights out of focus, he focused on faces. "In a sense, I believe, I was unconsciously trying to know people, to find something strong and universal about them," Richard wrote. He was "very pleased with the results."

Teachers remembered Nickel's enthusiasm. Richard, who most often wore a white T-shirt and army pants to school, carried out his assignments with "intelligence, precision, and some imagination," Siskind said. "His life seemed to be under fine control. This was what he was doing and he didn't seem to want to do anything else."

Callahan remembered that Richard was very aware of form and structure right from the start. To his classmates, Richard seemed straight, distant, and preoccupied. One friend, Mary Ann Lea, recalled how Nickel's photo of a dried brown leaf on floral wallpaper surprised her. "I just didn't think he had that kind of feeling inside of him," she said.

But it is by the Sullivan work that most of Nickel's classmates remember him. "At the start, I didn't have the proper equipment and had never given architecture a serious thought, and had never heard of Sullivan," Nickel wrote. "It proved to be an education." Years later, several former students half-jokingly wondered aloud if Richard had ever done any other work in college.

Nickel and his classmates soon decided to form a production company to photograph Sullivan buildings. To Siskind, an admirer of the documentary tradition of the 1930s, single photographs were not as significant as a series. "The first buildings we photographed were exciting and beautiful," said Richard's classmate, Len Gittleman. "We both wanted to dig more. Richard never wanted to stop."

The students were attracted to the architecture because Sullivan's ideas paralleled the philosophy of the school, Nickel wrote. Sullivan, like Moholy-Nagy, believed that mankind has a godlike power to create. "This idea of power extends from Sullivan's childhood to his death, and although we have his writings in evidence, we feel it is most clearly exemplified by his buildings," Nickel wrote.

Soon the class developed an "aesthetic," or artistic method, of photographing the buildings. The students decided to take only straight, factual, clear photographs of the architecture and ornament. Their goal was to describe the buildings as objectively as possible.

For each building they found, the class took a minimum of four shots: one general view, one environmental view showing the building and its surrounding, one detail shot of the building's exterior, and one interior view. "After that," Siskind told the class, "I suppose the best thing is to try to illustrate the essence of the individual buildings in any way you like."

Many of the buildings—such as the Auditorium and the Carson Pirie Scott store in the Loop—demanded days of work. "Photographing these buildings requires a genuine dedication to duty in the sense that the buildings are not so easily recorded," Nickel wrote. "Very often a student will figuratively shoot a building to death and accomplish nothing. Many times the use of offices in adjoining buildings is necessary and this is characterized by the fearful, questioning secretary who has never heard of Louis Sullivan and is not particularly concerned with assisting."

At first, the students did not have the right equipment, but they raised money by selling the first photographs in order to buy a view camera as well as wide-angle and telephoto lenses. The project expanded quickly, and Nickel, Siskind, and Gittleman began taking two- or three-day trips around the Midwest photographing Sullivan buildings. Siskind and Gittleman usually photographed the "arty" details while Richard took overall views showing the buildings in their surroundings. His goal was to record all that was there.

Siskind said he made Richard the leader of the Sullivan project because Nickel was the most committed. Nickel modestly suspected that he was given the project because he was the only one with draft-exempt status. Either way, Nickel's classmates moved on to other assignments while Richard was left to finish.

Nickel organized the result of the class's work in a 1954 photo exhibit of 75 of the 114 Sullivan buildings known to be standing. The exhibit showed Sullivan's work throughout Chicago as well as St. Louis, Missouri; Grinnell, Cedar Rapids, and Clinton, Iowa; Owatonna, Minnesota; Ocean Springs, Mississippi; and New York City and Buffalo, New York.

At the exhibit opening, Hugh Duncan, an Institute of Design teacher, called for a comprehensive program to photograph Chicago's great buildings before they were demolished or altered. "I think it bad taste on our part to attack businessmen for not saving art," Duncan said. "If we are so concerned about these masterpieces, we should use our energy to see them photographed, described, and analyzed so that future students can benefit from the documentation of a great tradition."

Today, Duncan's plea for a sort of historical preservation sounds meek. At the time, it gave Nickel a sense of purpose.

On a television program promoting the exhibit, Nickel discussed the need for documenting Sullivan's work.

> We believe our project to be a most necessary and timely task. We have already lost the Walker Warehouse to the Congress Street highway and can only speculate which will be next. In effect, we feel that the history of architecture and the force which Louis Sullivan had on that architecture will not be completely realized until our self-assigned work is completed.

Like many stories of modern Chicago, the tale of Richard Nickel has its origins in the flames of the Great Chicago Fire. In two days the fire of 1871 leveled 17,450 buildings in the city's central business district and surrounding neighborhoods and left 100,000 Chicagoans homeless. Fed by wooden cottages and swift prairie wind, the blaze that started at Patrick O'Leary's West Side barn in the early morning of October 7 spared few buildings in its fury. It put an abrupt end to Chicago's frontier past.

Only 76 years earlier the sandy plain at the southwestern tip of Lake Michigan had come under federal control. That control proved to be on paper only, for in 1812 Indians attacked and burned the government's outpost, Fort Dearborn, and once again took over the swamp they called Chicago, meaning "wild onion."

In the early 1820s, when New York was already an established metropolis, Chicago was still called a "mud ball" by pioneers, most of whom were just passing through. In 1830 "Chicago" was still a term used for the great prairie that extended westward from the lake. The city was platted and surveyed that year and became the seat of Cook County in 1831. The city's first bridge was built the following year, as was the Illinois and Michigan Canal. Chicago's first real estate boom ensued, then fell prey to the 1837 Panic and the depression that followed. It was also in 1837 that Chicago was incorporated as a city. Its idealistic founders adopted the motto *Urbs in Horto,* City in a Garden.

By the late 1840s, the railroad had finally put Chicago on the map. The city became the gateway to the West, and with swift transportation came factories. By mid-century Chicago had become "a brutal network of industrial necessities," in the words of historian Lewis Mumford. Factories meant profits, and by the 1870s speculators were again advising about boom-town Chicago: "Buy by the acre—sell by the foot."

The crippling 1871 fire brought both destruction and opportunity. What had been a frontier town was eventually rebuilt on a grand scale. The once-in-a-lifetime chance to build a great city attracted both established architects and engineers— including William LeBaron Jenney, Frederick Baumann, and Peter B. Wight—as well as young newcomers like Daniel Burnham, John Wellborn Root, and Martin Roche.

Nothing could stop the rebirth of Chicago, not even the Panic of 1873. "Big Crude Chicago!—destined to become the most beautiful American City!" wrote Frank Lloyd Wright. Within six weeks of the fire, construction began on more than 300 buildings. By the World's Columbian Exposition in 1893, Chicago had more than quadrupled its pre-fire population and size to become the nation's second largest city. Germans, Swedes, Irish, Poles, Bohemians, Lithuanians, Italians, Jews, and African Americans all migrated to Chicago. Their hard work made Chicago a physical town of slaughter and packing, of steel making and manufacturing—and of new, staggeringly tall buildings called skyscrapers.

The designers of the new Chicago had an opportunity to be innovative. Working with a palette of new technologies and materials such as metal framing, the elevator, electric light, and the telephone, many of Chicago's architects rejected the popular revival styles of the day. The straightforward structures were frequently referred to as the "Chicago Commercial Style" or the "Chicago School." But it was the graceful skyscraper that won the city worldwide attention. Before the turn of the century, Chicago had several buildings that laid claim to being the world's tallest. By 1891 James Maitland's *American Slang Dictionary* defined *skyscraper* as "a very tall building such as now being built in Chicago."

The most important early leader of the Chicago architects was Jenney, a confident former Union Army bridge builder who had come to the city in 1867 at the age of 35. "We are building to a height to rival the Tower of Babel," he said in

1883. Within a year Jenney had devised a system for hanging the exterior walls of the nine-story Home Insurance Building on an internal frame of iron and steel. From then on, the sky, it seemed, was indeed the limit.

It was to Jenney's office that Louis Sullivan came in 1873. Although he arrived with little professional experience, the 17-year-old Sullivan was filled with youthful experiences that would define his talented and tormented adult life. "Remember the seed germ," wrote Sullivan, explaining it is the seed germ, not the leaves, that determines how a plant will grow. "The germ is the real thing; the seat of identity," he wrote. The message of Sullivan's *Autobiography of an Idea* is that the seeds planted early in his life propelled him—and bound him—forever.

Henry Louis Sullivan, who later switched his first and middle names, was born on September 3, 1856, in Boston. His father, Patrick, had emigrated from Ireland in 1847 and opened a music and dance academy upon his arrival in Boston. His mother, Andrienne List, had emigrated to Boston from Geneva, Switzerland, in 1850. The couple married two years later and had their first child, Albert, in 1854.

Louis spent his childhood summers on the small farm of his grandparents, Henri and Anna List, in South Reading, Massachusetts. As he watched and began to understand the natural world, he felt as if he were taking possession of what was around him: first flowers, then grass, trees, orchards, cows, oxen, birds, rain, sunshine, the sky, and the clouds. "Was there to be no end to the sweet, clamorous joy of all living things?" he wondered.

Sullivan would later cite nature's influence in his architecture. He called his buildings "organic" because they were built along the same lines as the living forms he so loved. Sullivan wanted to create grace and beauty just as he saw it in the natural world. "Bring it alive, man! Make it live!" he would implore his draftsmen. He wrote:

> To vitalize building materials, to animate them collectively with a thought, a state of feeling, to charge them with a subjective significance and value, to make them a visible part of the genuine social fabric, to infuse into them the true life of the people, to impart to them the best that is in the people—such is the real function of the architect.

In nature Sullivan also found a rule to direct his architecture. His famous, albeit misunderstood, dictum "form follows function" was not a functionalist's call, for Sullivan was far too elegant to be considered a simple pragmatist. Sullivan was saying that architecture was the expressive sense of its reason. "Every problem contains and suggests its own solution," he wrote. "Don't waste time looking anywhere else for it." His point was an outgrowth of his observations. "Speaking generally, outward appearances resemble inner purposes," he wrote. The long, strong legs of a horse, for instance, permit it to run fast and far. Likewise, the shape and image of a good building should reflect its purpose. "This is the law," he said.

As much as the young Sullivan was stimulated by the bucolic farm setting, however, he was enthralled by the bustling city, with its trains, bridges, and shipyards. Thus inspired both by nature and by the capacity of people to create, Sullivan began a "natal dream of power."

Louis Sullivan in Ocean Springs, Mississippi, around 1900. He built a cottage there so that he could return to nature during his vacations away from Chicago. The photographer is unknown.

To achieve that dream, he became a self-described "mental athlete" at Boston's English High School and later at the Massachusetts Institute of Technology, where he learned the classic orders of design. Dissatisfied with the architecture school, Sullivan left MIT in 1872 and took his first job as an apprentice in the office of Furness and Hewitt in Philadelphia. There he received his first hands-on experience and learned the importance of color and ornament to building design. When the Panic of 1873 put an end to his job, he joined his parents in Chicago, where they had moved several years before.

Chicago awed the young man. Characteristically referring to himself in the third person, he wrote: "Louis tramped the platform, stopped, looked toward the city, ruins around him; looked at the sky; and as one alone, stamped his foot, raised his hand and cried in full voice: THIS IS THE PLACE FOR ME!"

Sullivan was particularly moved by the will of the city's leaders to rebuild. And he was oddly affected by pre-fire Chicago, a city he had never seen, but one that vividly existed in legendary perfection in his mind.

Sullivan soon found work at Jenney's architectural firm, where he stayed for about a year. Not satisfied that he knew enough to break out on his own, Sullivan set sail for the fountainhead of architectural training, the Ecole des Beaux-Arts in Paris. While the program eventually proved too rigid for *Monsieur* Louis Henri, it did increase his knowledge of proportion, detailing, classical arrangement, and the importance of a quick sketch.

Sullivan also sent back frescoes he designed on a free-lance basis for his friend John Edelmann, a Chicago architect who was working on the new Moody Tabernacle north of the Loop. The bright colors and originality of the frescoes caught the attention of newspaper architecture critics—and the ire of the

Bible-thumping followers of the building's sponsor, evangelist Dwight L. Moody. Finally, Moody himself had to calm his congregation by declaring, "The artist has done his job well." Sullivan had made his mark.

Perhaps the most important lesson Sullivan learned overseas was in Rome. He traveled there in April 1875 to see if Michelangelo's Sistine Chapel paintings had been created *en momentum*—in one creative stroke, without planning—as was the claim of Sullivan's Ecole professor. Sullivan spent two days studying the ceiling in the chapel.

He left empowered. "Here was power as he had seen it in the mountains," Sullivan wrote, again in the third person. "Here was power as he had seen it in the prairies, in the open sky, in the great lake stretching like a floor toward the horizon; here was the power of the forest primeval."

The ceiling of the Sistine Chapel convinced Sullivan that artists—if they depended on knowledge, instinct, imagination, and uncompromising faith—could create timeless work. Mankind's creative ability, he determined, is an extension of nature. "This steadfast belief in the power of man was an unalloyed childhood instinct, an intuition and a childhood faith which never for a day forsook him, but grew stronger, like an indwelling daemon." Remember the seed germ, Sullivan wrote. The seat of all power is the mind.

Upon his return to Chicago in 1875, Sullivan took short-term jobs with many of the city's major architects and soon developed a reputation as "that Irish-man with ideas." In the spring of 1880, Sullivan was hired by Dankmar Adler as a "draughtsman/designer" for the firm known as "Dankmar Adler, Architect." In May 1882 Sullivan was given partial partnership and the firm name was changed to "D. Adler & Company." Finally, in May 1883 Sullivan was given full partnership and the name was changed to "Adler & Sullivan."

They were a perfect team. Sullivan described the short, bearded, 34-year-old Adler as "built like a Byzantine church." Frank Lloyd Wright, who got his start working for the firm, wrote that "Dankmar Adler was a solid block of manhood, inspiring the confidence of everyone, a terror to any recalcitrant or shifty contractor." Adler, known as "the Big Chief," had been a partner in one of the city's leading architecture firms following the fire. He was an excellent businessman and engineer, but always needed design help. Adler gave Sullivan clients, courage, and an engineering cunning that made his ideas work. As Sullivan later wrote of the relationship, Adler was the "sturdy wheel-horse of a tandem team of which Louis did the prancing."

Together Adler and Sullivan produced nearly 120 buildings in 14 years. For a time, the relationship brought them wealth and fame, and gave Sullivan an opportunity to try out his ideas.

Architecture was not truly a creative art when the firm was formed. As Moholy-Nagy had complained on his arrival in Chicago, classical architecture still had a strong grip on Western civilization. Building owners, especially in the United States, demanded that their structures look "cultured," with classical facades. So architects resorted to stylebooks—guides crammed with architectural elements such as columns and pedestals—to produce new structures.

"We have Tudor for colleges and residences; Roman for banks, and railway stations and libraries—or Greek if you like—some customers prefer the Ionic to the Doric," sneered Sullivan about the architecture of his age. "We have French, English and Italian Gothic, Classic and Renaissance for churches. In fact we are prepared to satisfy, in any manner of taste. Residences we offer in Italian or Louis Quinze. We make a small charge for alterations and adaptations."

Sullivan's desire to embrace the new was radical. He used his creative power on the very first homes he designed with Adler on the city's South Side. Sullivan rejected the old forms and began designing buildings "out of his head," responding to time, materials, and place.

That made him suspect right from the start. The architecture critic from the *Chicago Inter-Ocean* wrote on August 12, 1882, that "Mr. Sullivan is a pleasant gentleman, but somewhat troubled with large ideas tending to metaphysics." The critic found Sullivan's originality troublesome. Unable to categorize the spectacular renovation of Hooley's Theater, the writer criticized the innovation rather than evaluating the work.

"I have no words to characterize what you see," Sullivan told the writer.

I have not given study to the nomenclature of the peculiar art forms developed in these boxes or carried out in that proscenium crown. These are unclassified forms, and stock terms will convey no adequate idea of the successful treatment under a formula that is a new phase in the art view of architecture. . . .I prefer that you speak of it as the successful solution of a problem. The vaguer you are in such matters the better I shall be pleased. It would be fatal to attempt anything like a discursive consideration of art in architecture in Chicago just now. People are not prepared for it.

In a newspaper interview following completion of his Kehilath Anshe Ma'ariv Synagogue on the South Side in 1891, Sullivan again resisted talk of style. "It is the 19th century school. That is all I can say for it," Sullivan told a *Tribune* reporter. "It has no historical style. It is the present. We have got to get away from schools in architecture. As long as we adhere to schools of anything there is no progress; nothing gained; no advancement."

In 1890 Sullivan gave form to Jenney's skyscraper. Although the 10-story Wainwright Building in St. Louis was far from the world's tallest building, the significance of its design loomed large in the myopic world of American architecture. Sullivan articulated and abstracted the edifice's skeletal frame with large windows and long brick piers extending from the two-story base of the building to the attic. "What is the chief characteristic of the tall office building?" Sullivan asked himself when he began work on the Wainwright.

It must be tall, every inch of it tall. The force and power of altitude must be in it, the glory and pride of exaltation must be in it. It must be every inch a proud and soaring thing, rising in sheer exultation that from the bottom to top it is a unit without a single dissenting line.

The design of the red-brick Wainwright was "sudden and volcanic," Sullivan wrote. According to architectural lore, he completed it in three minutes—*en momentum*. Frank Lloyd Wright called the skyscraper "a new thing beneath the sun." Nickel, who first saw the building in 1955, wrote: "If ever there was an original work of art, it is the Wainwright. I've seen Sullivan's other important works throughout the country, but the Wainwright is always overwhelming in its perfection."

Not all of the firm's buildings were this easy. The one that won Adler and Sullivan its international reputation was the Auditorium Building near Lake Michigan in downtown Chicago. Comprised of a 4,200-seat opera house enveloped by both an opulent 10-story hotel-office building and a 17-story office tower, the Auditorium took four grueling years to design and build. That it worked was "largely due to Adler's good judgment and restraining influence," wrote Wright, who joined the firm during the design years. But, he continued, "It was Louis Sullivan who made it sing."

When the Auditorium opened in 1889, tourists traveled to Chicago expecting to see it fall. Adler and Sullivan answered the skepticism by moving their office to the top of the tower.

All of Sullivan's buildings celebrated his ideals—that people had dignity, power, and freedom—as well as his ideas. Architecture is made up of the pier, the lintel, and the arch, he wrote. "The remedy to repetition is instinct and imagination."

Like all great builders, Sullivan wanted to create beauty. He used ornament—sculpture made out of terra cotta, cast iron, plaster and wood—to charge his buildings with meaning and impact. Buildings were much more than shelter to Sullivan. "A building which is truly a work of art (and I consider none other) is in its nature, essence and physical being an emotional expression," he wrote. "This being so, and I feel deeply that it is so, it must have, almost literally, a life."

Ornament, "like a sonorous melody overlaid with harmonious voices," helped Sullivan transform his piers, lintels, and arches into art. He most enjoyed using terra cotta, which he called "the primal plastic." A fired clay that could be easily molded and reproduced, terra cotta was durable, was much lighter than stone, and provided protection for the exterior. Wright wrote that Sullivan used it "to weave the stuff of his dreams."

Ornament was integral to Sullivan's work because it repeated the essence of his buildings in a powerful, poetic manner. Instead of looking "stuck on" to the exterior, Sullivan's ornament was "part of the surface," he wrote. It grew out of a building's soul and gave people a sense of what a building was all about. Like poetry, Sullivan's ornament could be appreciated on several levels. At a glance, it was lush and beautiful. Longer study revealed a reflection of a building's skeleton or the horizontal and vertical forces at work on a structure. And still deeper, Sullivan's ornament—his sculpted life forms molded from structural material—often returned to his favorite theme: the organic and inorganic. As with poetry, not everyone got the message. Those who did were deeply moved.

As Nickel delved into the Sullivan project, the young student sensed the impor-

tance of each Sullivan building. The buildings were more than just beautiful. Nickel realized that each contained an aspect of originality stemming from Sullivan's system of thought. Sullivan became a symbol through which Richard learned about the world. The essence of his education in design was based on the project to photograph Sullivan's architecture. Nickel realized he could not know everything, but he could know one thing well. Sullivan's buildings were worthy of his time, attention, and ultimately his life.

The Columbian Exposition, the world's fair held in Chicago in 1893, should have been a showcase for Adler and Sullivan. Instead, it unleashed forces that would defeat Sullivan's effort to create original architecture. The picturesque beauty of the "White City," much of whose architecture still resembled that of ancient Greece and Rome, delighted the crowds. Sullivan derided the fair as "naked exhibitionism of charlatanry." His colorful Transportation Building, one of the few original structures of the fair, was ignored by most critics.

"The damage wrought by the World's Fair will last for half a century from its date, if not longer," Sullivan wrote years later. "It has penetrated deep into the constitution of the American mind, effecting there lesions significant of dementia."

Two years after the fair, the firm of Adler and Sullivan dissolved. Adler left when he was offered a job as a designer for the Crane Elevator Company. When the job didn't work out, he tried to rejoin Sullivan, but was rebuffed. Adler died in 1900.

Sullivan's career also foundered. Arrogant and uncompromising with clients, he won only about 20 commissions in his last 30 years. He appeared to enjoy being a neglected renegade. "The Master," as Wright called Sullivan, was reduced to redesigning small factories, foundries, and cottages. Sullivan's office, which had once employed 50, was down to only one draftsman by 1906.

His career revived somewhat when Carl Bennett, vice president of the National Farmers' Bank in Owatonna, Minnesota, put him to work with instructions to design a new bank that was "simple, dignified, and beautiful."

Sullivan's 1906–08 National Farmers' Bank in Owatonna, Minnesota, photographed by Nickel in the mid-1950s.

The National Farmers' Bank was unlike any building ever built. Sixty-eight feet square and 49 high, it was a tall jewel box. The red sandstone exterior and huge arched windows protected the ethereal banking room, with its colorful murals and extravagant ornament. Most bank buildings reflect power and strength. The Owatonna bank reflects a peaceful heaven.

Word spread about the building and its architect, and Sullivan found himself in demand in Iowa, Wisconsin, Indiana, and Ohio. He would arrive in town, study a site for days, then sketch a building in minutes. Sad, lonely, and often drunk, Sullivan nonetheless managed to stay creative, designing radical buildings in conservative towns. His approach to architecture remained sober and serious.

His late buildings show little sadness. They are optimistic, majestic, bold swaths of masonry, stone, wood, and, of course, terra cotta. Shunned by the city,

Sullivan brought beauty and harmony to small towns. Sometimes he signed his name on buildings.

Sullivan was a model for Ayn Rand's hero Howard Roarke in *The Fountainhead,* a formerly renowned architect reduced to designing banks, homes, stores, and a church. Like Roarke, Sullivan refused to break because, as Roarke says in the book: "Every building is like a person. Single and unrepeatable."

Unlike Roarke, who made a successful comeback in New York City, Sullivan's life continued deteriorating. "As for me, the bottom has dropped out, and the future is bleak," Louis wrote in 1907. His eight-year marriage to Margaret Hattabaugh ended in 1909. A few days later, his valued draftsman, George Grant Elmslie, left him, too. Sullivan also became estranged from his brother, Albert, who had a successful career and family.

During the following few years, Sullivan lost his beloved cottage retreat in Ocean Springs, Mississippi, in a mortgage default. Ashamed, he wrote in his *Autobiography of an Idea* that the cottage was "wrecked by a wayward West Indian hurricane." He auctioned his library and household effects for $1,000.

"My crisis has, with varying fortunes, been steadily approaching during the past 17 years," Sullivan wrote in 1910. "I have all alone intuitively felt the cause lay in a flaw in my own character which I, alone, could not discover. So I had to pay the price." Later, he specified the flaw: "The simple, fundamental trouble that has caused all my unhappiness, bitterness, misery. . .is none other than my persistent lack of kindly feeling toward my fellow men." Sullivan was like his buildings, wrote biographer Larry Millet: "romantic and passionate on the outside but with an inner frame of cold steel."

During the final years of his life, the architect walked off jobs and lost commissions. By 1918—"that nightmare year," he called it—Sullivan was forced to leave the Auditorium tower for a second-floor office suite. "With the future bleak I am surely living in hell," he wrote to Wright. "To think I should come to this at 61."

After a struggle with depression and alcohol, Sullivan moved into a one-bedroom apartment and took a small office in a terra-cotta company. "If you have any money to spare, now is the urgent time to let me have some," Sullivan wrote Wright in 1920. "As I do not know how you are fixed, I cannot specify any sum; I can merely say that I am in a very serious situation: indeed it is now a sheer matter of food and shelter. So many of my friends are out of town on vacations that the situation has become very peculiar—I seem to have lost my way."

Sullivan's final jobs included designing the facade of a small store, a pedestal for a statue, and a platform for a potbellied stove. He also hung on to finish his autobiography, published in 1924.

Oskar Gross, who had painted murals for the Owatonna bank, told Nickel in 1959 about his encounter with Sullivan near the end of his life. "I saw him once—the big man—touching me for a quarter on Michigan Boulevard."

Sullivan died broke, sick, and lonely at age 67 on April 14, 1924. He was buried next to his parents in Graceland Cemetery on Chicago's North Side. Although his grave bore no headstone for five years, he died knowing he had made a mark on the world. He realized that his architecture—like the Sistine Chapel he had traveled to see decades before—was timeless.

"If you live long enough, you'll see all your buildings destroyed," Sullivan said in his last years. "After all, it is only the idea that really counts." In 1921 the distinguished landscape architect Jens Jensen predicted that Louis Sullivan's buildings, standing or not, would one day be properly appreciated. "They belong to tomorrow, the dawn of a beautiful life, American in conception," Jensen wrote. "Someday there will be pilgrimages to the tomb of Louis Sullivan."

For decades after his death, Sullivan's work was ignored. His book on architecture, *Kindergarten Chats,* enjoyed a cult following among forward-looking architecture students, but his work was all but formally repudiated in class. These were the years when the austere, sleek International Style was in vogue. Ornament, a throwback to the frilly Victorian years, was out of style, and Sullivan was considered—at best—a grand decorator. In 1949 Wright published a powerful tribute to Sullivan, *Genius and the Mobocracy.* Wright, however, was so far ahead of society in those years he was considered radical, so the book never caught on.

Sullivan's first true believer following his death was Hugh Morrison, an art historian who spent several years during the 1930s writing Sullivan's first full-length biography, *Louis Sullivan: Prophet of Modern Architecture.* "The Master" was an elusive subject. Details about his tragic personal life were kept secret by Elmslie, Sullivan's former draftsman and literary executor, who had thrown away Sullivan's memoranda and daybooks in an effort to direct attention toward his architecture. Ironically, even that, apart from the buildings themselves, proved elusive. Sullivan's office records—including the list of his commissions—were lost in a fire.

As a result, students at the Institute of Design could find little information about Sullivan or his architecture when Siskind's class began its project. They found the Morrison biography and used its directory of Sullivan architecture to scout out the buildings still standing. In 1954 Nickel started questioning the completeness of Morrison's book. The biography states that the Adler and Sullivan firm had designed 103 buildings and that Sullivan had designed 21 during his years alone. Richard's goal was to find the dozen or so Sullivan buildings mentioned by Morrison that were missing complete addresses. His first find was a small store Adler and Sullivan had built for Richard Knisely on Chicago's West Side. Morrison's book lists the Knisely store as being built in 1883 on Lake Street. Nickel drove slowly down West Lake until he found a run-down building with Sullivan's characteristic lotus stalk ornament. The keystone on the front facade bore the date 1883. Nickel photographed the building and returned to City Hall to verify the owner and date through city building permits.

His next find was the Ann Halsted House, listed in the Morrison book as being built on Lincoln Avenue in 1883. Nickel referred to each of the residences that Sullivan designed by the name of the original owner. When Nickel drove along Lincoln, he could not find any building that matched the description. When he found an "A. Halsted" listed at 710 North Park Avenue in the 1882 city directory and an "A. Halsted" at 490 Belden Avenue in the 1883 directory, Nickel guessed that the house must be on Belden because of its proximity to Lincoln Avenue. The city street numbering system having been changed in 1909, Richard converted the address to its modern number at the city's bureau of maps. The Adler and Sullivan house was waiting for him at 440 West Belden, just a few blocks east of Lincoln. "It is an excellent example of the dignity and monumentality with which Sullivan could endow even a simple residence," Nickel wrote. To his surprise, the owners still had copies of the original plans.

By talking to people who had known and had worked with Sullivan and by searching through books, serials, newspapers, city building permits, property records, and building journals dated from 1876 to 1900, Nickel soon located six more of the lost buildings Morrison mentions. Richard photographed the buildings, drew floor plans, and collected construction records.

The August 1883 issue of the *Inland Architect and News Record* led Richard to the discovery of the Aurora Watch Company Factory. The suburban Aurora building was Adler and Sullivan's first factory and a prototype for several other factories the firm later designed. Only a small section of the original plan was ever completed, but Richard found a rendering of the entire complex on a discarded watch certificate in the building's attic.

Although finding the buildings was fun detective work, understanding their significance was more difficult. What attracted Nickel most, he later wrote, was the architect's devotion toward his work. "I am doing this for Louis Sullivan," Nickel wrote in 1956, "the first inspiration of my life." He reveled in the beauty of Sullivan's creations and slowly grew to understand the reasons for Sullivan's martyred existence. He wrote William Gray Purcell, a Sullivan contemporary:

Regarding our lot in life. . .the whole business and struggle of trying to justify God's ways and ultimately understanding how he is made manifest. . .seems part and parcel of Sullivan's life, writings, and buildings. I think Sullivan never found it necessary to justify, but he glorified in describing how God is manifest. How he did this in his buildings is his greatness: I've told you on many occasions the degree of pleasure I get out of standing in the street and studying them.

In mid-1955, when Nickel began work on his graduate thesis at the Institute of Design, he thought he knew of all of Sullivan's commissions. By June 1957, when Richard completed what he described as a "thorough, painstaking re-investigation" of Sullivan's architecture, Richard claimed to have found nine of Morrison's "lost" buildings still standing, as well as 38 previously unknown commissions, 23 of which had been built.

Nickel's 232-page thesis was a continuation of the original Siskind assignment. He photographed all of the out-of-town Sullivan buildings that Siskind's class had failed to photograph and returned to buildings he felt merited more study. Finally, he unearthed long-lost details about most of Sullivan's commissions and corrected Morrison's mistakes.

To support himself Richard took a part-time job starting in July 1955 as the director of the Illinois Institute of Technology (IIT) audio-visual department. He also made money by photographing architectural models designed by IIT students. In September 1955 he began teaching basic photography at the Institute of Design and at Wright Junior College on Chicago's Northwest Side.

Although he daydreamed about life after the Sullivan project, Nickel never seriously considered leaving Chicago. In 1956 he applied for a grant to study motion-picture photography to document the architecture of Peter Behrens, Berlin's pioneering modern architect, in West Germany. But Nickel flunked his German class at Northwestern University night school. The following year he turned down a chance to teach full time at San Francisco State University.

The Institute of Design changed during the years Richard was there. It became a small department of the Illinois Institute of Technology and moved to the Mies van der Rohe–designed IIT campus in 1955. The school's new home was in Crown Hall, Mies's "iron Parthenon of the South Side," which design students shared with the IIT architecture department.

Nickel benefited from the merger because it gave him the opportunity to take courses from Alfred Caldwell, who taught a spellbinding class on the history of architecture. With intense eyes and a hawklike nose, Caldwell gave his lectures in overblown oratory. His message was that great architecture is the product of economic growth within the constraints of contemporary materials and technology.

He often started his introductory lecture by showing slides of a peasant house and asking: "Who decides the angle of this thatched roof? Who makes it this high and not that high?"

Caldwell paused after each question he posed for dramatic effect. "Is it because of the architect's personality? Is it because of fashion?" His raspy voice lowered, he gave the simple answer: "No, it is so the house will shed the rain and not the thatch."

Better than anybody, Caldwell put Sullivan's transitory ideas into words. "The tall buildings of Sullivan present simultaneously the two great developmental powers of man—imagination and reason," Caldwell told his students.

The imagination creates. The reason analyzes, directs. The clear, clean frame of the building, its logical construction was the way of the mind. The architecture, the expression was the way of the imagination.

The profane austerity of the Carson Pirie Scott building mass has stood alone for nearly 50 years. Save for the tall building construction of Mies van der Rohe, there is truly nothing in the world today in any way comparable. The vertical and horizontal members of the frame form a grid and the windows are simply the space between. The upper two floors, used as offices and hence requiring a lower ceiling, are with perfect assurance diminished. Just this one building would mark Sullivan as a great master of the rational. Here is a skeleton frame so reasonable that the question of reason never occurs. The overhanging roof, since removed, once cast a deep shadow of solemnity. Skeleton frames there are today, but not like this one.

The reason of a Sullivan building was inherent reason. It was not reason on the surface, but reason in the depths. It touched everything in the building; it was the building, its plan, its use, its construction. The building and the reason were inseparable. Thus the reason was organic reason, the reason was wisdom. This is the reason which is only unlocked by imagination. Plato called it idea. Idea then is the true reality.

So Sullivan was defeated in his life and work and he knew it. Yet he never gave an inch. He made a war in which he was slain.

The acceptance of Sullivan today raises the question whether the war is forgotten and all is forgiven or whether the war was won posthumously or whether his fame is simply part of the idiocy of time, touching us as in a trance, one man by the sleeve out of the multitude.

Besides refining Nickel's understanding of Sullivan, Caldwell broadened Nickel's capacity to evaluate and appreciate all architecture. Out of class, Caldwell taught Nickel how to make architectural plans and think like an architect. And he taught Nickel about what was worthwhile and what was worthless.

The lessons went well beyond architecture. In 1960, during the height of the fight to save the Garrick Theater, Nickel wrote to Caldwell, "There is no question about it now—your talks are having their effect on me."

Slowly, Richard established himself as a commercial photographer. His photographs of contemporary buildings for architecture firms appeared in trade maga-

Adler and Sullivan's 1890 Dooly Block in Salt Lake City, Utah. The photograph was taken during the 1950s.

zines such as *Progressive Architecture* during the late 1950s. The editors of *Forum* magazine invited Richard to show them his portfolio in 1957, but Nickel wrote he didn't have time. His Sullivan pictures, along with those taken by Siskind and Callahan, were lavishly displayed in the Italian architecture journal *Casabella* in 1955. Three of Nickel's photos of the poet Carl Sandburg, in town to gather material for his Chicago poems, were published in the *New York Times* in 1957. They were among the few non-architectural photos he ever had published.

In 1955 Nickel took two cross-country journeys in search of Sullivan architecture. On June 14 he went West. "As I recall, I travelled like a madman to make this trip as quickly and economically as I could: driving long days and nights, sleeping in the car (or trying to)," he wrote. He spent the first several days in Salt Lake City photographing Adler and Sullivan's six-story Dooly Block office building at 111 West 2nd South Street. "Just finished the Dooly, and am headed for Mississippi—after something cool to drink," he wrote Siskind. "Expect good results—even some sensational stuff (I hope). What a paradise this is—*dolls* all over the place. Who was it who said, 'Go West, young man?'"

From there, Nickel swung southeast to photograph Frank Lloyd Wright's "Prairie Skyscraper" in Bartlesville, Oklahoma. Then he drove to New Orleans to see Adler and Sullivan's 1892 train station. The station, described as still standing in Morrison's book, had long since been demolished. Tired and dirty, Nickel pushed on to Ocean Springs, Mississippi, to look for Sullivan's cottage.

Sullivan designed and built bungalows for himself and his friends, the Charnley family, as vacation retreats in 1890. The vacation house was a reward to himself after the years struggling to design and build the Auditorium Building. Sullivan's T-shaped cottage, tucked away in the woods on the west shore of Biloxi Bay, was where the architect traveled for inspiration. Here he could return to nature, cultivate his rose garden, and walk the paths he had carved through the surrounding thick growth.

Nickel knew that Ocean Springs would require days of study and work, but he was exhausted. He arrived late and needed the police to show him the way through the woods. After spending a miserable night trying to sleep in the car battling mosquitoes, Nickel took only a few photos of the cottages and left for home.

"The Sullivan and Charnley cottages have been painted over and the stables have been demolished and all that remains of Sullivan's proud rose garden is an elliptical scar of dead shoots," Nickel wrote. "The tall pines and the exotic plants, once controlled, now grow wild but the care once rendered this place is easily sensed."

In August Nickel made the eastern leg of the Sullivan trip, traveling with Hinman Kealy, a fellow Institute of Design student. Their first stop was at the Best

Sullivan's 1897–98 Bayard Building in New York City. The photograph was taken in 1955.

Jewelry Company in Newark, Ohio. It had been built by Sullivan in 1914 as the Home Building Association. There they were shown blueprints and building specifications. The store owner allowed Richard to photograph Sullivan's ceiling frieze, hidden by a dropped ceiling, and took him to the basement to see the original light fixtures.

They then traveled to Philadelphia to research and photograph the work of Frank Furness, Sullivan's first mentor, and to New York City, where they stayed for almost a week studying the Sullivan manuscript collection at Columbia University and photographing Sullivan's only Manhattan skyscraper, the angelic Bayard Building on Bleecker Street.

The pair also stopped in Poughkeepsie, New York, to meet Adrienne Sullivan, daughter of Sullivan's brother, Albert. She provided Nickel with letters from Louis and talked about her uncle for hours. She refused, however, to discuss the strained relationship between the two brothers.

On the way home, Nickel and Kealy drove to Buffalo, New York, to see the 13-story Guaranty Building, Adler and Sullivan's final commission together. The building, on the corner of Church and Pearl streets, was being remodeled, and the wreckers gave Nickel and Kealy dozens of doorknobs, chandeliers, push plates, and a few fragments of terra cotta. Kealy recalled that Richard preferred the nuts-and-bolts hardware to the terra cotta.

By 1956 Nickel's work slowed to a standstill. The Institute of Design travel fund was down to $40. But when the University of Chicago Press expressed interest in publishing a pamphlet or small book based on the Sullivan project and the *Journal of the American Institute of Architects* inquired about publishing an article, Nickel balked, saying he wanted to gather more information and take more photographs. In a January letter to *Journal* editor Henry H. Saylor, he wrote, "I feel we would be doing Sullivan an injustice by going to press with what we have now. . . even though it is of high quality. Also, I could not go on to other things knowing that I have not gotten the best out of Sullivan's buildings."

The project was revived two months later when editors at Horizon Press, the New York City publishing house of Frank Lloyd Wright's books, agreed to publish a book based on the Sullivan project. Richard wrote an excited letter to Saylor on March 19 with news of the proposal. "I am leaving my present job to work full time on completion of photography and research. . .which should take four or five months," he wrote.

Siskind signed a contract with Horizon Press on June 1, 1956. The agreement called for Siskind to deliver photographs from the class by July 15 and five pages of text by November 1. The plan called for the book to have 200 pages of black-and-white photos and 10 to 15 color plates. The book was to include an introduction by Siskind, reprinted essays by Adler and Sullivan, and a detailed list of buildings by both architects. Royalties were assigned to the Institute of Design, which received $1,000 in advance to pay for extra travel. The book, entitled *The Complete Architecture of Dankmar Adler and Louis Sullivan*, was given a $15 price tag and scheduled to be on the bookstands by the fall of 1957.

The editor behind the project was Ben Raeburn. "I want to tell you that your

prints of the work of Louis Sullivan constitute the greatest architectural photographs I have ever seen," he wrote Siskind. "Nobody, in my opinion, has ever approached the beauty of this work. Besides the incomparable quality of the photos, I think the proposed book, if adequately produced, will make a unique contribution."

It was obvious to Raeburn from the start that this was to be more than a business relationship. Nickel's job was to edit the photographs, prepare a building list, and write captions describing each building. The care and concern Nickel and Siskind showed when they began laying out the book with Raeburn convinced the editor that this was a cultural enterprise. The three men spent a week together making three complete dummies of the book at Raeburn's New York home in January 1957. Siskind and Nickel slept during the day while Raeburn went to work at his office. Then the three would work through the night.

The first stumbling block was compiling the list of Sullivan buildings. By mid-1956 Nickel suspected there were Sullivan commissions and buildings still to be found. Wondering whether Sullivan had more than six commissions in St. Louis, Nickel spent 12-hour days at the St. Louis Public Library reading the local 1890s newspapers page by page. Wondering whether Hugh Morrison of Dartmouth College knew of others, Nickel drove to Hanover, New Hampshire, to meet the professor. Morrison lent Nickel his research notebooks, but could shed little new light.

Nickel also drove to Taliesen in Wisconsin to interview Frank Lloyd Wright. Sleepy at first, the 85-year-old Wright later gruffly monopolized the conversation, offering little help and putting Nickel off. "About all I can honestly respect in him is his architectural ability," Richard wrote. "Shouldn't there be something more?"

A year later, Wright was much more helpful, reviewing Sullivan's drawings with Nickel and commenting on the building notes Nickel had prepared for the book. "The notes were pretty bad, but he was quite understanding and patronizing," Nickel wrote. "I left there that night feeling pretty good."

Wright must have been impressed by Nickel. He told Richard that his photos of the Bartlesville, Oklahoma, skyscraper were the best he had ever seen and seemed surprised that Nickel had discovered Adler and Sullivan's Loeb Apartments at 157-59 North Elizabeth Street in Chicago. "So you found that house," Wright snorted.

In May 1957 Nickel took what he thought was his last midwestern trip in search of Sullivan. He drove 500 miles north to the Upper Peninsula of Michigan to photograph Sullivan's remodeling of the First National Bank in Manistique, then 300 miles west to Owatonna, Minnesota, to interview residents about Sullivan's proposal to build an addition to the Owatonna High School. The trip should have

Sullivan's 1914 Merchants National Bank in Grinnell, Iowa, during the mid-1950s.

made Nickel feel good about coming to an end of his research, but the new finds indicated that the building list might be incomplete.

There was always something more to learn. He kept traveling. The contractor who worked with Sullivan on the Henry C. Adams Land and Loan Office Building in Algona, Iowa, told Richard that Sullivan was particular about how much mortar should be placed between bricks. John Van Allen, president of the John D. Van Allen & Sons Dry Goods Store in Clinton, Iowa, told Richard that his grandfather once made some design suggestions to Sullivan. "Well, I'll be goddamned if someone in the retail trade doesn't tell me how to put up a building," Sullivan shot back.

And something more important slowed down the project.

Adler and Sullivan buildings began to disappear. The Cyrus McCormick residence, which Sullivan remodeled around 1899, was demolished in 1954. In early 1955 Richard found that the John Borden residence, the first designed by the firm, was vacant. Richard entered the gloomy interior, but he was too timid to explore or make a floor study. When he drove back a few weeks later, the house was gone.

By the end of World War II, many of the early houses designed by Adler and Sullivan had been engulfed by the city's ever-expanding West Side and South Side slums. By that time, most of the residences—two- and three-story rowhouses and large homes—had long since been divided into small apartments.

In 1946 nearly one-third of all Chicagoans were living in what the government called "substandard housing." The following year, voters in the city approved a $15-million bond issue to bulldoze the slums. The plan was to concentrate the poor in new high-rise apartments and clear large tracts of land for private developers. The rationale was to make urban property values competitive with the wide-open suburbs.

It was a slow process, but by the late 1950s much of Chicago's worst slum property had been leveled. In a flurry of demolition, more than 5,860 buildings were torn down between September 1957 and April 1960. "The face of Chicago is being changed more rapidly today than ever before," said City Building Commissioner George L. Ramsey in 1960. Mayor Richard J. Daley promised he would wipe out the slums in 20 years. Few people objected.

As the Adler and Sullivan buildings were torn down, Nickel started saving ornament. "It gave me a particular thrill to rescue a piece (since this would otherwise be lost forever)," Nickel wrote. His efforts—at first—were not premeditated; he was simply there. Many Sullivan buildings were being lost. He was powerless to change that. He knew if the Master's ornament was to be saved, he would have to do it. So he went on commando raids, using ropes, chisels, and hammers to hack down the terra-cotta and stone ornament when nobody was watching. Soon he found there was no need to work in secret. Police would see him and drive right by. Nothing valuable here.

Actually, Nickel was not much of a saver by nature. The only thing his brother, Donald, recalled Richard ever saving was the magnesium wheel of a P-51 Mustang. They both witnessed the plane crash about three miles west of their Logan Square home during the late 1940s, and Richard brought the keepsake home.

During the 1950s Nickel tape recorded lectures by photographers Alfred Eisenstaedt, Arthur Siegel, and Ansel Adams at the Art Institute of Chicago. Prompted by historian Beaumont Newhall's statement that "every scrap of personal documentation is precious material," Richard wrote, "I do not see why we should depend on 'scraps' of information when it is within our power to accurately record talks like these."

But as late as 1957, Richard had only rescued a few pieces of Sullivan ornament: the items he picked up in Buffalo from the Guaranty Building; fretwork he recovered after the interior of the Albert Sullivan house caught fire on the South Side in 1954; and two heavy cast-iron columns he helped salvage from the Jewelers' Building during its 1956 remodeling.

The pieces Nickel saved were not just mementos or curiosities, but beautiful pieces of art. Sullivan's ornament, which showed his progression from the botanic and Egyptoid forms of his early work to the geometric forms of his later periods, were all original. They had to be, for as Sullivan had written: "It follows then, by the logic of growth, that a certain kind of ornament should appear on a certain kind of structure, just as a certain kind of leaf must appear on a certain kind of tree." The ornament, wrote Elmslie, was the final and logical flowering of the building.

"When I started saving Sullivan ornament from buildings being demolished— actively since 1957—it was only to keep it from being turned under," Nickel wrote. "As the collection grew, I envisioned a private Sullivan ornament museum. After all, I thought, if nobody cares about it, why should I share it? I wasn't being selfish in that, just venting my anger that I was always the only person at the wrecking site, even when a Sullivan building was being demolished."

The first building Nickel beat the bulldozers to was the 1884 Reuben Rubel residence, a three-story house on the Near West Side. With a sandstone base and red pressed brick, the front was sculpted with bold red terra-cotta ornament brimming with force and energy.

Richard discovered the house in the mid-1950s after he found it mentioned in an 1884 issue of *Inland Architect* magazine. "I'll never forget going to the site and finding the house still there, lurking in the shadows between some gaudy semi-modern buildings," he wrote, "but within a few years it was gone. I photographed it in detail as it was lathered with Sullivan ornament of very high quality."

By 1958 it had become the headquarters of the Journeyman Barbers Union. Because it sat in a neighborhood ripe for urban renewal, Nickel suspected that the house would soon be demolished. He asked union officials to tell him if they got word to vacate. On June 3 he received a cryptic postcard that read:

State Wrecking Company
333 N. Michigan
The above company will start wrecking the building at 320 S. Ashland about
June 9th. Please don't mention this note.

Nickel went to work just as the wrecking crews arrived. He carted away just about everything worth taking. Some of the pieces were too heavy to lift by hand,

so he convinced the wreckers to lend him a hand. The prize was a piece of sunburst ornament from the chimney. He also took ornamental copper trim from the roof, an iron window grille, plaster ceiling escutcheons, and wood trim. His only regret later was that he had not saved the doors, which he had ripped apart for the intricately carved cherrywood panels.

Next to go was the Knisely store, the three-story store and apartment at 2147-49 West Lake Street that Richard first discovered. In the early summer Nickel found out that a housing project was to be built in the neighborhood. He tracked down the wreckers and persuaded them to tell him when the building was to go.

Richard was determined to document the picturesque Knisely before it met its doom. He entered the building and made detailed floor plans, noting every important detail. "Most inner walls 6-inches thick and 11-inches where the doors slide in," Nickel noted. "Most doors 32-inches wide and 7 1/2-feet high with 17-inch by 32-inch transoms above."

In July Nickel began an exhaustive photographic record of the little building. In all its years it had never received such attention. He photographed the exterior, including its flat roof, and took interior photos of the fireplaces, stairway, and woodwork. Taking great pains to show the beauty of the building, he photographed the Knisely from nearby roofs so that it would not be obscured by the adjacent elevated tracks and showed the building from blocks away. His most haunting photo, however, was from ground level. Compressed with a long lens, the view shows abandoned cars—the bubble cars of the day with their hoods and trunks popped open—in a junk yard about a block away. Out of the background, with its ocular

third-floor window high above the neighborhood muck, the Knisely was a beacon in the vast wasteland.

The building was demolished later that summer. Its best feature, two ornate sheet-metal bays that projected from top floors, had rotted. Why so much sheet metal, Nickel must have wondered. Richard Knisely owned a factory that manufactured the material.

Looking back, Richard wrote that he did not save enough from the Knisely. "I suffered a great disappointment on that building because they failed to let me know when the wrecking would start. When I arrived on the scene one day, the building was one-half down and one-third of the big pieces of stone I wanted had been knocked off. You can imagine how I felt at that moment. After all this time, looking at it and negotiating to get it, I let it slip out of my hands."

He was most disappointed that the wreckers had ruined a spectacular ornamental spandrel panel that separated the second and third stories. With only a few lines incised into Bedford limestone, Sullivan created a vigorous design that reached toward the sky. The piece was cracked in half by the time Nickel arrived. Heartsick, he saved the bottom half and for years hoped to recreate the top half.

Determined not to lose other pieces, Nickel took action. His brother, Donald, helped him chisel off two massive ornamental projecting supports at the top of the first floor. They hired cemetery workers from the Kuper Monument Works in suburban Niles to hoist the half-ton corbels from the building and haul them to a limestone cutting yard, where the excess structural stone was trimmed off. Even then, each piece weighed 300 to 400 pounds. "After removing the remaining piece, I have no future doubts about what can and cannot be moved: Anything is possible if you have the sense to do it," Richard wrote. "In conclusion, God Damn It. I always learn when it is too late."

Next to fall was the Levi Rosenfeld Building, one of the earliest Adler and Sullivan buildings faced with terra cotta. It had been built in the early 1880s as a complex of stores, apartments, and a hotel. By 1958 the building was vacant and in bad shape on Skid Row just west of the Loop. Many of the interior walls had been torn down and much of the sheet-metal cornice, the projecting ornamental moldings, had been stripped away from the roof lines by previous owners. Although the orange brick was covered by a century of city grime, the brick, terra cotta, and sandstone of the facade remained largely intact.

Nickel could see beyond the grime. He saw the building as Sullivan had designed it, saw the interplay between the strongly emphasized vertical piers and the recessed horizontal spandrels. The first floor was an expanse of glass storefronts, with slender cast-iron box columns supporting the load of the masonry above.

"The facade of the building offers one of Sullivan's best solutions for the 'row' type store and flat building," he wrote. "The stores were fronted almost entirely by glass with a combination of slender round and square box-type cast-iron columns carrying iron lintels, which support the wall above. This is not a wall in the ordinary sense of masonry punctured by windows, but a rhythmic alternation of windows and projecting brick piers."

Nickel made drawings and took photographs of each floor in late October. He then hauled away a large load of terra cotta, stone, and ironwork, giving the wreckers $90 for their help. The superintendent was supposed to split the money but pocketed it instead. "He was really a rat about the whole thing," Nickel wrote.

Demolition picked up in late 1958. While Richard documented the last days of the Rosenfeld, three other Sullivan buildings—the Falkenau row houses, the Lindauer residence and the Henry Stern residence—were all torn down. An October 22 note shows the frantic pace.

> *Spent the early afternoon at the Rosenfeld where demolition of the east wing had begun by Speedway Wrecking Co. (Mr. Walter Holmes, supt.) Then drove to IIT at about 4 p.m. to see Aaron and together we worked at the Falkenau, which was almost evacuated (the copper was stripped from the south bay), and at the Lindauer. Aaron left at 6 p.m. and I at about 7:30, stopping en route at the Henry Stern residence, which I discovered was finally undergoing demolition. Using my flashlight I was able to find the two corner pieces of ornament from the top floor. The walls are being knocked in and these were lying right on the top floor. One hell of a job getting them down the littered steps.*

It was in the gloom of the Lindauer residence, a rugged, granite house within walking distance of the IIT campus, that Nickel first met John Vinci. Nickel had photographed the building at 3312 South Wabash Avenue in 1954 and knew it well. As soon as the residents moved out in mid-November, the Lindauer was raided by neighborhood scavengers and IIT architecture students. The scavengers took copper cornice trim, window guards, handrails, pipes, and radiators, then tore up the floor coverings in search of money and valuables. The students took stairway posts, handrails, and ornamental plaster for a Louis Sullivan exhibit at the school.

By the time Nickel arrived, the once-opulent interior was a shambles. Even though Vinci and fellow student David Norris had as much right in the abandoned building as did Nickel, they sensed that Nickel was hostile. His turf was being invaded, his booty taken.

With the help of Chuck Swedlund, an Institute of Design photo student, Nickel worked overtime at the Lindauer to save what remained. From the interior, they hauled away a wooden partition and plaster ornament. His prize was the band of terra cotta on the base of the chimney above the second floor. Without the proper equipment, in 10- to 15-degree weather, he took apart the chimney to pull out the ornament.

"On the site we found that the ladder would not reach the top of the chimney, or for that matter, even come close to it," Nickel wrote.

After trying for a while to figure out how it could be done, Chuck finally got the idea of knocking off the bricks of the front chimney with a long board from the roof top. This worked. Chuck stayed on the ground with a flashlight to watch for passersby and I commenced to knock the bricks off. It went pretty fast too. I tried to knock off big chunks. Unfortunately, as I learned later, the falling brick scathed some of the ornament on the way down. But this was inevitable as the stuff I wanted projected out slightly. Once all the brick was off, we put up the ladder and from the second or third rung from the top of the ladder I was able to look into the chimney hole. I commenced to break loose the common bonding brick and drop it within the hole. It was difficult to get the first piece loose as the binding mortar was still pretty tight. Using all kinds of tools, I finally got one loose but could not wiggle it out. Then I put myself on the spot by shifting three of them (these are the plastic leaf pieces) and setting them off balance. Rubble filled in after them and there I was holding up the three. Off balance and on a top rung as I already was, the only thing I could do was drop them. I stepped down a rung or two and hung onto one of them and slowly pulled it away. The other two came crashing down but did not fall off the roof... they wedged at my feet between the chimney and the slate wall, and were in pretty good shape. From then on it was a matter of just pulling them off. The corners were a wrap-around piece and were pretty heavy and as I remember it, we left one of them up there.

The whole job took a few hours and we had everything that we wanted down on the third floor by about 11 p.m. We had to make about 5 or 6 trips with the stuff and loaded up my car. A roving Land Clearance cop spotted us and took my name and license number but did not have much to say about what we were taking. He only said we shouldn't be in the building.

Swedlund drove home, but Nickel kept working:

I continued on to the Rosenfeld building where one of the metal face columns was knocked down and lying in the debris. I had brought along the proper tools to drill off the heads of the ornamental pieces which decorated this piece. It took some drilling but I got it off in an hour. By this time it was pretty damned cold too. I drove home via Milwaukee Avenue and unloaded the car the same night.

Nickel returned to the Lindauer later to draw a floor plan and take more ornament, but he found that the building had been gutted by fire a few days earlier. He tried to survey the building, but found it impossible to walk the floors that iced after the fire department hoses put out the fire. The Lindauer was razed in January 1959 to make way for the expansion of the IIT campus.

The next victim of urban renewal was Adler and Sullivan's 1885 Henry Stern house, at 2915 South Prairie Avenue, which was razed in late January. The two-story building (with a mansard third floor) had terra-cotta trim that Nickel considered the best of Sullivan's early years. Once again, Nickel's goal was to remove terra cotta from the roofline. And once again the job was difficult and dangerous. Nickel spent nearly six hours on a 20-degree night in late January dislodging and lowering the terra cotta. He broke several pieces and had to leave others in place because they would not budge. Tired and cold, he wrote, "Got home around midnight—all sooty."

By 1958 Nickel's progress on the Sullivan book had bogged down. The salvage operations were exhausting and time consuming. He spent many more hours keeping watch on his buildings once they were in jeopardy. The key to saving ornament was arriving at the right time on the right day. Arriving too early would arouse suspicion; arriving too late meant a total loss.

Nickel also suffered from writer's block. Lacking confidence, he was afraid of making mistakes—and was shocked by the number of published errors he encountered reading about Adler and Sullivan. He determined that "his" book would be as perfect and complete as possible.

"When somebody wants to know something about any of the buildings, especially in matters of design, or dates, or cost or dimensions, or sites or anything, I'd like to have them come to [my book]," he wrote in 1958. "I am not interested in a literary career. It is a matter of paying back a debt. This book is a token of my appreciation to Adler and Sullivan for that 'something' I have gotten from my interest in their work. It is an indescribable feeling of illumination, so to speak—and that is the only reason I am doing this."

Nickel wrote clearly and well and had received positive critiques from such people as Frank Lloyd Wright and Ansel Adams. But he still questioned whether he

A limestone panel from Adler and Sullivan's 1883 Solomon Blumenfeld Flat Building rests against the trunk of Nickel's car. The building was razed in 1963.

had sufficient skill to complete the project.

"The only reason the notes are not finished now is that the writing became a real obstacle," Nickel wrote his editor, Ben Raeburn, in 1959.

> *The library work became complex, and more and more I felt greater responsibility for completeness, accuracy and perfection in all the parts: photos, plans, text. Then there was the matter of understanding. How was I to write about Sullivan with only a meagerly art history and architectural training and no writing experience? It is probably our fault for never explaining that my work on Sullivan was the sum total of my experience. As I think about it now, I feel perfectly justified in not having the text ready. I was and still am overwhelmed by your confidence in my ability to do this and while any text I would have written could be 'cleaned up,' I cannot help but feel it would basically be superficial.*

Nickel told Raeburn he needed more time to produce a book with "good historic value."

> *You know what it is like to work in libraries for days on end, working with this goal, and getting nothing. Or of rushing through note-taking or reading and analysis so you end up with virtually nothing. I am perfectly willing to put in any number of years of work for a satisfactory result but I can feel you waiting. Yet rushing or shortcuts of any kind will not get us good text.*

Richard promised Raeburn on December 24, 1958, that he would finish the descriptions of each building within six months.

Yet he refused to be rushed. What should have marked the beginning of the end of Nickel's involvement with Sullivan had finally become an obsession. In 1959 he wrote Adolf K. Plaezek, director of the Avery Library at Columbia University: "I'm still struggling with the Sullivan book, which becomes more comprehensive every year and if I live so long, I think it will really be something." Similar frustrations filled a letter to a friend:

> Whereas I will give as many years as necessary to get the book done right, Aaron [Siskind] and our publisher want to get the book out. They often get fairly upset with me because I keep putting off the writing, but I feel inadequate and at the same time am struck with the ideals, commitments and when the book is reviewed, my neck will be out.

> Nobody seems to understand that I don't want any damned glory—I only want the book to be A-1 perfect. I'm trying not to cry over what cannot be changed, but you can imagine how I feel when I keep telling myself that I will never, never again associate with anyone or go to a publisher with a half-baked idea.

Nickel was not even satisfied with the layout of the book. He wrote Raeburn that the pages had either too many or too few photographs. "Aaron has a sociological interest ('then and now') and I have an educational interest to show the important things. . . .And I'm frightened to death of how we use details large and general views small. I'm for showing the architecture first and the ornamental details next. The chronological order has been for some time my main concern. I feel our notebook is very close to how it happened."

In late June 1959, Nickel drove west for more building research. He spent three days in Pueblo, Colorado, researching Adler and Sullivan's 1889 Grand Opera House, which had been gutted by fire in 1922, then spent three more in Salt Lake City re-photographing the Dooly Block and tracking down the sparse remains of the never-completed 300-room Hotel Ontario. With the help of a custodian, Nickel found and photographed the hotel's foundation.

"I was in the basement with Mr. Nielsen and observed the heavy foundation walls, upon which are presently the meager joists necessary for the present two-story building," Nickel noted. The joists created the floor slab of the new building. "Many solid stone walls run the depth of the building and these are apparently the walls of the hotel." No trace of Adler and Sullivan's work went unrecorded.

From Salt Lake City Nickel traveled to Pasadena, California, where he stayed for a week talking to William Gray Purcell, a Prairie School architect who had worked with Sullivan. Richard had corresponded with the architect since 1953. Purcell, who called Richard the "prairie boy from Park Ridge" and wrote to him as "Dear Lad of Sullivan," was very ill and was only able to talk every other day for two hours. Nevertheless, he gave Richard insight into Sullivan's work and critiqued the book. Purcell liked Nickel's writing but disagreed with some of his conclusions. He also criticized the book's symmetrical layout, which he said did not reflect Sullivan's architecture.

Nickel spent a week in Prescott, Arizona, with Frederick Sommer, a photographer Nickel had met the previous year during Sommer's stint as a visiting photographer at the Institute of Design. Born in 1905, Sommer now was a multimedia artist who combined photography with drawing, painting, and even music. Sommer, who was trained as a landscape architect, had long talks with Richard about the interrelatedness of science and art. He gradually helped furnish Richard with an intellectual philosophy upon which to work. Devoted to art, Sommer was an absolute perfectionist who might spend years scouting out a location to take a photograph and days to make just one perfect print. "Life is a wonderful flirtation," Sommer told his young friend. They talked about the rigor of dedication, the importance of aesthetics, and the pursuit of elegance. The two men understood each other.

Through the 1960s Sommer often stayed at Nickel's Park Ridge home when he traveled to Chicago. The visits invigorated Nickel. Sommer, like Moholy-Nagy and Siskind and Callahan, made art come alive. "You know," Nickel wrote Sommer's wife, Frances, in 1969, "I hold Fred in awe."

After Richard's return to Chicago in 1959, another Adler and Sullivan building was razed. The narrow, three-story Samuel Stern row house at 2963 South Prairie Avenue was one of the last structures standing in a multiblock area tagged for urban renewal. Nickel's long description, which he placed in the building files he maintained of his salvage effort, characterizes the way he worked. On September 8 he and a friend found the house partially demolished.

I did not feel when we turned off at 31st Street that the status of the Stern residence would be changed as I had been told by a former owner, and the woman who managed the place (a kind of boarding house) said that they would be there through the forthcoming winter. To my astonishment in looking down Prairie Street, I saw the windows all broke in and realized the building was empty. I had my friend immediately drive there and behold, the doors were off their hinges and were lying right in the doorway. I was overjoyed and stood them both up against the wall and just as we were about to get them up and to the car, a negro fellow from across the street claimed that the wrecking company had left him in charge and he wanted to know what we were doing there. He obviously saw the opportunity to make a few bucks but I answered simply that I was writing a book on architecture and would be back later to draw a floor plan.

So we had to leave the doors right there and I was very nervous about them while I waited for my friend to finish his job interview. When he did finish we drove back but approached by the rear of the building and parked. I jumped through a rear window and walked through the house, carrying each door back through to a car side window. When I had the two there I called my friend and handed them down to him. They were quite heavy and it was a real effort to lift them up and get to the rear of the building. When they were both outside and lying against the south wall we lifted them individually and carried them back to the car, where we quickly loaded up and drove away. So I got the doors. I had been watching them for several years, with the desire of getting this third one to go along with my Henry Stern and Reuben Rubel panels.

Nickel returned to the building the following day to make floor plans, take photographs, and remove the ornamental triangular sheet-metal pediment above a window in the dormer. The piece, which featured unique, interlocking metal spirals, was important because it foreshadowed the Auditorium ornament. To get at it, Nickel had to break through the front hall and roof above the third floor.

"This was a messy job," he wrote. "There was a strong wind, it was hot in there under the roof and dirt was flying at every moment. But I worked at it until I felt I had it whipped." He left the piece in place, because he wanted to take a few last photographs before he removed it.

Nickel returned the next day to finish the floor plans, take the final pictures, and bring his piece home. After returning from lunch, he was approached by two well-dressed men who appeared to be government workers.

One of the first questions they asked was whether I knew about the doors and I naturally answered that I had them. They explained then how they had been keeping an eye on the building, waiting, etc. I said I was sorry and that I had been doing the same thing. . .that if I hadn't promised away the second door long ago, they could surely have had one. The conversation went on and ended with my inviting the guy out to the house to see the ornament collection I had. He said he was due to go to Europe in about five weeks, and that he would call soon. He said if I was willing to part with any ornament he might like, that he would be happy to pay for it. I answered that if he saw something he liked that I could part with, that he could simply "have it."

As he and his friend were leaving, he asked whether there was any sense in going up to the third floor. This, of course, was where I had been working on the wall to get at the metal ornament. I stumbled in answering his question because I feared the inevitable. And sure enough, they came down a minute later asking about the metal ornament. (You could see it from up there by going out on a small balcony.) I explained that I had bust the hole and was going to take it as soon as I completed a few more exterior pictures. His answer was something to the equivalent of: "You got the door panels, we're taking this!" And they walked off quite quickly. I followed them to that front door room a minute later when they were pounding at it from the inside, attempting to knock it down to the street. They were dressed and didn't know what they were doing and asked me how to get it down when I remarked they were going to ruin it. I said you have to rope it and lower it and that pounding

Demise of the Samuel
Stern row house at
2963 South Prairie
Avenue. The first
photo shows the house
intact. The second,
taken from the same
angle in 1959,
shows the start of
demolition with the
neighboring house gone.
By the time this photo-
graph was shot, Nickel
had taken the doors
and the triangular
sheet-metal pediment
on the third story.

it loose would not do, that someone would have to get up in there and work it loose without impacting it. So they got a wire to lower it with and eventually hired a negro bum to go in and break it loose. I walked away having told them what to do, being too disgusted with them for commandeering what I felt was mine.

Next thing I knew, the fellow came in and said they had gotten it down, and asked if I thought I could get it home in my car. I asked what the sense was of talking about my moving it when they took it and he replied that he had decided I should have it.

The men had apparently decided that the piece was too big, too rusty, and too dirty for them. They helped Nickel lift it into his car and left.

"I was relieved to have it but sorry I hadn't taken it sooner," he wrote. He never found out who the men were.

By then, the ornament collection was becoming a burden. In 1958, his big year in gathering artifacts, Nickel admitted that the backyard at his parents' Park Ridge house was beginning to look like an archeological field, filled with limestone, terra cotta, wood, and metal. The yard was so jam-packed that Nickel moved some of his finds into the garage, displacing his car. "If I don't get in the habit of slowly getting rid of it all, it will consume me. You know what I mean? It's beginning to govern my life," Nickel wrote in 1959.

By 1960 about 60 pieces—from small wood medallions to a 1,500-pound pediment—were scattered around the yard, and his neighbors were complaining. He wrote: "Suburbia: Houses where I am separated by about 15–20 feet. Learned last week that the neighbors to the north went to the neighbors to the south asking whether they would agree to cooperate in making a complaint about the unsightly appearance of our yard. It is full of big and small hunks of bright terra cotta ornament. The neighbors to the south said they would make no such complaint. I suppose it is kind of unsightly but when it is gone, I don't know what is going to look much better. To their eyes, maybe the rows of garages, or the chrome plated cars, etc. Oh, well."

Nickel could not understand why others did not grasp the significance and beauty of the ornament.

When he visited the University of Illinois campus in 1959 to see ornament salvaged by an architecture professor from the razing of Sullivan's Walker Warehouse, Nickel compared the huge slab of damaged limestone to the broken hull of a ship. Saddened to see the ornament ignored in a courtyard and weathered by rain, Nickel turned to an architecture student and said: "Great architecture has only two natural enemies: water and stupid men."

Nickel protests the
destruction of the Garrick
on June 8, 1960. The
photograph was taken by
Chicago Sun-Times
photographer
Ralph Walters.

WHAT IS A CYNIC? A MAN WHO KNOWS THE PRICE OF EVERYTHING, AND THE
VALUE OF NOTHING.

Oscar Wilde, *Lady Windermere's Fan*

The destruction continued.

In late 1959 a window bay was removed from a residence built for Max M. Rothschild at the southwest corner of Indiana Avenue and 32nd Street. Workers at the site used sections of the bay for firewood, but Nickel managed to cart away a six-foot wooden panel for his ornament collection. The house was one of three neighboring residences that Adler and Sullivan built for Rothschild. The chipped and broken panel was the only remnant Nickel saved from the entire complex, which was razed five years later.

A sadder loss was the Henry Babson mansion, the victim of changing times, not urban blight. Completed in 1909 on a 23-acre estate in the west suburb of Riverside, it was one of only a few houses Sullivan designed after his break-up with Adler. With a low-pitched roof and overhanging eaves, the long, horizontal lines of the Babson house reflected the parallel paths of Sullivan and Frank Lloyd Wright. But the inlaid terra cotta and ornate overhanging second-floor balcony were pure Sullivan.

Nickel tracked down Babson himself to get a first-hand history of the house. Babson told Nickel that he had hired Sullivan after overhearing a group of architects at a downtown restaurant, complaining about their lack of work due to bad economic times. One of the architects had said how sad it was that even "the Master" could not find work. Babson asked whom they were talking about, and hired Sullivan.

Demolition of the Babson mansion to make way for the Walter S. Baltis subdivision began during the last week of January 1960. Alfred Caldwell called the razing a "cultural crime." In late February, Richard, his brother, Donald, John Vinci, and David Norris salvaged what was left. "It was zero degree weather and we were trying to take photos and remove ornament," Vinci wrote. "His shutter would freeze and he would get angry because the ornament removal was going faster than the photo documentation." They spent days disassembling a major section of the second-floor balcony and driving it to Norris's home. It was the largest assembly that Nickel had ever taken.

Sullivan's 1908–09 Babson House in suburban Riverside, Illinois. The photograph was taken during the 1950s.

"I often think it is the most important thing I am doing," Nickel wrote about the salvage work.

It is not an intellectual accomplishment, but simply a recognition of the importance and great beauty of Sullivan's work, and [of] being able and interested in saving it. Honestly, I'm more at home in a wrecker's environment: dirty clothes, using rope and pinch bar, moving weights out in the air and wind. Very exhilarating, especially when you get a choice piece of a building up high and then take it home and look at it in various kinds of light. Ah, Sullivan!

But Nickel was also growing bitter. Adler and Sullivan's three-story Victoria Hotel, in the south suburb of Chicago Heights, was cleared away after it was destroyed by fire. Plans were announced to raze several other early Chicago School skyscrapers in the Loop. "Now I am pulling out of it," Nickel wrote after weeks at the Babson house. "Buildings are coming down on all sides."

Two weeks later, Nickel returned to the Babson mansion for one last look. As he approached, he could see no sign of the house behind the still-barren spring trees that lined Longcommon Road. The house had been flattened. He hadn't thought it would go so fast.

The turn of the new decade was a difficult time. Ben Raeburn at Horizon Press still believed in him and the Sullivan project, but Richard was making little progress on the book. He moved into Siskind's apartment at 615 North LaSalle Street on the city's Near North Side to focus on the book. "The idea was that I should take an apartment to be free of the home disturbances, be closer to my work, the libraries, etc.," Nickel wrote, "but the arrangement did not work." When Siskind returned with a new wife and her daughter, the apartment was too crowded and it was obvious to Richard that he should move back home.

He was also having financial trouble. "I pondered the problem a week. . . . started looking at want ads and trying to figure out what kind of job I wanted. The next Monday morning I went to see Siskind at his apartment to tell him I was about to give the whole thing up," Nickel wrote. But Edgar Kaufmann, Jr.—son of the Pittsburgh retailer for whom Frank Lloyd Wright had designed several buildings, including the Fallingwater home in Bear Run, Pennsylvania—came to the rescue with $5,000 to keep the Sullivan project alive.

In late January of 1960, Nickel learned that Adler and Sullivan's "soaring tower," the 17-story Garrick Theater Building in the heart of the Loop, was to be demolished. David Wallerstein, president of the firm that owned the building, Balaban and Katz, told newspaper reporters that the building was being sold. It was losing too much money and was too old-fashioned. It was to be replaced by a parking lot, he said.

"Oh well, guess it is time to get out the old pick axe again," a friend wrote Nickel. But the Garrick was the one Sullivan building that Richard could not bear to see demolished.

The commission for the Garrick, to be built at 64 West Randolph Street, had come to Adler and Sullivan in late 1890. Like the Auditorium, the Garrick was a theater ingeniously surrounded by offices. Originally named the Schiller Building, it was built primarily to serve as an opera house for German Americans. The offices were meant to financially support the German Opera Company.

In 1898 opera gave way to vaudeville and the name of the building was changed to the Dearborn. Five years later the name was changed to the Garrick when the Shubert Brothers purchased the building and made it the "Flagship of the Shuberts' fleet" of theaters. From 1910 to 1950, the Garrick building was leased, subleased, sold, or put into receivership a half-dozen times. Throughout the years, the theater remained a popular stop on the vaudeville circuit, becoming the Chicago home for such stars as Mary Pickford, Al Jolson, Lionel Barrymore, Sophie Tucker, Jimmy Durante, Eddie Cantor, and Bob Hope.

Between World War I and the Great Depression, the two-block stretch of Randolph Street between State and Clark streets was a national center for popular sheet-music publishers. About 50 pluggers filled the Garrick and neighboring buildings, selling their new material to traveling vaudevillians. Chicago's Tin Pan Alley was where Leo Friedman wrote "Let Me Call You Sweetheart" and Gus Kahn wrote "Yes Sir, That's My Baby."

In 1950 the theater was closed and converted into a television studio. Seven years later, the Garrick was sold to Balaban and Katz, a theater company, and reopened as a movie theater with new sound and projection equipment, air conditioning, and new seats for the Midwest premiere of "Fear Strikes Out."

When Chicago officials announced in 1959 that the city would build a square-block Civic Center across the street from the Garrick, Wallerstein determined that the Garrick's future was limited. He made a deal with the operator of a Loop parking lot to wreck the Garrick and build a new garage. Instead of losing money

by running the office building, Wallerstein figured that Balaban and Katz would receive a minimum $135,000-a-year profit in rent from the garage. When he hired the Atlas Wrecking Company to tear down the building for $140,000, Wallerstein never thought that anybody would object.

The once-noble Garrick was dilapidated by 1960. Cheap rents attracted private detectives, phrenologists and ne'er-do-well attorneys. Many of Sullivan's exterior details, such as the top-floor cupola and cornice, had been removed or covered over. The entire exterior entrance area had been disfigured from remodelings. An ancient boiler heated the building and stag movies were shown in the 13th-floor lodge hall at night.

The idea of saving the building must have baffled most anyone who took notice of the Garrick. All that most passersby saw of the building was the fake 1950s Permastone facade of the first-floor Ham 'n' Egger restaurant and its flashing "Always Open" and "Never Closed" signs. Declaring the Garrick pretty was like saying a West Madison Street bum was handsome. All you noticed as you approached the Garrick was its stinky, ragged suit. The building's light brown terra cotta was covered with dirt.

The Garrick had been built in the Sullivan tradition. The bottom two floors formed a base to attract the eye. The wide-open first floor served as a grand theater entrance. Above, the facade reflected the location of the building's 342 offices. The building tower rose 211 feet above Randolph Street, and was topped by a columned arcade and several feet of overhanging terra cotta.

The six-story theater served as the base for seven stories of offices. Iron trusses, two stories tall, sat atop the theater to carry the weight of the upper floors and suspend the graceful plaster arches of the theater below. Each truss carried a 300-ton load.

Although unnoticed and unappreciated by 1960, the Garrick had long won acclaim. In 1894 English architect Bannister Fletcher wrote that the Garrick design was as important to modern architecture as was the Parthenon design to Greek architecture. That same year, U.S. critic Barr Ferree called the Garrick "one of the most beautiful and impressive high buildings in the world."

Decades later, Hugh Morrison appraised the beauty of the Garrick's theater as equal to any other by Adler and Sullivan. Sullivan biographer Willard Connelly wrote that the Garrick would be forever significant on a national scale. "With the Schiller Building the era of the American skyscraper firmly caught the public fancy, and the East began to talk of the multiple-storied architecture of Chicago," he wrote.

Nickel, too, saw beauty and greatness above the Ham 'n' Egger. The Garrick, he believed, was the culmination of Sullivan's early architectural ideas. The building was a brilliant solution to the problem of designing a skyscraper on a fairly small urban lot in the center of a block, and foreshadowed the "set-back" skyscrapers of the following decades. By the 1890s it was possible to clad entire buildings in terra cotta—which is just what Sullivan did. Taking advantage of the material's plasticity and adaptability, Sullivan treated the facade of the Schiller as a fluid, undulating skin, shaped as if the entire building were sculpted out of a single lump of moldable clay. The effect was heightened by contrasts: light-and-shadow, straight lines to curved lines, and the relationship of the building's flat wall to three-dimensional terra-cotta ornament.

"The form of the building answers the need for light and air—which ruthless real estate operators and money-hungry clients were not so prone to recognize," Nickel wrote.

As his eyes followed the piers rising to the top of the Garrick, Nickel sensed great power in the Randolph Street facade. As Sullivan had said, it was designed "without a single dissenting line." Wrote Nickel, "The Garrick is Adler and Sullivan's tallest building. What would the world say were we to destroy the accomplishment of the man who gave esthetic expression to the tall building?" To Nickel, the building was a bold piece of sculpture.

Richard also loved the theater space. Although it was not the tour de force of the Auditorium Theater, the cozy Garrick had its own charm. "Vision was unobstructed; acoustics were near perfect; scale and spatial relationships were exactly calculated to give a sense of intimacy while preserving the necessary spaciousness of a large theater," Richard wrote.

The theater was basically a great masonry box within which was hung and applied a shell of plaster, which, like terra cotta, is moldable. The interior was a column-free span detailed with a breathtaking progression of plaster shapes and forms that interplayed in different relationships as one moved through the room.

In the early 1950s Nickel and Siskind took exquisite photographs of the wide spans of the theater's ornamented semi-circular ceiling arches. They showed the beauty of the space despite the clutter of klieg lights and apparatus of the TV studio. "Even in its final state, the proscenium vault was equal and maybe greater than any Gothic cathedral I've seen," Nickel wrote.

Nickel's first response to news of the Garrick's planned destruction was to finish documenting the building. Preoccupied as he was with the Babson house, however, Nickel did not focus on the Garrick until early 1960. On March 28 he wrote, "In the last week, as I've worked about the building, gathering data and making record photographs, I realize that the Garrick is one of Adler and Sullivan's most important works."

During that month, when Balaban and Katz began ousting tenants, Nickel wrote a note to himself detailing how the Garrick could be converted to government offices, artists' studios, a hotel, or a school, and how the theater could be turned into a showcase for art, foreign films, or legitimate theater.

"I say the Garrick would still do its job if it was maintained as any good office building deserves and if it was kept up to date," he wrote. "That there are no toilets on all floors, that it still uses DC current, that it is still coal stoked (by hand) etc., etc., suggests mismanagement or, as Caldwell states, 'They want to bleed every last dollar out of the building and then scuttle it.'"

Nickel did not make his thoughts public. He had received permission to enter and photograph the building and did not want the privilege taken away.

His priority was to photograph the exterior. He worked so hard and for so many hours that he never even took time to make proof sheets of his negatives.

Nickel tried to photograph calmly, taking pictures in his most objective manner. However, his frustration showed. Unlike his early work, almost all of Nickel's photographs of Garrick ornament were shot off-center. His pictures of the front facade were unusual because he did not crop out the building's glitzy theater marquee. Instead of showing the busts of European philosophers and artists on the Garrick's second-floor balcony in the context of when they were built, Nickel photographed them cynically hovering above the first-floor restaurant. His picture "Beethoven looking over the Ham 'n' Egger" was one of his favorites.

But he also photographed everything in the interior, taking pictures of the lobby, elevators, stairways, lodge rooms, and many of the Garrick's offices. He even took photographs of a messy supply room. Siskind taught his students to find order in disorder, and Nickel—who produced arty views of the supply room's chaos—showed that he had learned his lesson well.

To photograph the theater he usually arrived after the last movie around midnight and stayed until dawn. He took exploratory pictures with a small-format camera and returned during the last week in March with his large-format camera so that he could capture as much detail as possible. Nickel's 4-by-5-inch Linhof camera was heavily worn by years of use. The standard was so loose on the track that Richard was never sure it was parallel to the back. "It is easy to check that visually in bright light, but when you light a huge theater, it is still pretty dim and wide-angle lenses are only f8 maximum aperture, the good ones," he wrote. Nickel was working with one 1,000-watt and a few 500-watt flood lights, exposing Tri-X black-and-white film at f16 for about eight minutes. Although working under difficult circumstances, Nickel promised himself that he would not stop until he was satisfied. "I find myself having to retake many pictures nowadays," he wrote. "Something always goes wrong the first try. . . .it is fantastic the things that can go wrong, or make petty nuisances. Photography requires a strong back too."

The late treks proved worthwhile. One night, he discovered a stencil pattern under layers of paint near the wainscoting, the wood paneling in the gallery. It was the first hint of a horde of hidden treasure he was later to uncover.

Richard caught a cold the weekend of April 15–16 while shooting the theater gallery. Because of union regulations, the building manager would not let him pass through the projectionist booth to the closed gallery. Undeterred, he went outside and climbed into the gallery from the roof of the neighboring Greyhound bus terminal through a door on the fourth floor of the Garrick.

"This involved being in and out, setting lights and then running back to the camera," Nickel wrote. "Then back to set the lights, and so on. It was warm enough out, but damp. Well, I'm paying for it now. What annoys me more is that some of the negatives do not have a focus in all parts to satisfy me, after days of effort."

Nickel's black-and-white photographs helped others appreciate the Garrick, particularly its 1,286-seat theater. By 1960 Sullivan's plaster ornament had been painted over in garish colors. The woodwork was painted red, which made it glow like a Christmas tree, and the arches were steeped in tones that ranged from salmon to wine purple. But the bad paint jobs disappeared in the black-and-white pictures.

Structure and form once again took center stage.

Richard took dynamic pictures of the seating arrangements and of the ornament inside the theater. Again, he demonstrated what he learned from Siskind. The photographs are like abstract art, exploring shapes, textures, and patterns. Like Siskind, who had taken beautiful pictures of Sullivan's Walker Warehouse before it was destroyed in the early 1950s, Nickel pulled his camera so close that the Garrick ornament flowed in and out of the picture frame. He also took great effort to show how the room worked. He climbed above the theater to photograph the trusses, and pointed his camera down to show the ironwork rods and framework that held up the magical, floating theater arches. Backstage, he revealed the secret of the rigging loft, four tremendous wrought-iron Phoenix columns, rising from the basement to the eighth floor.

The condition of the theater saddened Nickel. The stairway system leading to the main room had been changed to work just the opposite from the way it had been planned. The vestibules, once framed with oak and ornamental trim panel, had been hideously refinished. Part of the wooden floor had been relaid with concrete, and extra seats had been added to the main floor and the foyer. The lights, recessed into the plaster walls to give the room an elegant gold tone, had been replaced with cheap light fixtures. The statues in the boxes and the balcony paintings were long gone and the stairway to the gallery had been closed.

"As I look back, the building was a mess," Nickel wrote in 1965. "You wouldn't find a better example of planned obsolescence even in Detroit. However, this was not planned. It was a simple matter of making any concession to a tenant or prospective tenant in order to make a buck."

Finally, on April 22 with the photo work completed, Nickel took action. He wrote Arnold Maremont, a millionaire philanthropist and a patron of the arts, requesting financial and political help to mount a campaign to save the Garrick. "I appear to be fighting a lone battle in the cause of this building," Nickel wrote. "Everybody, and I only speak of people who should care, says 'It's a matter of economics.' Well, isn't architecture a public art too?" Maremont, who had political aspirations, wrote back that he had no time to help.

"What is going on in Chicago?" Nickel wrote a few days later. "The Walker Warehouse went uncontested to the best of my knowledge and what a jewel of a building that was! And since, many smaller insignificant Adler and Sullivan buildings have gone, but now the Garrick. Something should be done about that."

Nickel decided that, despite warnings that his fight to save the Garrick would be fruitless, he would forge ahead. "Nothing developing in the papers on the Garrick," he wrote on April 27, 1960.

Looks like we are going to lose the fight. I am still working in the building (finding out how green I am as a photographer) and so do not want to stick my neck out by writing to the newspapers. But will in another week or 10 days. I am hot to write the essay on the Garrick but the photography comes first, also the measuring and note-making. Photographing interiors is a back breaker; I may come to love using my mind yet.

The proscenium arch
rises above television
studio lights at the
Garrick Theater during
the 1950s.

The same day, Balaban and Katz signed its lease with the Garrick Garage Corporation. Nickel found out from the building engineer that the building was scheduled to come down on June 1. He could wait no longer.

In late April, he sent off dozens of letters to architects all over the world asking for help and suggesting they write protest letters. He wrote Sullivan's old associate, William Gray Purcell, in Pasadena:

Your plea to save the Garrick could be very effective and I wish you would jot something to the Voice of the People, Chicago Tribune, 435 N. Michigan Ave. If you do want to help, here are some items worth taking up:

1. That you've heard of the Chicago Landmarks Commission but what is its function if a building as important as the Garrick is allowed to be demolished? (A member of this committee has invited attacks to clarify what they are doing.)

2. Your visit to the theater after being away from Chicago for a number of years, and finding it fresh and "right." (I believe you have something in your files on this subject).

3. The fact that you had the privilege to work for Sullivan.

Because of the Garrick's early connection to the German community, Nickel wrote to the German consulate general, the *Abendpost-Sonntagpost* newspaper, the Germania Club, the German Old People's Home, and to anyone else with any possible reason to support his cause.

Saving the Garrick soon became full-time work. Nickel's monthly phone bill reached nearly $50 in mid-1960. On May 2 he wrote, "I am not doing anything in the cause of my book these days, but I am having one grand time—and learning a lot—trying to save the Garrick."

The idea of officially preserving architecture dates back to ancient Rome, when Emperor Majorian issued an edict to put an end to the destruction of the empire's monuments. The order, proclaimed about A.D. 460, was aimed at builders who, instead of traveling to distant quarries to gather material, plundered stone from standing statuary.

During the centuries when space was plentiful, buildings were generally left to stand until they collapsed. By the 19th century, however, congestion in large cities began to take its toll on architecture. In 1830 King Louis Philippe of France appointed a commission to inventory his country's worthwhile buildings. Soon after, architect Eugène Emmanuel Viollet-le-Duc was hired by the government to restore many of France's great buildings. In England, such private groups as William Morris's Society for the Protection of Ancient Buildings formed the vanguard of the movement to save architecture.

No laws to save buildings existed in the United States until 1906, when Congress passed the Antiquarian Act, thereby designating certain monuments on federal property worthy of protection. Until then the only designated landmarks in the United States had been buildings where great Revolutionary period events had taken place, such as the Old South Meeting House in Boston and Independence Hall in Philadelphia; or where great people had lived, such as President Washington's Mount Vernon in Virginia.

The effort to save Chicago's great buildings began in March 1957, when Frank Lloyd Wright arrived in the Hyde Park neighborhood near the University of Chicago to fight for his Robie House. Swinging his cane as he inspected the house at 5757 South Woodlawn Avenue, the 87-year-old Wright characterized as "barbarism" the Chicago Theological Seminary's plan to raze the Robie and replace it with a dormitory. Wright called the Robie House the "cornerstone of American architecture" and promised to build a "a charming dormitory which would win the admiration of the world" if his house were left in place.

"To destroy it would be like destroying a great piece of sculpture or a great work of art," he told reporters. "It would never be permitted in Europe. It could only happen in America, and it is particularly sad that professional religionists should be the executioners."

Wright loved the fight because it gave him a chance both to promote his architecture and to attack organized religion. He blasted the Protestant seminarians for not appreciating the Robie, and declared, "It proves that you cannot trust theologians with spiritual matters."

Wright's visit sparked a worldwide protest against plans to tear down the Robie House. In late April 1957, the newly formed Chicago Commission on Architectural Landmarks named the Robie House the city's first landmark. Although lacking any legal authority, the commission recommended that Chicago make every effort to preserve the Robie House, and requested that the seminary reconsider its plans. On April 26 city building commissioner George L. Ramsey issued orders to block a wrecking permit of the Robie until he received instructions from the city's law office.

Arthur Cushman McGiffert, Jr., president of the seminary, stood firm. He wrote the landmarks commission that he would give the house to the city if it agreed to move it to the nearby Midway, an open area of green space. "What they ought to do is build a nice model of the Robie House and put it in the Museum of Science and Industry or the Art Institute," McGiffert said. "Then the architects could all go look at it without the roof leaking on them."

Wright retracted his earlier offer to repair the Robie House, citing the "graft" of the seminary. "The house is really in marvelous shape considering the abuse it has suffered," Wright wrote Samuel Lichtmann of the landmarks commission. "The students came in here and made whoopee, you know." Eventually, however, the Robie House was saved. The house was purchased, repaired, and turned over to the University of Chicago.

Few other buildings had received such immunity from the dreamers and builders of the new Chicago—not even historic Fort Dearborn. The fort, built in 1812 to replace the city's first military outpost, was demolished after years of neglect. Thirty-four downtown buildings, including William Le Baron Jenney's trailblazing Home Insurance Building, were razed from 1925 to 1940. Little was spared, not even George M. Pullman's grand house, Cyrus Hall McCormick's huge mansion at 675 Rush Street, Potter Palmer's castle on Lake Shore Drive, or the Wright-designed Midway Gardens on the South Side. During the seven years of the Depression, more buildings and houses were torn down in Chicago than were built, prompting one tourist to remark: "A visitor to the heart of Chicago must wonder what has happened to the metropolis of the Middle West."

A rare exception was the Water Tower. A venerable 128-foot-tall standpipe that survived the Great Fire, the Water Tower was called a "bottle neck" by city planners in 1918 and was targeted for demolition. It was saved by Mayor William ("Big Bill the Builder") Hale Thompson when he ordered that the new Michigan Avenue be built around the tower. Decades later, it survived a proposal to tear it down for an apartment complex and later outlasted a 1948 plan to raze it for an arts center.

By 1960 economic growth had wrought even more destruction. Plane and jet traffic broadened the city's economic base and increased its business activity, making Chicago a powerful force in world trade. The new Inland Steel Building and Prudential Building heralded a new Chicago. Before the end of the year, the D. H. Burnham Great Northern Office Building and Theater as well as Holabird and Roche's Republic and Cable buildings were doomed.

But the mood of Chicago was changing. Few of these buildings were torn down without at least a nostalgic protest letter in the local newspapers. In late 1955 Hyde Park resident Thomas Stauffer held meetings with civic leaders, architects, and newspaper reporters to introduce his idea of establishing a city commission to preserve "the architectural wonders of Chicago." Stauffer's friend, Alderman Leon M. Despres, prepared an ordinance designed to protect city landmarks. "Since the ordinance presented no threat, but glorified Chicago, it passed," Despres wrote. On January 18, 1957, the City Council voted 48-0 to create the Chicago Commission on Architectural Landmarks.

Mayor Richard J. Daley ushered the commission's eight members into his office and delivered a short speech on the importance of their work. Nine days later, the commission declared the Robie House the city's first landmark.

The Garrick was one of 13 buildings cited as primary landmarks by the commission in 1959. A plaque was presented to the owners of the buildings at a formal dinner.

Nickel was not involved in the early effort to create a landmarks commission, but he was aware of Stauffer's work. Nickel saved all of the newspaper articles on the proposed commission starting with Stauffer's first letter to the editor in 1955.

In May 1960, Nickel wrote Stauffer a letter introducing himself and asking for his help in saving the Garrick. Before Stauffer had finished reading the letter, he called Nickel and invited him over to work out a plan.

The 43-year-old Stauffer was erudite but abrasive. He had attended the University of Chicago from kindergarten through graduate school. He received his bachelor of arts degree in 1936 but never received his Ph.D. because he was unable to finish his doctoral thesis. Working as a classroom and television instructor of social sciences and humanities at Chicago City Junior Colleges, Stauffer seemed to be the perfect front man for the Garrick fight. With a professorial demeanor and a gravelly voice, he could quote from Aristotle and Le Corbusier. But his gruff demeanor turned many off. "He's like an air-filled balloon, shooting about the place and hitting everything, but often not on target," Nickel wrote.

Stauffer, who had grown up in Hyde Park, had become an architectural junky when his father told young Tom that the nearby Robie House was built to resemble a steamship. This was enough to tickle any boy's imagination. After four years in the army as an intelligence officer and five years overseas in the State Department foreign service, Stauffer returned to Chicago in the early 1950s. He served as a special assistant to his local congressman and worked as a behind-the-scenes leader in the movement to integrate his Hyde Park neighborhood.

The Garrick was not important to Stauffer; he was not even sure if he had ever been inside the theater. But he saw the Garrick as a means to an end, a way to keep the landmarks fight alive while pushing for laws that would protect Chicago's architectural past. Although he had a genuine interest in preservation, he was not necessarily concerned about saving specific buildings. "It was not this man and that, creating this or that building that is the miracle," he wrote, "but collective man building the human city."

Stauffer wanted to convince City Hall that architecture was worthy of public protection—through tax relief, grants, and laws to prevent destruction. He knew he must first take the issue to the public. He later mused: "If Lincoln would have taken a piss in the Garrick, we would have had no problem saving the building."

Nickel, meanwhile, saw the Garrick as an end unto itself. Although grateful for Stauffer's efforts, he at first had little interest in working for laws to protect architecture. Instead, he preferred a rear-guard action, saving buildings one by one as they were threatened. He would have been content to close up the Garrick and take tours through it from time to time. Richard never pretended to be practical. Money issues, however familiar, were irrelevant to him. "Caldwell gave me that crap about 'economic expediency' as if I didn't know it already," he wrote during the height of the Garrick fight.

Because of their differences, Nickel and Stauffer were never friends. To Richard's chagrin, Stauffer called him "Dickel," for Dick Nickel. And Richard once characterized Stauffer—to his face—as being "as brusque as a truck driver." But as Stauffer later noted, there was no need for friendship; like Goethe and Schiller, he and Nickel were bound by work and purpose.

After meeting Stauffer, Nickel wrote the landmarks commission asking for a "holding action" and sent Mayor Daley a two-page letter defending his position.

Daley didn't respond. Samuel Lichtmann, the commission's vice president, wrote Nickel on May 5 to say that the city was powerless to stop the demolition. "There are economic circumstances beyond our control," Lichtmann replied. "We have no money and no legal powers other than working through the city building and other departments." A few days later, landmarks commission president Augustin J. Bowe wrote Nickel and Stauffer that he had been advised that the theater was structurally "obsolete" and that the office building had outlived its usefulness. "We must recognize the socio-economic factors that affect our society today," Bowe wrote.

That same day, Nickel sent a letter to the *Chicago American, Chicago Daily Tribune,* and *Chicago Sun-Times.*

> *The face of Chicago is being transformed. There is no questioning it, and apparently, no stopping it. This sad fact compels me to write an appreciation of one of architect Louis H. Sullivan's most noble buildings. The Garrick, a combination theater and office building erected in 1891 as the Schiller, is threatened with demolition.*
>
> *What will come in its stead no one knows, perhaps nothing more than a parking lot. But what will be taken from me is perfectly clear.*

I no longer will be able to stop momentarily at the foot of the building and exult in following it from base through shaft upwards to its mighty tower.

My fascination with the fenestration—the square static windows, at once suppressed by the tower and expressive of it, and the bay windows, perfectly formed as the facets of a diamond—will be ended.

The idea of the building, its form, will remain only in memory for it will not be there to feel 'in the round.'

Sullivan's glorious ornament, whether formal or surging of the life of the building, will have been broken formless in the fall to the ground.

And the beautiful proscenium vault, which ravishes and strikes one speechless in its rise and sweep. . .it is hard to believe we would allow this to be destroyed!

Nothing can replace the joy and satisfaction this single building has given me. No new building in Chicago, be they of the finest materials, appears to offer what the Garrick does—the mind and heart of a great man.

I only hope that those who condemn the building can justify its loss. "Economic circumstances" can be resolved but this symbol of American culture of the 1890s can never be replaced.

By mid-May, telegrams and letters of protest that Nickel had sought began pouring in—to Daley's office, to the landmarks commission, and to newspapers. Sullivan's colleagues, architect A. O. Budina and sculptor Alfonso Iannelli, reached Daley by mail. Olgivanna Wright, Frank Lloyd Wright's widow, sent Daley a plea by telegram. "What marks the degree of culture of other countries in the world is chiefly and most obviously their architectural monuments," she cabled. "Would it not make us all gasp if we heard that Notre Dame was to be destroyed for a parking lot?" The French architect Le Corbusier wrote Daley, "The 'Chicago school' was of the highest importance. To demolish these works therefore seems to me truly a sacrilege. Being a city planner myself I know that it is possible to preserve the life and usefulness of such buildings. It is a question of imagination."

Nickel solicited and received letters from Arthur Drexler, director of architecture and design at the Museum of Modern Art in New York, Harvard University architecture professor Jose Luis Sert, and Lewis Mumford, who later wrote, "Please carry my warm admiration to Richard Nickel for his valiant lonely effort."

In a letter to the newspapers entitled "The Prodigal City," Nickel's former teacher at the Institute of Design, Alfred Caldwell, declared that the Garrick is "part of the cultural inheritance of the nation and does not belong to individuals to destroy."

The assertion that this building is old-fashioned is curious. Nothing will be old-fashioned quicker than the overwhelming majority of sleazy buildings being built today. In reality, a good building is never old-fashioned. Are the 12th-century French cathedrals old-fashioned, or the Parthenon?—or to bring matters to relatively recent times—is Berlage's great hall at Amsterdam or the Brooklyn Bridge old-fashioned too? Or Frank Lloyd Wright's Robie House on Woodlawn Avenue? To ask the question is to laugh. Fashion is simply the huckster's sales talk.

After the first barrage of letters from the architectural community, non-architects came to the defense of the Garrick in letters to newspapers and the landmarks commission. One man suggested turning the building into a courthouse; another suggested converting it into the Chicago branch of the University of Illinois. A John Switalski wrote, "Chicago allowed Louis Sullivan to die in abject poverty. But since his reputation as the 'father of modern architecture' is now universally recognized, it is incredible that the influential people of this city are so indifferent to the fate of his building." Jacob L. Getty wrote, "The proposed destruction of the Garrick Theater for a parking garage is another typical example of the cultural decay of Chicago."

Suddenly, the Garrick was a potent public issue.

The controversial building's last picture show, a double feature of "Masters of the Congo Jungle" and "When Comedy Was King," was shown on May 27. Anticipating that Balaban and Katz would soon file a request to demolish the building despite the public outcry, Leon Despres, one of the few aldermen not aligned with Daley's machine, introduced a resolution that day in the City Council to withhold a wrecking permit. "Unfortunately, it is not likely to stand there much more than a few days longer," wrote Despres. The proposal was sent to the Committee on Rules, a traditional burial ground for gadfly requests. "Thus the resolution has become an epitaph," Despres wrote Nickel.

But hope remained. When the theater company filed for a wrecking permit on June 1, Building Commissioner Ramsey refused to issue it until the legal status of the Garrick was determined.

Balaban and Katz's Wallerstein was baffled. He called Daley, who told Wallerstein that he planned to hold a public hearing on the Garrick. "There's nothing I can do about it now," Daley told Wallerstein. "It's too hot to handle."

Meanwhile, Bowe's landmarks commission held a special meeting and determined that it was "not feasible" to save the Garrick.

Nickel lashed out at Bowe. "I have been fighting to save the Garrick from demolition," he wrote,

but find, due to the negative stand which the Commission on Chicago Architectural Landmarks has taken, that the battle is futile. At every turn in my efforts, I am confronted by the judgment of the commission that the building is "uneconomical" and that, in effect, it cannot be saved.

While this may be true in the case of the present ownership, I believe it can be remodeled; the building should really be put into the hands of a capable management firm. In any case, I intend to continue the fight, for the architectural value of the Garrick is the main thing.

On June 7, 1960, Nickel began a demonstration against the demolition of the Garrick Building. Carrying a sign that read "DO WE DARE SQUANDER CHICAGO'S GREAT ARCHITECTURAL HERITAGE," he marched down Randolph Street with his friend Chuck Swedlund. This was the day attorneys from Balaban and Katz rode up and asked Nickel, "What the hell do you think you are doing?"

He was joined by Thomas Stauffer and about a dozen other friends the following day. Stauffer, the first to arrive, remembers that he and Nickel felt more lonely than brave as they readied picket signs in the alley. "As unlikely a crew of agitators as ever assembled are whooping it up (sedately, of course) in front of the Garrick Theater these days," wrote Mervin Block in a *Chicago American* story entitled "Picket Garrick Razing: Eggheads Plead for Culture." He wrote: "Doctors of philosophy, Phi Beta Kappas, professors, architects, and others of that intellectual ilk were picketing, passing out handbills, circulating petitions, and declaiming yesterday."

Nickel and his cohorts marched for four or five days and gathered 3,300 signatures protesting the demolition. Joining them were Aaron Siskind; architect Philip Johnson, who was in Chicago and said he wanted to go around a few times; Chicago Art Institute curator Hans Huth; and 82-year-old Sarah Adler Weil, Dankmar Adler's daughter. Mies van der Rohe did not march because he was ill, but sent word he was "100 percent" behind the effort.

John Vinci arrived with a sign that read "Mayor Daley destroys buildings as Hitler destroys Jews." Stauffer, who had procured the marching permit, told Vinci he could not join the line if he carried the sign. Vinci refused to back down and picketed by himself nearby.

After the picketing, the *Chicago Sun-Times* kept the Garrick issue alive. Nickel had sparked the paper's interest when he approached reporter Ruth Moore in early May asking to get publicity for his salvage work so that he could create interest in the Garrick. "I've devoted a fantastic amount of time, money, gas, etc. on this project and received little recognition," he wrote her. "It is either the usual pat-on-the-back from people who appreciate it or the attitude that I am a 'screwball' from those who don't. Any article you would do would at least give me a little stature." Moore and the paper took on saving the Garrick as a cause, publishing articles almost daily during the summer.

Like a happy St. Bernard puppy, Nickel's emotions showed all over his face, recalled Moore, who covered the city for several decades. With his genial, trustworthy, approachable appearance, Nickel appeared to her as a little boy grown tall. When Nickel took Moore on several tours of the Garrick, she was struck by his sincerity and by the beauty of his photographs. "He had an unwavering conviction that this great art had to be saved," she said. "He talked well, quietly and modestly, and never threatened or made exaggerated statements like most people with a cause. He was reasoned and reasonable. He really cared, and backed his feelings up with intellectual and artistic understanding."

To Jacob Burck, the *Chicago Sun-Times* editorial cartoonist who won a Pulitzer Prize during the 1940s, Nickel was a "ray of hope," a young, vital person who was telling the blind city to open its eyes. The first of Burck's many cartoons on the Garrick fight showed tourists walking through the ruins of the Acropolis and remarking: "If We Had This In Chicago, We'd Knock It Down And Make A Parking Lot." The following day the paper came out strongly in favor of the Garrick with its "It Couldn't Happen In Athens" editorial. "To destroy it would be as sensible as throwing out a Rembrandt because it had gotten dirty."

Mayor Daley responded to the Garrick publicity in June by inviting about 100 people to the City Council chambers for a hearing on the building's fate. Leading the fight was the Chicago Heritage Committee, a group founded by Nickel and Stauffer to rescue and rehabilitate the Garrick and push for legislation that would save the city's great architecture.

Stauffer, who presented petitions gathered during the picketing, was the first of 15 people to speak in favor of the Garrick. He suggested that Chicago issue revenue bonds to buy and renovate the building as had been done in New York City to save Carnegie Hall. The New York concert hall was saved from demolition at the last moment by state money and by a campaign started by violinist Isaac Stern that raised more than $4 million. Stauffer said the Garrick would cost an estimated $1.5 million to buy and more than $1 million to renovate. The bonds, he said, could be paid off from rents from the building.

Balaban and Katz attorney Arthur Goldberg countered the arguments. The company was losing $400 a day operating the Garrick, he said, because real estate taxes and maintenance costs far outran income from office rentals.

> *We cannot operate the present Garrick building except at a loss and we are positive that no one else can operate this building except at a loss. We believe that however desirable it may be to preserve this building as a landmark, it is impractical to try to preserve an expensive commercial building such as this after it has outlived its commercial usefulness.*

Balaban and Katz had decided to tear down the building for a parking lot long before "any agitation" to save the building began, he continued. "We believe that the fact that Mr. Sullivan designed this building is not a legal or proper reason to stop its demolition after it has outlived its usefulness and has become an economic burden."

Only one person, George R. Bailey of the Building Managers Association of Chicago, joined Goldberg in his assessment that the unprofitability of the Garrick

Carl Sandburg and Mayor Richard J. Daley look over a document at City Hall during Sandburg's 1957 visit. Paul M. Angle, president of the Chicago Historical Society, looks on.

should cause its destruction. "Keeping the Garrick is like keeping an elephant for a pet—very expensive," he said. Blueprints and old photographs would be an adequate reminder.

By holding the meeting, Daley raised hopes that the Garrick still had a chance. "I am sure that not only those in the audience, but the people in Chicago are wholeheartedly behind any program that seeks to demonstrate to the world the genius and ingenuity of Chicagoans," Daley said in his opening remarks. No matter how vague, the words lent legitimacy to Nickel's cause.

At the hearing's conclusion, Daley appointed a 14-member committee to find a solution to the Garrick problem. "I'm sure that a way can be found, must be found, and will be found to accomplish what we are striving for," Daley said.

Nickel, who was too shy to speak, called the public hearing a "smashing success." Afterward he wrote an out-of-town friend, "We are very close to being able to save it. Watch *Time* the next few weeks. We are raising hell here."

The only chance to save the Garrick, Nickel knew, was to convince Daley, for the mayor was the ultimate power figure. By law, Chicago was run by the mayor and 50 aldermen, but in 1955 the mayor had taken control when he told the City Council members that he would veto any measure "harmful to the people." Within a few years, Daley had gained power over the budget, over all city favors from jobs to zoning, and over the Cook County Democratic Party. "Make no small plans," he told his advisors, a reference to Daniel H. Burnham's celebrated planning credo. Nobody had the guts to tell Daley that the correct quotation was "Make no little plans."

Daley is largely responsible for the way Chicago looks today. He both preserved and disturbed the city. During his 21 years as mayor, he propelled it into a major economic force by building highways and the world's largest airport and convention centers, as well as by demolishing many square miles of slums. The argument that Chicago was the "city that works" required clarification. Chicago worked primarily for a powerful few.

By 1959 the city worked for those few as well as it ever had, moving Daley into the role of undisputed city boss. The St. Lawrence Seaway opened, connecting Chicago to the Atlantic Ocean; and the city played host to the International Trade Fair, the Pan-American Games, and Queen Elizabeth. Even Daley's beloved White Sox won the pennant that year. "We stand on the threshold of a great future, of tremendous expansion, and our destiny is to be one of the great cities of the world," Daley proclaimed.

Daley loved Chicago like he loved his family. He pointedly ignored the City-on-the-Make allusions by such literati as Nelson Algren, and snapped back at magazine writers who took uncomplimentary pokes at his "Lady of the Lake." Although he did not appreciate Chicago's architecture on an intellectual level, he was impressed by the people who cared and sensed that the city possessed a lode of worthwhile buildings.

Yet Daley was not a sentimentalist. He was a tough, practical, Machiavellian character who very ably sat on the sidelines while conflicting forces played out their cards. "That's a good way to run any business," he told *Life* magazine, and that is how he handled the Garrick fight. Wounded by the anti-intellectual charges hurled at him over the years, he realized there was something to be gained by playing ball with these architectural know-it-alls. But he owed his first allegiance to city developers who had helped him gain power. That is why Wallerstein was so surprised at Daley's cavalier attitude about the wrecking permit.

At the first meeting of his Garrick committee, Daley sounded magnanimous in his intentions to save the Garrick. He announced that he would ask the Public Building Commission to include the Garrick in its $67 million Civic Center project. "If the Garrick can be preserved, and I think that it must and can be, it would add a beautiful auditorium to the center where Chicago will receive its most distinguished guests and hold its civic ceremonies," he said.

The speech may have been only window dressing, because it soon became obvious that the Public Building Commission did not have the extra $2 million to $3 million needed to buy and restore the building.

For the following six months the fate of the unsinkable Garrick bobbed in the waves of big-city politics as aldermen, judges, civic leaders and the mayor took up sides for or against Nickel and his followers. There was no question on whose side stood Alderman Matthias "Paddy" Bauler. The former saloon-keeper, who was best known for his assessment that "Chicago ain't ready for reform," plunged right into the Garrick fracas with an opinion that must have been shared by many other Chicagoans: "Tear it down before it falls down."

Daley's early optimism was burst by a study that stunned everybody at the Garrick committee's second meeting. The report, issued by the Building Managers Association, concluded that the Garrick was "economically unsound." Repairs—including new tuckpointing, toilets, windows, sashes and frames, elevators and new plumbing, heating and electrical systems—would cost $2.1 million, more than rental income could ever recoup. Even if the Garrick were nearly fully rented after its restoration, it would lose about $105,000 a year.

For committee member Jack Randall, the report put an end to any hope. "I am still very sad for our great big bumbling boy of a city," he wrote the following day.

Nickel, too, was depressed, but he still hoped that the Public Building Commission, which Daley headed, would rescue the Garrick.

I am not sure who was the first to suggest making the Garrick a part of the Civic Center, but that is what will happen, I hope. Big business, realtors, are all convinced that when a building hits 50 to 70 years of age, it is wiser to tear it down and rebuild. They see no reason for being concerned about the historical or architectural value. I talked to Mies [van der Rohe] about this and he thinks the best thing is for the city to slowly gain control of important buildings.

In early July, Daley announced that the Public Building Commission could not purchase and restore the Garrick. Although prospects looked bleak, Nickel was a different man. "This campaign has changed my life. . . .I'll explain how one day," he wrote architect William Gray Purcell on June 27. "It's difficult to get back to work after the fight, but I am convinced of what I must do. . .what will be really meaningful."

The following month, he sent Alfred Caldwell a photo of a woman named Janice, whom he was dating. "Look at the pretty girl I met at the International Trade Fair," he wrote. "Aspiring model (ugh, again). Need some diversion." Nine days later, he wrote:

Janice is something all right, but what has cleared my skies is the fight for the Garrick! All this time I was going along thinking no one really cared, didn't know the difference, nothing could be done, etc. About everything, too. And so our near success, and the earlier effort for the whole building, changed my whole outlook, almost the way you describe the turn-around of architecture in the 1890s. (Before the Garrick I'd have admired the girl from afar and that's all.)

Nickel kept up his letter-writing campaign to keep the Garrick in the public eye. "It has been assumed by many that the removal of Adler and Sullivan's Garrick Building for a parking garage is simply part of the consumer process, like a carton which we use and throw away," he wrote the *Chicago Daily Tribune*.

We have to realize that the architect is a creator and endows a building with meaning. No attempt is made to give meaning to a milk carton, that it carries the milk without leaking satisfies us.

The expression a great architect achieves has continuing value, just like any work of art. Because architecture is three-dimensional and functional it can be saved, logically, by saving the whole building.

Once we learn to appreciate what our architects give us, we will not be so prone to allow the destruction of our great buildings. Keeping them useful and maintaining them is a problem which will be solved in great part by our enlightenment in the spiritual realm, which is what life and architecture are all about.

Balaban and Katz filed a lawsuit demanding that the city issue the wrecking permit on July 15, while Daley was at the Democratic National Convention in Los Angeles. Wallerstein did not want the bad publicity of a court case, but felt he had no other choice.

The Garrick went on trial on July 28. Before the hearing, Nickel brushed shoulders with Wallerstein outside the courtroom.

"Where do you get the money for your research?" Wallerstein asked Nickel.

"Edgar Kaufmann, Jr.," Nickel replied truthfully.

"That's all I wanted to know," Wallerstein said.

"He's probably going to snitch on me to Edgar," wrote Nickel to his friend, former Institute of Design student Kazimir Karpuszko. "Boy, they have it in for me."

The case was assigned to Superior Court Judge Donald S. McKinlay, a lifelong Democrat who could see the upper floors of the Garrick through his courtroom windows at City Hall. Although McKinlay, 72, knew little about architecture, he impressed Nickel on the first day of the hearing as a "very wise, liberal judge."

Edwin A. Rothschild, attorney for Balaban and Katz, thought the case was decided in the first two minutes when he asked city attorney Edward W. Parlee if the theater corporation had properly requested permission to wreck the building.

"Yes," Parlee replied, "we have examined all of these instruments, we have checked the code, and there is no question that the petitioners in this case have fully complied and shown everything that is required for the issuance of the permit."

Rothschild told McKinlay that Balaban and Katz, therefore, had a "clear legal right" to demolish the Garrick. "We are a corporation with obligations to our stockholders," he told the judge.

We are being forced to hold an empty shell on which we are losing several hundred dollars a day. We cannot continue to hold it until some day in some way someone may somehow think of a way to put it to use. To say that the owners should be compelled at their own expense to continue to hold the building indefinitely is fantastic.

Parlee told the court that the city needed more time to save the Garrick, and disputed Rothschild's claim that there was no legal precedent for courts protecting great architecture.

There is a growing need for a new principle of urban continuity so that the connective tissue of architectural design—buildings such as Sullivan's Garrick—can be saved in order to remove the raw edges, heal over scar tissue and link the present to the past and the future. To save what is best and salvageable from the past is not only an economic, but a strong esthetic necessity.

Several people took the stand to testify on behalf of the Garrick. Nickel watched, but did not testify. Rothschild would later confide that he felt as if he were fighting "a ghost," an invisible legal opponent. Instead of arguing law, he was forced to argue whether Sullivan was a great architect or whether the Garrick was a masterpiece.

Finally, Rothschild called to the stand William Horowitz, the architect commissioned by Balaban and Katz to design the garage to replace the Garrick. Horowitz did not want to testify. He admired Sullivan's work and had tried to convince Balaban and Katz to retrofit the building when he was first approached. Yet the parking lot was one of his largest commissions, and Horowitz did not want to lose the job.

Horowitz told the judge he would incorporate Sullivan's ornament in the new garage and install a plaque as a tribute to Sullivan. He argued that the Garrick was not functional. "It no longer does the job Sullivan wanted it to do," Horowitz said. "Again, it's conjecture, but it is my opinion that he would say 'Take it away.'"

But Horowitz's heart was not in his testimony. After telling the judge it would cost millions to restore the Garrick, Horowitz was asked by Parlee, "Even if it cost $5 million—we are not talking about $2 million now—do you think those ideas of beauty and culture and the spirit of Chicago should be preserved?"

"Yes," said Horowitz.

"That is all," said the lawyer.

After adjourning the hearing twice, Judge McKinlay visited the Garrick on August 10. He was accompanied by Nickel, Garrick committee member Jack Randall, and Arch Trebow, Balaban and Katz supervisor of buildings.

The theater was empty, dirty, and dark. Building inspectors had gouged holes in the walls and ceiling to conduct structural tests. The architects used flashlights to point out the ornament on the nine proscenium arches and the balcony.

"Magnificent," said Randall.

Trebow agreed, but said: "The iron beams behind the plaster are rusted out and there's practically nothing holding it up." He said the wooden floor made the understructure unsafe.

Nickel disagreed. He said he had walked on the superstructure holding up the vaulting and found no rust.

On the upper floors, Randall directed the judge's attention to the window frames, decorated with terra-cotta designs. Trebow said the terra cotta was falling off and impossible to repair. Again, Nickel disagreed.

After the tour, the judge said the building was "a pretty gruesome-looking place." But at the following hearing, he again held off a decision in the hope that the city could find a way to save the Garrick.

While McKinlay was deciding, the Chicago Heritage Committee held a rally for the Garrick in the Auditorium Building's Ganz Hall. About 175 people filled the recital hall to hear Alfred Caldwell, whose oratory kept the crowd spellbound. "Free enterprise," he said,

> is on trial here just as much as in its production of goods. This, too, is competition with Russia. All over the world, the enemies of America will be watching to see what is finally done about the Garrick Theater building, the Stock Exchange, the Monadnock Block. Our enemies will ask how real is a wealth that cannot take care of its own property; that witlessly tears down a Marshall Field Warehouse, mighty as the Kremlin, to make a parking lot; that levels the fabulous Midway Gardens of Frank Lloyd Wright to make a filling station; that assassinates a great building by Sullivan on the word of a bookkeeper.

Caldwell was at his best as he showed slides of the Garrick, Sullivan's Carson Pirie Scott store and Gage Building, and other Loop buildings.

> In these buildings, the Chicago architects left behind them the ludicrous mimicry of the past. Using steel and glass they created a new architecture as distinct as though it were another civilization, as in fact it was.

> These buildings revealed a new logic and a new depth of expression. By coming to grips with the real problems of building, renouncing the trivial and fictitious, the academic mish-mash of historical styles, a genuine style resulted, a veritable new architecture with all the old forces and clarity of ancient buildings.

Sounding like a gospel preacher, Caldwell brought the meeting to a foot-stomping conclusion. "If we tear down the Sullivan buildings we are in effect serving notice on the world and on ourselves that we repudiate the life of the spirit, and that we intend a belly-and-fashion civilization. We repudiate all the propositions by which men have always lived."

Judge McKinlay made his decision on August 23. For only the third time in 32 years as a judge, McKinlay wrote out his opinion. "It is difficult for one who has recently seen the inside of this building on busy Randolph Street to visualize what some artists and architects see in the structure," he stated.

> I don't doubt their sincerity, but I am sure millions of persons have passed it and are passing the building without especially noticing it.

> Part of the reason for this is that it is now deserted and badly in need of cleaning and repairs. Standing alone and appearing as when built in 1892, it was probably a very imposing edifice. The cornice has been removed and a

wall of plain new brick crowns the structure. The theater entrance is not as it was, in shape or material. The inside is very dirty as the tenants left it, with holes in the plaster, etc. Other things are different from the original although both on the exterior and interior still remain many fine designs in terra cotta.

The issue, he said, was whether the city could deny the wrecking permit if it compensated the owner. He concluded, "I cannot overrule the discretion of the city in refusing to issue a permit for wrecking the building unless the refusal is based on some unlawful or arbitrary act. And I fail to find anything unlawful or arbitrary in their denial of the permit."

Rothschild was so surprised he was not sure he heard McKinlay's opinion correctly. The lawyer announced immediately that Balaban and Katz would appeal.

The following day, Daley wrote attorney Parlee congratulating him on the victory. Daley said it was a great advance toward preservation throughout the country. Randall wrote Nickel: "Congratulations! Congratulations! Congratulations! and best regards. Where do we go from here?"

Nickel was cautiously optimistic. Suddenly sounding like the legal-minded Stauffer, he wrote Kazimir Karpuszko, his friend from Institute of Design days, that he hoped to set "good solid law" and save the Garrick.

Many important people around town have told us our achievement is fabulous and we think so too, but are wise enough to know we have gotten many good breaks.

The Garrick is still not saved but we are hopeful. The latest trend around town is to create a new image of Chicago—you know that line, I'm sure—and we actually have gotten support by a recent rape of a visiting school teacher. Also the fact that there are only three legitimate theaters left but some 8,000 saloons. They all say "Are we going to let Chicago become an asphalt jungle?" etc., etc., etc., all to the benefit of our cause.

Karpuszko wrote back: "Your latest achievement is pure history; even if the Garrick should go, you've done your work in the style of a great scholar, a 'struggling man without a fortune,' who cannot possibly be responsible for the ignorance and stagnation of other people."

Indeed, Nickel found there was little he could do as the Garrick case worked its way through the appellate process. The Garrick was boarded up in early September to prevent vagrants from sleeping in it as the weather got colder, but Nickel snuck in to clear the drains of the second-floor balcony system so they would work during the winter.

By the fall of 1960 Nickel had acquired a substantial reputation. The *New York Herald, St. Louis Post Dispatch,* and several architectural magazines all published articles about the Garrick fight. "The Garrick means little to most people in Chicago," explained Peter Jacobi in the *Christian Science Monitor.* "But those who love its beauties, who understand its importance—just like a larger group might understand the importance of a Babe Ruth or Knute Rockne—are trying to keep the wrecking crews away." *Variety* summed it up in *Variety*-ese: "With the newspapers milking it with fastidious round-by-round coverage, this town's latest *cause célèbre* has become an empty Loop landmark—the Garrick cinema. . . . It's been reprieved from scheduled razing (for a parking lot) because the town's architecture buffs raised a successful clamor for a display of cultural conscience."

The articles and radio and TV programs about the Garrick boosted Nickel's morale. The fight was front page news in Chicago. Ada Louise Huxtable, the architecture writer for the *New York Times*, wrote often about the Garrick, giving the fight national significance. Finally, *Time* magazine traced the legal victory's roots directly to Nickel: "As a result of a feverish crusade started by a 32-year-old architectural photographer named Richard Nickel, the case of the Garrick went before the Cook County Superior Court. The ruling could well be a historic one for Americans concerned about saving landmarks."

Nevertheless, the momentum to save the building slowed. Nickel took City Council members on a Garrick tour that "demoralized" him. "There were no signs of historical sympathy whatsoever," Nickel wrote, "only clever remarks about the distress of a still noble building." The aldermen came away more convinced that the Garrick was a fire and safety trap than a landmark. "I came, I saw, and I'm for demolishing," said Alderman Thomas F. Fitzpatrick. Even George Ramsey, the building commissioner who had withheld the Garrick and Robie House wrecking permits, showed little sympathy. He pointed to a stain on the balcony front and said it indicated moisture. Nickel agreed, but said it was caused because the balcony water drains had been closed. "The building commissioner and the commissioner of city planning thought I had an angle and just couldn't believe that anyone would raise such a fuss, especially for such a dumpy building as the Garrick," Nickel wrote. "I think these building commissioners still can't figure it all out."

The *Chicago Sun-Times* continued its support, publishing an editorial calling for the city to purchase and restore the Garrick, but Daley took no action. "At the moment we are very hopeful," Nickel wrote in September, "but there is always the possibility that it is all politically predetermined."

A panel of three state appellate court judges heard arguments on the Garrick case on November 1. A city attorney told the judges that the city needed a year to work out a way to save the Garrick and promised that a permit would be issued if the city decided not to purchase the building.

Rothschild, the Balaban and Katz attorney, argued that the city had no right to prevent demolition merely to "satisfy the aesthetic or cultural desires of miscellaneous members of the public who have no official status or financial responsibility in the matter." McKinlay had ruled "without a semblance of legal or legislative authority," leaving Balaban and Katz with a building that could not be used, sold, or demolished. "We are being made involuntary guardians of a shrine," he concluded.

The judges sided with Rothschild, voting unanimously to reverse McKinlay's opinion. They wrote that the theater was obsolete and a potential fire hazard. The city had 15 days to file the petition for rehearing and 55 days to appeal the case at the state supreme court.

The *Chicago Daily News* heralded the decision by running an editorial suggesting that photographs, drawings, and written descriptions of the building might be enough to remember it by. "To be honest about it," the piece ran, "our heart does not go as violently pitty-pat at the sight of the Garrick as some of its devotees consider proper."

Nickel wrote back, saying that photographs would be inadequate because architecture is a spatial art. "If we cannot experience works of art, they might as well not be created," he wrote.

With the city as yet undecided regarding the appeal, Stauffer and Nickel knew that the Garrick's fate was now in Daley's hands. Stauffer wrote the mayor a letter demanding that he live up to the city landmarks ordinance. The law, Stauffer wrote, was strong enough to save the Garrick. The building's imperiled status had been caused by the city's failure to come up with a plan.

Nickel wrote Daley a more positive letter, once again pointing out the significance of the Garrick by enclosing testimonials from books and journals. "The effect of saving the Garrick will be as exhilarating as the accomplishment of McCormick Place and the Northwest Expressway," he wrote.

> *It would evidence that Chicago has a cultural conscience—and heart and a soul which is above the singular money interest of a conventional city. Whatever happens to the Garrick, it will remain a symbol, either of our self-respect and recognition of our greatness, or of a day when enlightened and concerned citizens said, "We care" and the city of "I will" was irresolute.*

The tone of the letter concealed Nickel's waning confidence. He wrote Purcell in early December: "I fear that we have lost the Garrick. Not enough people really care, especially the architects."

It was time to start thinking about salvage work. This time, Nickel wanted to save the whole proscenium vault. He envisioned that the dome could be lifted from the building by helicopter as was done to transport Buckminster Fuller's geodesic domes. "I am going to prepare a prospectus on the project and try to get support for the idea," Nickel wrote to Purcell. "Mad, but I am convinced it can be done. If I sent you dimensions and description of metal frame and parts, thickness of plaster, etc. could you figure out the weight?"

The idea was naive. The dome was much too heavy for such a move. By itself, moreover, the proscenium would have little significance.

Nickel was quiet during the last few weeks of 1960, and again the Adler and Sullivan book played on his mind. In April he had written publisher Ben Raeburn that the book should be divided into two volumes, one on the firm's architecture and one on ornament. "Ben, our early work on Sullivan architecture was really pretty superficial," Nickel wrote.

In December he wrote Raeburn apologizing for his lack of work during the year. He said he had gotten carried away with the Garrick fight and with photography work for the landmarks commission. "Is the date of Dec. 31, 1961, for text completion satisfactory?" Nickel asked.

Raeburn responded bluntly:

I have your letter of the 7th and cannot tell you what a shock it is. Aside from the irrecoverable damage that the Dec. 31, 1961, date portends for Horizon, I don't know how we can explain such extreme violation of our promises upon which we secured the large extra sums of money to enable you to finish it some time ago.

I at first read your date as 1960, which after the long delay seemed natural to me; having thought you were making the notes all along and assumed that they'd need a couple of months of editing here. Allowing six months for all the

Wreckers remove ornament from the Garrick in 1961.

engravings, corrections, printing and binding, our production schedule would have just made publication in the fall of '61, which we have been crucially counting on.

Reluctantly, Raeburn agreed to Nickel's new schedule.

Nickel replied: "I view the 'Complete Architecture of Adler and Sullivan' as a monument, which is the reason for the struggle, the delay and the 'violation of promises.' The ideal is always a step ahead of my capabilities—but I will do that work."

Nickel did little more to save the Garrick. He wrote Daley about a fire that had broken out on the third floor of the Garrick, but had been contained with little damage. Nickel advised that the theater was in danger of more fires as long as the first-floor doors were left open. The city boarded up the entrance and the fire department put the Garrick on a 24-hour watch.

Finally, Daley met with the Garrick committee on January 5, 1961, and told the group that Chicago could not come up with $5 million to save and restore the Garrick. "What do you want me to do?" he asked.

Everybody except Randall voted to end the fight. "The meeting decided everything," Nickel wrote, "and outside of the principals, nobody knows who was there, what was said, etc. Jack was so disheartened by it then that he wouldn't even talk about it."

Later that day, Daley announced "with deep regret" that the city would not appeal the Garrick case. He said he would issue the wrecking permit without delay.

There was little left to do. Stauffer sent President-elect John F. Kennedy a telegram asking him to intervene. "The loss of the Garrick Building from the cultural heritage of mankind is another instance of the self-defeat of our urban culture: Every day our cities become uglier, every day more people leave them," he wrote. On January 6, the day the wrecking permit was issued, Stauffer led 30 picketers back to the Garrick. Nickel did not march.

Demolition started three days later. Wreckers removed the doors and elevators inside and started tearing down the marquee.

Nickel watched the work. "What has been revealed by the removal of the Garrick Theater marquee makes the imminent demolition of the landmark even more heart-rending," he wrote in a *Chicago Sun-Times* letter.

Looking up from the foot of the building one sees now how the projecting arcade forms a floating base for the movement and soaring qualities of the tower. It is an amazing and inspiring aerial conception, and strictly modern.

Underneath the gaudy porcelainized and plastic facing which for years defaced the entrance, other wonders are revealed. Above one of the entrances to the original basement beer stube a low relief figure has come into view, and on the ceiling a string course of beautiful star-like ornament. The fine scale and proportion of the theater entrance will never be more exposed than it is now just before the end.

Top stories of the Republic
Building. Nickel stood on top
of the cornice for his self-
portrait.

CHAPTER FIVE

DON'T IT ALWAYS SEEM TO GO THAT YOU DON'T KNOW WHAT YOU'VE GOT TILL IT'S GONE?
THEY PAVE PARADISE AND PUT UP A PARKING LOT.

Joni Mitchell, *"Big Yellow Taxi"*

The Garrick was not the only building Nickel mourned in 1960.

Two buildings by the Chicago architectural firm of Holabird and Roche had been condemned during the height of the Garrick battle. Neither the Cable nor the Republic buildings went unnoticed.

The handsome 10-story Cable, built in 1899 at 57 East Jackson Street, was a fine example of the Chicago School with its bold windows and sensuously fluted terra-cotta skin. The building's fate was sealed in mid-1960 when the Continental-National Insurance Company announced plans to replace it and three of its neighbors with a huge, 22-story office building.

Nickel conceded that the Cable was not worth fighting for.

"It would be unreasonable to hinder a $15 million improvement for a building which was notable but not as significant as the Garrick," he wrote. But he did want to document the building before it was demolished. In September he waited for an official assignment from the city landmarks commission. "Has the commission discussed what is to be done in the way of recording the Cable?" he wrote Joseph Benson, commission secretary. "Am I to do photographs only. . .or do you want me to go all the way? (I don't mean try to save it either!) I think an attempt should be made to search out old building records, clips, newspapers, photo blueprints and interview old tenants."

Benson made arrangements for the city to pay for a book with photographs and historical data on the Cable. Support for Nickel's work also came from D. E. Mackelmann, commissioner of the Chicago Community Conservation Board. After reading an article about Nickel, Mackelmann wrote Mayor Daley suggesting that the city identify and save "relics" from important structures about to be razed and install the ornament in parks, schools, playgrounds and shopping centers. Mackelmann's offer of city help lured Nickel. "I am against this," Nickel wrote members of the Chicago Heritage Committee concerning the proposal, "believing the ornament belongs in a museum. But this plan offers an interim solution."

In early October salvage work on the Cable began with Nickel directing a crew from the Speedway Wrecking Company. It was one of the first times any U.S. city had embarked on a program to save architectural ornament. Nickel and the wreckers removed sections of terra-cotta facade from the first, second, third, fourth, and tenth floors and transported the pieces to the city-owned Navy Pier for storage.

Nickel spent much of October documenting the Cable. He photographed all of the building's elevations and took photos of important details, from the roof to the boiler room. He tracked down executives and employees of the Cable Piano Company in order to gather a historical record of the construction, additions, and renovations. Paid by the city, Nickel prepared a book on the Cable that included measured drawings by Naess and Murphy, the architectural firm contracted for the new project. He also photographed the Continental Center building that replaced the Cable. Remarkably, it was one of few modern structures that Nickel thought was even better than the original.

Nickel was more saddened by the loss of the majestic 19-story Republic Building. With a white glazed terra-cotta facade that gleamed in the sunlight, and a sweeping bronze and marble arcade, the Republic was a gem. "This building sings of the steel skeleton construction," Nickel wrote to *Chicago Sun-Times* reporter Ruth Moore on September 25. "We hope to tackle that once we save, or they save, the Garrick (fingers crossed)."

Built in the early 1900s, the Republic was one of the reasons that State Street was a great street. An innovative, multilevel shopping center, it was a forerunner of the modern shopping mall. "Talk about spaciousness and finish, it is really something," Nickel wrote architect Purcell. "It is going to be torn down for replacement by a Skidmore building. I'm getting a headache thinking about it. Goodnight."

The building was purchased for $2.5 million in 1958 by the Home Federal Savings and Loan Association. The directors first intended to remodel the building and use the first several floors for the main banking room and offices. However, in 1960 they announced plans to replace the Republic with a 15-story tower.

The decision was architectural arrogance, according to Nickel. There was little wrong with the Republic. The building was structurally sound and in excellent condition. Only the windows and the elevators needed attention.

"May I inquire what is so grand about a glass slab with aluminum strips running down the sides," Nickel wrote Skidmore, Owings, and Merrill a few days after the architectural firm's plan was unveiled. "I think the architects are selling a bill of goods like the automobile industry sold the tail fin. The new buildings are *gaudy and superficial,* their only merit being mechanical improvements like air conditioning, automatic elevators, etc."

Richard asked fellow Chicago Heritage Committee members in September if the organization should fight. "We don't want to jeopardize our progress with the Garrick, but we have to be consistent: The Republic is a fine building and is in fine shape," Nickel concluded.

He wrote the *Chicago Sun-Times,* "Up and down the street are structures which should be demolished— if the aim is to improve the central area. Why do they always wreck the finest buildings?"

That question—Why do they always wreck the finest buildings?—was one that Nickel asked often. He never received an answer.

Too shy to speak out in public, Nickel asked and was invited to voice his concerns about the Republic Building in November 1960 at Skidmore, Owings, and Merrill, which Frank Lloyd Wright had dubbed "Skiddings, Own-More, and Sterile." Nickel's early Garrick victories had apparently convinced Skidmore's William Hartmann that Nickel was a power to reckon with. As a general partner in charge of Skidmore's Chicago office, Hartmann was accustomed to telling clients what was best for them. He was an imposing corporate figure: confident, straightforward, and, eventually, overbearing. He listened briefly to Nickel's objections and presented counter-arguments, trying to show that the new building could gather higher rents while providing more efficient space at the same cost. Nickel was unyielding. Soft-spoken and single-minded in his opinions, he argued simply that the Republic was a fine classical skyscraper that should not be destroyed.

Sensing an impasse, Hartmann sent Nickel to George Sample, an architect who had helped design the Home Federal building. Sample liked the Republic Building. When the commission had first come into the office, he had been enthusiastic about preparing drawings to show how Home Federal could convert the lower floors of the building into banking facilities. However, the directors had soon become more interested in tearing down the old building for a new one. The grand arcade entrance, which split the main floor in half, and the circular staircase limited banking space. The directors wanted an efficient expanse for dozens of tellers and new account desks. Instead of seeing the charm of the building, they only saw what was missing: modern bathrooms, enclosed elevators and stairs, new windows, and air conditioning. In their eyes, the building had too many things going against it.

So what was the Skidmore firm to do? Sample asked Nickel. Nickel replied that Skidmore should have taken the case to the American Institute of Architects, the Society of Architectural Historians, the mayor, or the landmarks commission. The firm could have distinguished itself. Instead, Nickel charged, the firm made facts suit its own needs.

"He kind of shrugged at this," Nickel wrote of Sample's reaction, "and I suspect he thought I was simply naive to think such things happened—or maybe it sounded so simple he wondered why they had missed it."

Actually, Nickel's words had a great effect on Sample. But he was a loyal employee of a growing firm, so he continued to defend Skidmore's position. He knew Home Federal was not interested in preserving the building. The directors wanted a swank palace that would help Home Federal become the largest savings and loan in the state. The Skidmore partners could have convinced the Home Federal directors that remodeling would pay off, but they never bothered. The architects manipulated numbers to convince themselves as well as the Home Federal directors that remodeling the building would cost between $6 million and $7 million, the cost of a new building. The new building had a smaller floor area and was four stories shorter.

Sample reluctantly went along with the decision to tear down the building because he believed in the firm. This was an exciting era to work for Skidmore, he later said, because the firm was building what architects considered was "the new environment." Year after year Skidmore designers were designing exciting, structures—the Alcoa Building in Pittsburgh, the Crown Zellerbach Building in San

Francisco—which would hit the magazines and be a boon for the client, the firm, and the city. The Skidmore partners wanted to create the most successful architecture firm in the world. "Skidmore was looking for big bucks and big glamour, and you don't get that by remodeling old buildings," Sample said in an interview years later. "The firm's approach was tear down and build, build, build."

Several days later, Nickel sent Sample a letter, which Sample kept for years. Nickel wrote that he knew Sample cared about the Republic, but chided him for not making a better case for it.

"Everybody has been talking about the Republic and nobody has done anything about it," Nickel wrote. "Table talk salves the conscience, but it certainly doesn't save the building, and the building is the important thing."

Nickel's offer to photograph the Republic Building for the landmarks commission was accepted, and he received permission from the Skidmore firm to gain access to the site in November. As a token gesture, Skidmore drew floor plans and elevations of the Republic and prepared a book on the building containing Nickel's photographs.

Wrecking began in February 1961. Sample, who helped design the free-standing tower that replaced the Republic Building, said the tower was an attempt to bring New York's modern Lever House skyscraper to Chicago. "You certainly cannot call the new building 'distinguished architecture,'" Sample later said. "About the best you can say about it is that it is 'nice.'" Sample left the firm a few years later.

Nickel never got over the hurt he felt over the destruction of the Republic Building. In 1964 he wrote journalist Ruth Moore:

> I had a good look recently at the Home Federal Savings and Loan building, which replaced the Republic several years ago. That looms in my mind now as one of the great tragedies. . .or rather as one of the most willful unnecessary destructive acts to Chicago School heritage. I'll never forgive Hartmann and SOM for that. The Republic was a work of art, and the new building is nothing, maybe some tinsel.

Meanwhile, Nickel began figuring out how to save the best ornament of the Garrick. He made a list of the most significant pieces, and persuaded the city to contribute $10,000 to the effort. Then he wrote letters to museums and universities telling them that Sullivan ornament would be available if they sent requests to Mayor Daley.

Nickel was in his prime. His letters, simple and sincere, were effective. By the time Atlas Wrecking Company finished putting the scaffolding in place around the Garrick, hundreds of requests for ornament had been forwarded to the mayor's office.

Nickel next called David Wallerstein, president of Balaban and Katz, and cajoled him into donating more. Wallerstein donated $5,000 from the theater company and even convinced Field Enterprises Educational Corporation, the sister company of the *Chicago Sun-Times*, to match his contribution. A total of $26,000 was eventually raised, but the wreckers said they would charge $50,000 to salvage the ornament on Nickel's list. Nickel offered to do the job for substantially less, and on February 9, 1961, he took charge.

Nickel hired John Vinci and David Norris, his old salvaging partners from the Babson House, to work with him. Vinci, 24, had just been laid off at Skidmore, Owings, and Merrill, and Norris, 23, was trying to finish his architecture studies at the Illinois Institute of Technology.

They began in the 13th-floor banquet hall, near the back of the Garrick. Working on a scaffold, they stripped off a large pre-cast plaster frieze surrounding the upper wall of the room and ornamental plaster ventilator grilles. They wrapped the plaster in burlap for protection and trucked the pieces to a city-owned warehouse at Navy Pier, just east of the Loop on Lake Michigan. From the start it was a race. They worked 16 to 18 hours each of the first days to stay ahead of the wreckers, who were making their way down from the tower at the front of the building.

The work was dangerous because the scaffold was positioned next to a huge hole in the banquet hall floor. The wreckers had gouged the hole there, and in the six floors directly beneath, so they could dump debris straight down through the rigging loft to the main stage on the first floor.

Nickel, Vinci, and Norris tried not to think about the hole, but when they glanced down the 13 stories, they could not avoid a sense of vertigo. It was like working next to a chasm, Norris said. He closed his eyes and imagined he were

Demolition of the cornice atop the 13th floor of the Garrick.

A staircase in the tower of the Garrick Theater Building during demolition in 1961.

somewhere else, but he could feel a physical pull. The three never discussed the danger, even after a wrecker fell 11 stories to his death. They convinced themselves they were on a "divine mission," and they learned how not to look down. As he chiseled out the plaster ornament on the ceiling of the banquet hall, Norris thought about a 19th-century chromolithograph he had been given as a boy. It showed two young children walking across a foot bridge under the watchful eye of an angel.

The longer they worked, the more resolute Nickel's team became to beat the wreckers down the building. As weeks passed, the dangerous race became a children's game, a capture-the-flag of sorts. The two sides were not outwardly hostile, but they viewed each other's motives and purpose with suspicion. As Nickel, Vinci, and Norris watched the wreckers smash the oversized sculpted head of a warrior up on the roof, and saw them drop an organ through the gaping hole of the banquet hall, the three realized they must stay in the Garrick as long as there were treasures to save. The organ was particularly sad for Norris, an accomplished musician, who had hoped to take it apart and save it. He suspected the wreckers dropped it just to spite them.

From the 13th-floor banquet hall, the three started work in the unheated theater, which still stank of greasy popcorn. Their prime targets were the ornamental star-pod plaster on the underside of the theater's magnificent nine arches and the ornamental plaster from the front of the balcony. Working under the glow of photographic floodlights, Nickel and Vinci could reach only a fraction of the ornament. Wearing crash helmets, they used a yard-long homemade tool to pick at and wedge the repeating patterns of plaster on the ceiling. The ornament on the front and underside of the balcony was firmly anchored. Nickel and Vinci tried to save as much as they could by climbing ladders or reaching over the sides. They pried and pried, but much of the ornament came down damaged.

It wasn't all work. Sometimes they swung from the balcony onto the stage, Tarzan-style, on a rope that had been rigged from the arches. But most of their time was spent at hard labor. Nickel discussed the tediousness of the work in a letter to a friend describing how he had salvaged a small chunk of Garrick plaster.

It is from a ceiling "string course" or "panel frame" in the ceiling above the two balcony murals. You should have seen John Vinci and I on our bellies inside the suspended t-bar and metal lath ceiling getting these off. I busted a hole through the lath adjoining the piece and when John could get his arm out under each section, I would pound it evenly with a heavy hammer. Sometimes we got two at a time—and sometimes even extra material stuck on which John could barely hold up. Then we pulled it out together. Then we would move down the line. There couldn't have been more than 24 inches to wriggle in. We must have 30–50 of these pieces in varying condition.

Then there were the stencils. While photographing the theater gallery with strong floodlights from the sides in 1960, Nickel had found a faint outline of stencil work beneath layers of paint. He had initially thought the stencils were original, but later learned they were added in a remodeling. The mistaken identity caused Nickel

A self-portrait showing Nickel as he photographs the mosaic stair landings discovered during the last days of salvage work at the Garrick in 1961.

to remove other wall slabs while working in the Garrick during 1961. Using a scalpel, he chipped away the nine coats of paint and found gold-on-beige, leaf-and-tendril stencil designs on the sloping gallery ceiling. As he looked around, Nickel realized the theater was full of Sullivan's stencils.

The three worked furiously through May and June to remove the Sullivan stencils from the flat walls of the theater. Norris was crude, using abrasives and detergents to remove the paint, or cutting off huge slabs of the flat walls and shipping them to Navy Pier so they could be uncovered later. Vinci was meticulous, using small pieces of tape and glue to remove each layer of paint individually.

In May Nickel and Norris made another important find. Norris chipped the asphalt off two semi-circular stair landings leading to the balcony and found the leaf-and-tendril design repeated in mosaics. To save the mosaics, Nickel hired stone masons to cut the three-ton landings into a few sections. With no time to separate the mosaics from the landings, Nickel and the stonemen jacked up the landings and carted them out of the Garrick to waiting trucks. Years later, Nickel wrote he would never forget how hard they had worked, starting at noon one Sunday and finishing at Navy Pier the next morning at four.

Nickel usually worked 12-hour days at the Garrick. Much of his time was spent directing the Atlas Wrecking Company crew to salvage terra-cotta ornament on the exterior of the building. Up high, the ornament was massive because it was proportioned to be seen from ground level. Bonded to brick and hooked to the metal superstructure, the terra-cotta removal proved costly and difficult. The Atlas Wrecking Company received close to $10,000 of the $26,000 budget. The crews saved the foliate terra-cotta frieze from the 17th-floor tower, the long frieze from the side of the 13th floor, a window bay from the ninth-floor, and much of the terra cotta from the second-floor arcade.

In the months Nickel was in charge of salvaging the Garrick, he took hundreds

G A L L E R Y   O F   P H O T O G R A P H S   B Y   **RICHARD NICKEL**

The 1883 Richard Knisely
Store and Flats building.
The photograph was taken
during 1958, the year it
was demolished.

OVERLEAF:
Self-portrait of Richard
Nickel atop Holabird and
Roche's Republic Building,
completed in 1909 in
Chicago's Loop.
The photograph was
taken in 1960, the year
before the building was
torn down.

Louis H. Sullivan's 1914
Home Building Association
in Newark, Ohio,
taken in 1955.

ASSOCIATION ♦ 1917 ♦

Sullivan's 1916–18
People's Savings and Loan
Association Bank in Sidney,
Ohio, in 1955.

Carl Sandburg takes a
quick nap during a visit
to Chicago in 1957.
Nickel, on a free-lance
assignment, followed
Sandburg during the
writer's three-day stay
in Chicago.

Adler and Sullivan's 1892
Wainwright Building in
St. Louis, Missouri.

Frank Lloyd Wright's 1908–10 Robie House. Nickel and Aaron Siskind took turns leaving the car on a cold winter day and pressing the shutter to make this side elevation. The photograph is a combination of two prints.

Sullivan's Schlesinger
and Mayer store, in
Chicago's Loop. Now
known as the Carson
Pirie Scott store, the
building was
constructed in two
stages from 1898 to
1904.

The demolition of
the proscenium and
stage of the
Garrick Theater
in 1961.

C. F. Murphy Associates'
1962 Continental Center
takes its place in
Chicago's Loop. The
skyscraper replaced
Holabird and Roche's
1898–99 Cable Building,
which was demolished in
1961. Nickel took
photographs of the
building for the firm
during its construction.

Interiors of Burnham
and Root's 1886–88
Kansas City Board of
Trade in Kansas City,
Missouri. The
photographs were taken
in 1967 before the
building was
demolished.

Rehabilitation of
Adler and Sullivan's
1886–89
Auditorium Theatre
during the
mid-1960s.

D. H. Burnham Company's 1894–95 Reliance Building surrounded by towering modern buildings in downtown Chicago. The Reliance was one of the world's first glass towers.

Looking down at
Chicago from the
Republic Building.

The second-floor log-
gia behind the mar-
quee of the Garrick
Theater. The photo-
graph was taken in
1960 or 1961.

of pictures, many of which were technical. He showed the exposed tile arches in the floors, the girders, the brickwork and plasterwork, the rigging loft and Phoenix columns behind the stage, the framework and truss support of the theater, and just about every unique feature in the building.

Richard enjoyed the Garrick even during its dance of death. The pain he felt must have been overshadowed by this singular chance to see—and show—what made it great.

Of all the photos he took, one in particular captures both the building's beauty and Nickel's sense of helplessness and anger. It is a view of the theater taken from deep within the ravaged structure in early May. Thrown open to sunlight by the razing of the back stage wall, the Garrick has, once and for all, become an icon, sacred in its destruction. The powerful sweep of the proscenium arch is still recognizable, but tons of rubble have been heaped onto the main floor and a bulldozer crouches where the stage once stood.

In the background, barely more than a speck on the negative, a man stands with his hands in his pockets. It is unclear whether this solitary figure, who peers back into the Garrick, is the operator of the bulldozer or simply a bystander. It doesn't really matter.

The dismantling of ornament ended on June 15, 1961, when the city's insurance policies on Nickel, Vinci, and Norris expired. For the next month Nickel transported all that remained in the Garrick to Navy Pier. By mid-July, 200 to 300 pieces were safely stored at the pier. "The storage room resembles an art treasure trove, with rows of panels and pieces, each a striking thing in itself," wrote reporter Ruth Moore.

Nickel was exhausted. The work, he wrote, had become a mental and physical drain. "It has become harder and harder to go back into the building, and I avoided discussing it whenever I could."

The terra-cotta and plaster pieces, wooden doors, and trim had long since displaced his 1954 Chevy in his parents' garage, and now he was responsible for the tons of material at Navy Pier.

He loved the ornament. Living with the pieces made up for watching the demolition, he wrote. During the summer, he sat in the garden to watch the sun play shadow games on the "sunburst" terra cotta taken from the Rubel house. "The ornament," he wrote, "is not just ornament—or even the variations of a theme, beautifully handled, but a meaningful depiction of the life-growth process, an attempt to stimulate that nebulous creative capacity or emotional (not in a trite sense) force in us, and an attempt to develop empathy between the live and the non-living (organic and non-organic)." In other words, the ornament was Sullivan.

Since 1959, when Nickel contacted the Chicago Historical Society about his collection, he had sought a permanent home for the ornament. In the early 1960s he approached officials at the Museum of Science and Industry, the McCormick Charitable Foundation, and the Art Institute of Chicago about establishing an architectural museum, but nobody was interested.

John Vinci sits among salvaged sections of the Garrick Theater in 1961. The pieces were stored at Chicago's Navy Pier (*above*). Atlas Wrecking Company workers cart away a piece of the mosaic stair landings (*right*).

His first choice was the Art Institute, which had by then developed an international reputation. Unfortunately, curators there feared that a permanent Sullivan-based architecture display might be viewed as provincial. They were interested in acquiring a few of the fragments, but not Nickel's entire collection, and Nickel did not want to split it up.

In late 1961 the need to find a home became more acute when the Navy Pier collection—which now included pieces from the Garrick, Cable, and Republic buildings as well as Nickel's own ornament—had to be moved to another section of the pier. The move took five grueling days. Ornament was chipped and weakened as the collection was compressed into a smaller space. "It looks like a pile of junk," Nickel wrote.

What may have been worse was the prospect for the future. Nickel was told by city employees that the ornament would need to be relocated in another two years. "Any further moves of this sort makes the whole ornament salvage idea rather questionable, if not plain stupid," he wrote.

In early March the Garrick's plaster walls were carefully transported to architect Crombie Taylor's home so that the Sullivan stencils could be stripped and restored from beneath the layers of paint. But Nickel was disheartened at the condition of the material. He felt partly responsible for the damage. "I wish you all could have been there today when we moved the remaining water-logged, flaking and generally disintegrating Garrick stencil slabs from Navy Pier," wrote Nickel to those involved in the salvage work. "We're not better than Rosen & Horowitz, George Ramsey, SOM, Paddy Bauler, the City Council, Society of Architectural Historians, the American Institute of Architects, Adolf Hitler, and anyone else dumb and ugly that you can think of."

The following month, a piece of his own ornament was stolen from Navy Pier. Angry, distressed, and disheartened, Nickel wrote city officials that he could not understand why anyone would take the material. It had no value to anyone else, he wrote. "To me, the pieces are important as the skeletons of early humans which are always being dug for. It is a 'link' in my study of architect Sullivan's ornament." He wrote a friend: "I must have been insane to move it to the pier."

In June Nickel persuaded *Chicago Daily News* reporter Georgie Anne Geyer to write about the need to establish an architecture museum. Geyer, who accompanied Nickel on a salvage expedition and later sailed with him, remembered he sounded defeated and worn out by the effort to find a home for the ornament. With the exception of the Garrick ornament, which he and the landmarks commission had agreed would be distributed to anyone who wanted it, he was offering to give his collection away free to any institution that could keep it together.

Richard took a break in early July for a trip to Europe. "All my friends have been over so I thought I'd give it a try," he wrote relatives after flying to Paris.

He traveled there with a friend, Shirley Courtois. They spent five weeks driving to Venice and on to Yugoslavia, then sailing to Greece and flying to Cairo. He most enjoyed seeing the ancient sites in Athens and Egypt, and photographed the Step Pyramid at Sakkara, the Luxor Temple, and Der El Bahri. Afterward, Nickel and Courtois, an art historian, ferried back to Italy, where they went their separate ways. Richard had no romantic interest in Courtois, but years later he wrote that he was let down by the news that she planned to marry somebody else. "What a failure I am," he wrote.

After touring Florence, Rome, and Turin on his own in August, Nickel felt saturated by art and architecture, as much as by buses and planes. He had spent most of his time taking slides, which he later sold to the Art Institute and the University of Chicago. He saw everything through Sullivan's eyes. Two Nervi buildings, for example, were disappointments. "Inner shells are beautiful but nothing else related, no outer expression to speak of," Nickel wrote. In Paris he spent 10 days researching and photographing the life and work of Emile Vaudremer, Sullivan's teacher. The trip was not eye-opening for Nickel. Rather, it confirmed what he had suspected: that Sullivan was the equal of Michelangelo, Bernini, Brunelleschi, and other European masters.

Back in Chicago, Nickel became consumed with his old concerns. His first order of business was distributing the Garrick ornament. He remained on the city payroll until 1963, making $3 an hour as a curator for the Municipal Reference Library.

Requests for Garrick pieces came in from all over the country. One man asked for a section of the proscenium arches. "I plan to use the relic as an attractive underpiece under plate glass as a cocktail table and any help you could give me would merit many drinks from atop the table once it is constructed," he wrote. Also requesting ornament were Geyer, soon-to-be architect Stanley Tigerman, several city officials, and even Balaban and Katz attorney Edwin Rothschild. Plaster star pods, mounted on burlap, were sent to about 30 people. Ada Louise Huxtable, who was given a fragment, wrote Nickel: "I have never been so surprised or thrilled by a gift. This is one of the nicest things that has happened to me."

About 30 colleges and organizations—from Beloit College in Beloit, Wisconsin, to the Museo Internazionale d'Architettura Moderna in Milan, Italy—requested and received ornament. Curators chose pieces through a catalog prepared by Nickel. The Art Institute was given first choice, but eventually requested only small samples of terra cotta, plaster, and the mosaic stair landing.

The largest shipments were sent to the Yale School of Architecture and the Fogg Museum at Harvard. Architect Paul Rudolph, dean of the Yale school, traveled to Chicago to pick ornament for Yale's new architecture building. A mold from a plaster frieze ended up in Rudolph's home.

The largest assembly, a 16-by-22-foot section of the loggia, a great open balcony that curved across the second-floor facade, was given to the Frank Lloyd Wright Foundation for reinstallation at Wright's summer home at Taliesin in Wisconsin. Another section of the loggia was sold by Atlas wreckers to the Second City comedy troupe and used as the trademark entrance for its theater in the Old Town neighborhood on the Near North Side.

Nickel was pleased by the high demand for the pieces, particularly for the heavy terra cotta. "The whole project has been very satisfying and educational to me as well as the confirmation of the value of the ornament by all the institutions," he wrote in 1963. "The appreciation of the ornament shows through their willingness to take assemblies of pieces too, rather than just fragments."

Nickel kept many pieces of the Garrick for his collection. The last pieces of the city-owned Garrick ornament were shipped out in August and the distribution was completed in early September, when Nickel submitted his final report to the landmarks commission. He was kept on the payroll for a few weeks longer as a reward for a job well done and because his pay had been so low. Nickel, Norris, and Vinci ended up splitting about $6,000. Nickel's mother made four open-faced pies—apple, peach, plum, and mixed fruit—to celebrate the end of the Garrick work, but Richard had turned bittersweet on the experience.

He wrote a wistful note later that month reflecting on the work. The tone was bitter at first as Richard complained about the success of his Institute of Design classmates such as James Blair, who worked as a *National Geographic* staff photographer, and Len Gittleman, who taught at Harvard University. "I got diverted into scholarship and architecture and history and my vocation slowly but surely became my avocation," Nickel wrote. "I'm not sorry because these have been very good years, and even the Garrick effort was very worthwhile."

There were, of course, many other Adler and Sullivan buildings to worry about. He took ornament from the Victoria Hotel, the Chicago Heights rooming house gutted by fire in 1961, and from four residences on the 3500 block of South Ellis Avenue—three row houses built for Dankmar Adler, his mother-in-law, and a family friend and a home across the street built for Adler's uncle. These houses were victims of urban renewal in 1961. Two years later Nickel spent several days collecting pieces from the fire-damaged 1884 Martin Barbe home on South Prairie Avenue.

As he completed the Garrick work, two more Adler and Sullivan buildings fell prey to the wrecking ball. "The Hammond Library was wrecked this week, and the little Blumenfeld House will go in 5–6 days," Nickel wrote to Nancy Boone, an Art Institute librarian. "The way it's going, I have no fears about anyone doing a comprehensive book on Adler and Sullivan. I've got the last photos, and the ornament in a warehouse and I see them dismembered."

Boone replied: "There is no doubt about it—you have a corner on the Adler and Sullivan market and soon as you say, you will have all there is. You must admit it is a novel approach to art history; never before have things happened with such speed that one person has the possibility of encompassing a field."

That was the remarkable aspect of Nickel's work: the Sullivan buildings kept coming down right before his eyes.

The Hammond Library, built for the Chicago Theological Seminary in 1882 about two miles west of the Loop, had been vacant for decades, except for the pigeons who lived in and fouled its upper floors. Nickel prized the eccentric ornament from the building because it hinted at the influence on Sullivan of Philadelphia architect Frank Furness.

The slender, three-story 1883 Solomon Blumenfeld Flat Building—with its vertical emphasis and flaring, lotuslike piers pushing through the parapet—shared some design characteristics with Sullivan's commercial buildings. Nickel bought one of the powerful pier tops for $10 from Three Oaks Wrecking Company wreckers, who threatened: "$40 or we'll smash it."

What bothered Nickel almost as much as the demolition of the buildings was the city's failure to do anything about it. "A hydrogen bomb couldn't move the Chicago Commission on Architectural Landmarks to action," he wrote. "They're doing the very minimum and it simply isn't enough."

He noted that the Blumenfeld's colored-glass windows and all of the wood from the triple-window bay eventually found buyers. "So you see," Nickel wrote, "enough people care about the pieces, at least, of Sullivan's buildings, much more than the commission realizes. Several people stopped to comment that they had passed the building for years but had never noticed the fine treatment of the facade and its ornament. That's life!"

Yet despite his passion for the work, Nickel was a reluctant salvager. Until he started salvaging, few had saved ornament for its artistic value. What was saved—

mostly murals or mosaics from doomed buildings—was, in itself, great art.

Nickel saved Sullivan ornament because it was important evidence of a crucial turning point in American architecture. Picking up the pieces from buildings such as the Hammond library or the Blumenfeld house was not a ghoulish pursuit. Like the 15th-century chapels in Florence, which showed the transformation from Medieval to Renaissance architecture, the Sullivan buildings promised the coming of a new age. Nickel saved the ornament because he was the only person there when the buildings were wrecked. If he didn't save what was left, nobody else would.

He was also a reluctant preservationist, forced into action through the apathy of others. "You probably realize that much of my time has gone into preservation efforts," he wrote an editor at *Forum* magazine. "Not that I'm so interested in it, but that no one else is."

When Nickel gave British journalist and politician Thomas Driberg a grand tour of Loop architecture, Driberg announced: "Most people in Great Britain don't realize there is any great historic architecture in Chicago."

"Most people in Chicago don't realize it either," Richard replied.

"Here in Chicago," he wrote, "they cover up the lower floors of buildings with slabs of granite that make storefronts 'modern.' In fact, this ruins any elegance a building has and destroys the unity of lower floors to upper. When this kind of so-called improvement goes soon out of date, they rework it again until finally it is such a mess they say 'obsolete,' 'old-fashioned,' etc. and find it can only be wrecked."

Nickel preferred sitting on the sidelines, making his preservation points by writing letters. When he heard rumors that the epochal Reliance Building, the inspiration and forerunner to the modern glass skyscraper by the architectural firm D. H. Burnham and Company, was doomed, Nickel wrote Thomas Stauffer, "Twice the effort that went into the Garrick should be given to Reliance. A real noise should be made."

Nickel fought any way he could. To Salt Lake City Mayor J. Bracken Lee, Nickel protested plans to tear down Sullivan's Dooly Block. "How many buildings of equal architectural merit do you have in Salt Lake City? Instead of being proud of this building, you ignore it. Instead of offering tax relief to the owner, or cleaning the neighborhood up, the city government is silent."

To *Forum* editor Walter McQuade, Nickel suggested the magazine examine the transformation of the Mies-designed Illinois Institute of Technology campus. "I'm sure you are aware of the situation," he wrote. "They have every architectural Tom, Dick and Harry adding to the campus now, with buildings styled after Mies. Trouble is, they can't even copy Mies well. IIT takes great pride in the fact that the campus was built in a slum, but they don't realize a new slum is in the making."

To the editor of the *American City Magazine,* Nickel wrote a critical letter about the magazine's June 1963 "The Touch of Lace" article, which praises the parking lot that replaced the Garrick Theater. "What about the lines 'the new building pays graceful tribute to the memory of Louis Sullivan?'" Nickel wrote. "They wreck one of his masterpieces, and you conclude it is a tribute? How? Why? Would you say that if someone wrecked St. Peter's Cathedral in Rome and erected a garage on the site, using some statues and whatever, that that was a tribute to St. Peter?"

Through the years, Nickel remained an idealist. He was unwilling to compromise, and that may have been his fatal flaw. As long as he was so unbending, he got little accomplished. Instead of finishing his book, he kept researching and rewriting. Instead of saving buildings, he was left with the scraps.

His preservation philosophy was spelled out in a letter to the building managers of the Monadnock Building after they proudly showed him changes they had made to "update" the building. Richard wrote that he was "shocked" by the alterations. Painting iron grillwork was "inexcusable," he wrote, for it destroyed the silhouette and lacelike quality of the building. "There's nothing like a standard," he wrote. "People respect you for it, at least the good people do." The managers of new skyscrapers will not lower office ceilings, so why is it allowed at the Monadnock? he asked. "If you need internal air conditioning, or a luminous ceiling, lower it a minimum. Who said low ceilings were modern and tasteful? I've always felt these cramped conditions were forced on us for economic expediency."

Nickel argued that the modern aspects of Chicago School buildings have been rejected or misunderstood.

If the Carson Pirie Scott store was erected today just as Sullivan did it in 1902, we would all be amazed. For transparency (lots of glass area), richness of materials, functionalism, beauty, and so forth, the building was a high point. But look at it today, it's only a shell of its original quality and greatness. What's needed here is more knowledge, and a good dose of faith.

In a similar vein, he praised the "heroic struggle" to rehabilitate the Auditorium Theatre, but criticized architect Harry Weese for not using historians and archeologists as consultants. "My feeling is that if it isn't as Adler and Sullivan left it in 1890, in essential character, then it's better to be abandoned," Nickel wrote.

During the early 1960s, Richard decided not to play an active role in any preservation group. "For anyone interested in architecture to sit around and discuss anything else while our fine Chicago School work is being defaced with mediocrity is incredible to me," he wrote about the Society of Architectural Historians. He refused to join the effort to save Jane Addams's Hull House on the Near West Side or to join the Chicago Heritage Committee's 1962 fight to save public sculpture.

The heritage committee, led by Stauffer, directed most of its effort toward passing laws to protect landmarks. Nickel, not interested in politics, offered his support but little real help as Stauffer spent years pushing a landmarks bill through the state legislature. In 1963 Chicago was given the power to designate and preserve landmarks.

"Chicago finally has a law to protect its architectural past," wrote Huxtable in the *New York Times*. "The new legislation is the result of the biggest, noisiest, most dedicated and desperate campaign waged in any American city on behalf of the great old buildings that are being knocked down like tenpins for massive urban renewal and private rebuilding projects."

To Nickel, only direct action mattered at this point. On April 6, 1963, he was arrested for taking leaded-glass windows from the Oscar Steffens house, a Frank Lloyd Wright–designed home under demolition at 7600 North Sheridan Road.

Nickel had been told about the windows by Philip Gardner, an architect with Skidmore, Owings, and Merrill who had met him during the Home Federal Savings dispute. Gardner, who lived near the Prairie School house on the North Side, kept watch on the building as the demolition began. By the time the pair started work, many of the first-floor windows had been shattered by rocks thrown by neighborhood children. Only 10 or 12 of the windows were still left on the second floor.

Nickel and Gardner removed six of the windows and stored them inside. It was near dusk and Nickel was on the eaves dismantling another window when the police pulled up.

"Be quiet, they'll go away," Nickel told Gardner. The pair stopped work and kept still. The police left and Nickel and Gardner went back to work.

A short while later, they heard sirens and saw a paddy wagon approach with a couple of squad cars.

"I think we better hide," Nickel said.

Gardner refused.

When the police hollered to come out, Gardner came to the window. Nickel was disgusted with him, but followed.

The police lieutenant asked them what they were doing.

"I'm saving these Frank Lloyd Wright windows," Nickel said.

"Who's Frank Lloyd Wright?" the lieutenant asked.

Nickel's explanation did not satisfy the officer.

"Do you have any tools?"

"Sure, we were taking these windows out," Nickel replied.

The lieutenant sent a patrolman into the house, who ran out moments later holding a hammer and chisel.

"Lieutenant, I found them! I found them!" the proud patrolman said.

"Good. Bring them with."

The police frisked, photographed, and booked the pair at the Summerdale station, but the lieutenant lost interest when he found that Nickel and Gardner had no criminal record. If they had been previously charged with a burglary, they could have been brought to trial on charges of possessing burglary tools.

Nonetheless, they were placed in the lockup, which they shared with a drunk. Gardner had neither identification nor money. Nickel had $15 to cover the bond for one. He paid to release Gardner, who went home and returned with enough money to release Nickel. Nickel immediately asked Gardner if he wanted to go back to the house and finish the job.

"I'm not going near that place," Gardner said. "The last thing I want to do is get caught a second time."

Nickel returned to pick up the windows that had been hidden. The following day, he and Gardner appeared in court.

The judge dismissed the case as soon as they told their story.

"Get out! Get out! Of all the silly things to bother me with."

Nickel was proud of the incident, which was mentioned in a 1965 *Time* magazine article entitled "The Gargoyle Snatchers." Later, when he lectured about his work, he often opened with the arrest story. And when they met, Richard warned his young friend Tim Samuelson: "You know, you are traveling with a jailbird."

The joy Nickel felt about distributing the Garrick ornament contrasted with the depression he felt in 1963 about finding a home for his own collection.

"My concern and hopes in architectural matters are at an all-time low. I'm sure it shows," he wrote in June. He had hoped that Navy Pier would be the final place for his 50 pieces of ornament before they were installed in a museum, but was told that the area where the collection was stored would be demolished soon.

"My asking around for help in finding a storage place for my Sullivan ornament gets more hopeless every day," he wrote. "They all pat you on the back and that's exactly what I do not need. I know what I am doing in saving the ornament. I watch the buildings. I make the payoffs to wreckers. I work and get dirty dragging it off of the building, and I carry it away. All that I really need is a storage place to put the things."

In late June, Nickel's storage problem appeared to be solved. An architect put Richard in touch with a client who agreed to allow Nickel to store the ornament in his South Side warehouse. "The main reason I prefer to put it in a warehouse and forget about it is that I am a photographer, not a curator of ornament," Nickel wrote. "I want to save it, but not move it around every other year to suit somebody. I get no income from renting trailers and moving it."

Richard spent the first two weeks of August transporting the ornament from Navy Pier to the warehouse at 45th and Racine. He made two trips a day. "My ugly mood tonight is from days and days of getting dirty and tired from hauling this stuff, gaining nothing from it all, and knowing that hardly anyone cares," he wrote in August.

The move's difficulty only increased with the news that the Hammond Library was being demolished. "I was hoping for a relief, but Hammond's time has come," Nickel wrote. At one point, the shaken Nickel confronted city planner Ira Bach and architect John Entenza and asked them: "Why am I doing it?" He received no reply.

The ornament was not the only cause of Nickel's bitterness. He was most concerned that he had lost any other life outside architecture. He wrote art historian Rachel Baron Heimovics, a friend, on August 20, 1963:

> I realized finally what a fool I must be. No control!! So I'm going to change things, but meantime I'm hard and miserable on everybody. I'm sorry to see the Hammond demolition come in the midst of this, as it has thrown me back into the pit. Well, living with Sullivan's lush ornament makes up for it all in great degrees but there is my life too. The gist of the problem is: why am I horsing around moving the stones from one warehouse to another while everybody else is making a dandy living, have their own lives and apartments and houses, etc. It's even a problem for me to buy a car, while most people can buy one every year or two if they like.

The 1891 Albert W.
Sullivan Residence on
Chicago's South Side.
This photograph shows
the house still fully
intact during the 1950s
before vandals stripped
a copper window bay
from the second story.
The house, built by
Adler and Sullivan for
Sullivan's family, was
where Nickel seriously
considered living.

On a 3-by-5 card stapled to the same letter, Richard wrote, "Through all this I've drifted into a dependency on my family. What a mess. I guess I'll have to write myself a code of conduct and live by it."

The following month, he wrote in a letter he was considering leaving Chicago. "I've been playing with the Garrick ornament for three years now, and I'm at my wits end."

Nickel stayed. In late 1963 he considered purchasing the Albert Sullivan house in the heart of the South Side black ghetto at 4575 Lake Park Avenue. Paid for by Louis Sullivan's brother, Albert, Louis had designed it in 1891 for their mother, Andrienne, but she died a few months before the house was finished the following year. Louis moved in and lived there until 1896, when he was forced to leave following a dispute with Albert and his family.

The two-story house was especially important to Nickel because of its Sullivan connection and the deceptively simple composition of its street facade. Nickel considered the house a shrine. Here Sullivan showed how a modest dwelling in a dense urban area could be graced with elegance. The facade was clad with a slablike plane of light gray limestone, its flat, two-dimensional quality offset by a projecting ornamental copper-clad bay and cornice at the second story, and deeply recessed first-floor windows set behind a cleanly cut rectangular opening divided by columns. The entrance consisted of a wide, ornamental wrought-iron door, above which sprang a lightly delineated stone arch filled with a carved limestone panel. It was identical to a motif used in Sullivan's great, lost Transportation Building at the World's Columbian Exposition in 1893. Clearly, this was one of Adler and Sullivan's most attractive city homes.

The house was remodeled into six or eight apartments during the 1950s. Nickel visited several times, looking for any clues of the original house. By October 1963 the house had been evacuated and vandalized and was put up for sale for about $4,000. Nickel wanted to purchase it and fix it up. By late November he had worked out an ingenious plan in which he hoped to establish a Sullivan museum. Once again, Nickel appealed to Arnold H. Maremont, whose Kate Maremont Foundation had inaugurated an effort to rehabilitate slums. In a letter to landmarks commission member Joseph Benson, Nickel wrote:

> He [Maremont] could buy the house, and implant me and my collection there; the ornament on the first floor and "little me" living on the second! Perhaps it could be worked that Maremont would pay all the bills and I would work there rent free in return for my services as chief curator. This probably sounds like I'm feathering my nest (and I am!) but I've put tons of time and effort into Sullivan ornament. It's one of the reasons I have nothing!

Nickel met with the foundation director, who offered Nickel the chance for a "relaxed loan" from a local bank if Nickel bought the property. The following

The bronze tympanum screen installed under the Stock Exchange Building arch in 1964. Nickel fought hard against the screen because it was not an original feature of the building.

month, Richard decided not to buy the house, even though the price dropped to $2,000. His parents were against it, and Richard depended on them. The house needed new heating, plumbing, and electrical systems, and Richard needed his father's help to make the repairs. His family, including his brother and an aunt, tried persuading Richard that the neighborhood was too rough. The police finally convinced him not to make the move. They told him the house would surely be vandalized if he ever went away on long trips.

Although he did not purchase the house, Nickel kept an active interest in it. In late 1963 he wrote Augustine Bowe, head of the landmarks commission, that the house was doomed with both winter and vandals threatening. The owners had replaced the broken windows with flimsy plywood, and the concrete balustrades had already been chipped.

Sooner or later the commission will have to act, and a small house seems to be an ideal place to exercise whatever powers you have. The often expressed excuse that the commission has "no powers" is wearing thin. I feel that a minimal effort, particularly in this case, will bring results. At least it will be evidence to all concerned that the commission sincerely cares about the buildings.

Bowe requested the police give the house special attention, but that was far from enough. Vandals stole the light fixture in the front vestibule and took half of the front fence. Around New Year's Day, they stripped every piece of copper window bay from the house. Before the house was wiped clean, Nickel and Stauffer took the wrought-iron front door, placing it in "protective custody" until a new owner was found.

Eventually the house was purchased by a not-for-profit social welfare group called the Lake Park Project House. The new owners planned to form a neighborhood arts and crafts community center, which would restore the house. Nickel was doubtful about the plan, but he eventually saw that the front door was returned.

The next building that occupied Nickel's attention was far different from the Albert Sullivan House. In April 1964 plans were announced to modernize the Stock Exchange Building at 30 North LaSalle Street. The work was being done by Nickel's long-time friend, architect Daniel Brenner of the firm Brenner Danforth Rockwell, in whose office Vinci was now working.

Nickel agreed with most of Brenner's plans for the building, but objected to the decision to change the look of the arched entrance with a new bronze grille filling the arch.

"I've seen the latest screen on 30 North LaSalle and, uh, I still don't understand why anything has to be done there," Nickel wrote Brenner. "The original segmenting looks fine to me. It delineates the shallow arch inside. . .and it is original."

Brenner replied that he was using a new screen so that it related to the new revolving doors. Sullivan's entrance was built for hinged doors and a staircase that was no longer used, the architect wrote. "As architects, not archeologists, our concern is with current solutions not restoration." He said the new arch was based on Sullivan's famed Golden Door entrance for the Transportation Building.

Nickel couldn't accept the answer. He knew that Sullivan saw each element of each building as a solution to an individual problem. Justifying the arch treatment as "Sullivan-like" was an insult to Sullivan's architectural philosophy. He was angry at Brenner and at Vinci, who spoke out against the Brenner plan at the firm but did not quit. Vinci, assigned to render the detailed drawings of the new arched panels, was viewed now as an enemy.

"Oh, it's so God Damned hopeless: you don't deserve to polish Sullivan's shoes and here you are bastardizing his buildings," Richard wrote Vinci. "Well, let me tell you I am on earth in his behalf, and I have only begun to fight. 30 N. LaSalle won't be screwed up so easily. Fear for your lives. You think I'm joking?"

The criticism by Nickel, whose photography and dedication was admired by all the firm's partners, was considered, but not taken seriously. "He did not presume to be an architect and had no idea how to solve his concerns," said partner H. P. Davis Rockwell. "It was sort of like having a bad boy in the classroom that you love. He may misbehave and do impossible things, but you love him anyhow. So you laugh, throw up your hands and are glad to see him."

Before Nickel left for a summer trip to the East Coast, an angry Vinci told him, "Well, Richard, when you return, 30 N. LaSalle will be changed."

Nickel took one parting shot. "Unless we're fighting the sea or sharks," he wrote Brenner,

the image of the defacement will haunt me all vacation. So little is involved. I only ask the retention of the original elements of the exterior so it will remain a Sullivan building. I accept the door changes as function.

Perhaps you feel that there is nothing to lose and something to gain by this change, but I think nothing can be gained by defacement except inevitable destruction.

You know what happened to the Sullivan house, the Garrick, to Carsons bit-by-bit. Why help that kind of thing along?

After his return, Nickel asked the landmarks commission to investigate the remodeling. Commission vice president Samuel Lichtmann responded by saying that the Brenner firm was "highly sensitive" to preserving the building and that the very thin sections of statuary bronze should attract attention to the building rather than deface it.

Nickel scrawled "Hopeless" over Lichtmann's letter.

True to his promise, Nickel never did forget. In 1967 he wrote that architects like Brenner have no consideration for historical fact. "They'll mess around with anything, but yet Brenner is a great art lover and if you propose putting a mustache on a Picasso painting (if there wasn't one already!) he'd be petrified."

Ironically, Brenner Danforth Rockwell hired Nickel to photograph the new

Stock Exchange entrance after it was completed. Surprisingly, he took the job. The photos helped the firm win a national award from the American Institute of Architects.

However, that proved nothing, Nickel maintained.

"I want you to know that I'll never forgive you for installing that substitute tympanum in the entry arch at 30 N. LaSalle," he wrote Brenner a few years later. "And the more I see it, the more I question the suitability of that Egyptian tomb-like character you gave the vestibule. And those ruined elevator lobbies which Jack Randall is largely responsible for. You've all done wrong to that building."

Richard spent most of the summer of 1965 away from Chicago teaching a basic photography course at Harvard University. Len Gittleman, now a professor there, had secured the two-month job for his old college friend. Richard, who drove East in his Chevy Chevelle, found Cambridge, Massachusetts, to be a pleasant relief. He especially enjoyed the "sweet smelling, briefly attired 19- and 20-year-old girls from Radcliffe, Gloucester and Barnard" who made up most of his summer classes. Nickel worked four mornings a week at Harvard's Carpenter Visual Arts Center and earned $1,800. He spent his free time hunting down traces of Louis Sullivan—his birthplace in Boston and his grandparents' farm in Wakefield, Massachusetts—as well as the architecture of H. H. Richardson, the East Coast architect whose career inspired Sullivan.

"Life is good, high salary, little work, no worries, driving to pine-scented mountains of New Hampshire to look for Richardson work," he wrote to friend Rachel Baron Heimovics. Nickel did not think Richardson was as original or as creative as Sullivan, but he loved the big, bold buildings with their "heavy rock arches. . .[implying] sex and power."

Unlike Sullivan's work, almost all of Richardson's buildings were well documented in text and photography, so the hunt was more of a hobby for Nickel than serious work. During the two summers he spent teaching at Harvard, Richard photographed all of Richardson's buildings east of the Mississippi River. Once again, Nickel sent dozens of inquiries to historical societies and chambers of commerce to determine when and where to photograph. By August he was receiving three to five letters a day from "old lady historians" and civic promoters. "Fun to be loved!" he wrote.

In the midst of his new mission, Richard toyed with the idea of producing a traveler's guide to Richardson architecture, but his proposal to publisher Raeburn—still waiting for *The Complete Architecture of Adler and Sullivan*—was duly ignored.

Nickel ended his New England summer by sailing on Gittleman's leaky old yacht around Cape Cod Bay from Gloucester to Narragansett Bay, Rhode Island. The previous year in Chicago, Nickel had purchased one-half interest in a small wooden sloop, and learning to sail had been rough going. In 1965 Richard loved sailing around Cape Cod despite having to pump water from the boat throughout a long storm. He thought it was wonderful to be cut off from civilization.

Meanwhile, progress on the Adler and Sullivan book was painfully slow.

In 1961 Nickel had told Raeburn that he felt he was two years away from finishing. With the Garrick fight over, he had expected to make quick progress. Amazingly, Raeburn remained loyal to Nickel despite all of the broken promises and years of inaction. The New York publisher wrote in late 1964: "Re your question about publication: I need not stress to you Richard, that my interest in the Sullivan project is as strong—stronger than ever."

Nickel felt rusty. "I am not a trained architect or historian, and my enthusiasm has waned in recent years," he wrote in 1964, "so that I am losing the vocabulary I once gained. Damn it." He felt his usual lack of confidence.

To help himself get back to work, Nickel gave a series of lectures about Sullivan at the University of California at Los Angeles and at Valparaiso University in Indiana. "I don't like any of this, but I'm going to do it in an attempt to stoke the fire again," Nickel wrote.

In May 1964 architectural historian Paul Sprague suggested that he work with Nickel in producing a two-volume book on Adler and Sullivan. The idea seemed ideal; it would have provided the intellectual backing Nickel so badly felt he needed.

Sprague had first met Nickel in 1962 while working on his Ph.D. dissertation about Sullivan ornament at Princeton University. For almost two years, Nickel kept the graduate student at arm's length, maintaining their written correspondences at a "Dear Sprague" and "Dear Nickel" level. Sprague finally won Nickel's respect, however, by discovering a few Sullivan commissions on his own and by convincing Nickel that he was no threat to the opus.

Sprague proposed that their first volume contain a preface by Aaron Siskind describing the origin of the work and an introduction by Nickel detailing the research. Sprague would then write an analysis of the architecture and ornament, illustrated by the Institute of Design photos. The second volume would be a photographic look at the commissions.

Nickel must have initially accepted the proposal, because on May 5, 1965, Sprague wrote asking if he could announce their collaboration. Hesitating, Nickel asked Sprague to wait. He then wrote Raeburn and Siskind about the proposed two-volume set and indicated he was against the idea.

To Siskind, Nickel wrote he that he wanted to keep the book "ours," and suggested they seek foundation support. "There's so damned much money around for this sort of thing, we should take advantage of it. We've got a good thing and we deserve support. God knows we've done enough on our own peanuts."

Two days later, he wrote Sprague an off-putting letter that indicated he was not willing to work at Sprague's pace. "I simply cannot imagine finishing my book in a year, the way I want to do it. I would be lucky to have a finished manuscript and illustrations of architecture and ornament by September, 1967."

The following month, Nickel made a firm decision to keep working on the book by himself. "Forget about Sprague!" Nickel declared in a letter to Raeburn. "Only important thing is a finished manuscript."

Nickel finally found a home for his ornament in 1965.

It was Jack Randall, the emotional architect who had testified for the Garrick Building in 1960, who helped Richard sell his collection to Southern Illinois University (SIU) at Edwardsville.

Randall had moved from Chicago in 1961 to become the associate architect for the new state school about 50 miles east of St. Louis. In mid-1964 he convinced university officials to consider purchasing the Sullivan ornament and installing it in the university's Lovejoy Library. SIU officials met with Nickel in Edwardsville and in Chicago during the summer. They discussed the possibility of buying the collection and hiring Richard as a part- or full-time curator on the new campus.

Nickel wanted to keep the ornament in the Chicago area, but was tired of moving the collection. He desperately wanted to get the pieces on display—perhaps in a museum or in a large room by themselves—so they could make a case for Sullivan. Richard's last choice, ironically, had been a college or university. "I refuse to give it to a school," he had written earlier, "where some freshmen will rub their greasy hands on it, and where a change in administration will have it put in the alley."

But he was lured by the enthusiasm Randall and his colleagues showed, and returned to Edwardsville in late October. "I normally don't leave when our buildings are coming down, but this is important," he wrote, referring to the demolition of Adler and Sullivan's Charles Kimball mansion at 22 East Ontario Street. Nickel met the university's president, Delyte Morris, who made a tentative offer of $15,000 for the ornament. The offer, subject to review by the university's art consultant, also included a $10,000, one-year salary so that Nickel could ship, prepare, and install the ornament, as well as a $2,000 annual salary thereafter so he could expand the collection in the future.

The offer was withdrawn, however, after the consultant, *Saturday Review* art critic Katherine Kuh, submitted her report. She wrote that the collection was not of "great monetary value" without pertinent letters, drawings, and papers and said the ornament would be very expensive to restore, store, and display. Its only suitable home, Kuh wrote, was at a major museum in a large city or at an architecture school.

"The more I ask advice and the more I think about it, the less possible I think it is for SIU to take on this vast undertaking," she reported. Kuh suggested dividing the collection and selling it to different institutions. "The Edwardsville campus is definitely not geared to such an enormous project."

Nickel was nonplussed.

"The more I read Katherine's letter, the madder I get, because it seems she never did understand what it was all about and now she is not willing to accept if for what it is," Nickel wrote Randall.

Richard assailed Kuh's criticism point-by-point:

1-Monetary value without the archives. I don't understand. If I could pick a piece off the Parthenon, I should worry about the documents?

2-It doesn't matter if it is more archeology than art. It should not be categorized. It is unique.

3-They could have been the envy of (every) art department in the nation.

4-It is not such a vast undertaking.

Nickel knew it was impossible to put a value on the ornament because no other collection like it existed. In a note marked "Thoughts and Considerations," Richard made it clear that he wanted compensation for the time and money he had spent to gather the pieces.

> *If I was an "operator" I suppose I could have interested someone in paying to have the ornament saved. Instead I just did it myself. This does not mean I did it inexpensively. Time spent watching buildings (from day to day often) and then actually being there to get the material has kept me not only from writing about Sullivan, but from making a reasonable living. In addition to time there is the payoffs I made to wreckers for the material and the help often given to load up the car. I usually did the work myself wherever possible, to avoid payoffs I couldn't afford. Once in a while I had to hire a truck with hoist to move pieces and a few times I had excess bulk stone cut from pieces to make them manageable. Finally, the storage and moving of pieces (from warehouse to warehouse) has been a spiritual and physical burden I prefer not even to think about it's so horrible.*

Six days after receiving Kuh's report, Nickel wrote that he was considering withdrawing the collection. "John Vinci, who knows all I have gone through with the ornament, agrees with me that it is bordering on the absurd now, and that it might be better to not offer it to anyone anymore," he wrote. "Just save the best myself and abandon the rest. Easier said than done."

Kuh convinced many Southern Illinois University officials not to buy the collection, but Randall lobbied hard for Nickel. In May 1965 the university offered Richard $12,000 for the collection, but withdrew the additional offer as project curator.

Randall, who considered the offer insulting, warned Richard that the new curator would probably have total control. Siskind advised Nickel to take the offer and withhold some of his best pieces, or to wait for a better deal, perhaps from an East Coast institution that had more money and more ability to handle the collection.

Nickel had different concerns.

"What worries me a little is the income tax on this, which may leave me with very little in the end," he wrote architect Ben Weese, a friend. "And I keep looking at the choice pieces and wondering if I'm really anxious or desperate to sell. I think I would like to dispose of it, but I want a guarantee that it will be well used and possibly expanded, that I will get a fair money deal."

Richard mulled over the offer through the summer at Harvard and back in Chicago. He had hoped that the interest shown by SIU would spur some last-minute Chicago interest, but that did not happen.

On October 9 Nickel wrote that he would accept the offer. He said his greatest concerns were that the ornament stay together and remain well protected, and that the collection be expanded as more Sullivan buildings came down.

"As the collection grew and occupied my time to the extent of halting my research and writing, I came to feel that the collection would be more important than any book I could write or any photograph I could make," he wrote.

Ultimately, he sold the collection because he wanted to get on with his own work and personal life. "Only one concern I have now, that everybody should forget it ever existed," he wrote. "I'm certainly going to, and it will be easy with it 400 miles away. Well, it's near the Wainwright Building anyway."

On October 18, the day he finalized the SIU deal, Richard rejected an offer from a former Institute of Design professor, photographer Frederick Sommer, to work for him as an apprentice in Prescott, Arizona. Nickel greatly respected Sommer, but he had other ideas.

"I would like to return to photography. I haven't made a picture since Aaron started me on Sullivan. And lately I've been wondering how I would proceed," he wrote Sommer.

That day, October 18, 1965, Nickel bought out sailing partner Lee Timonen's half-interest in the little sailboat they shared. Nickel made a low offer in the hope of being bought out by his partner, but Timonen accepted. "I'm not passionate about it, can take it or leave it, but it will be handy on those sultry summer evenings," Richard wrote.

On February 21, 1966, 37 pieces of masonry (including terra cotta or limestone), 14 pieces for masonry assemblies, one piece of plaster (marked: "DO NOT UNDERESTIMATE WHAT LIES BELOW THE PAINT"), 11 pieces of pressed or soldered metal, 10 pieces of cast-iron, and 25 pieces of wood were shipped out of the South Side warehouse to SIU.

"Think of me that day!" Nickel wrote Sommer a few days before. "It will be a day of mixed feeling but definitely of great relief. It was an interesting adventure but I'd never do anything like it again."

To another friend, Jerry Sinkovec, Nickel wrote about his first ornament: "When I carried that rock to Wright Junior College that time the farthest thing from my mind was that I'd ever get solid money for it. Indeed, most people thought I was a screwball!"

Although the SIU agreement stipulated that Richard give up his entire collection, he kept several other pieces that he could not bear to part with. He received his $12,000 check from SIU the following month.

"I've never seen so much money, only piles of rocks," he wrote sarcastically.

Looking down from the
roof of the
Bayard Building in
New York City in 1955.

CHAPTER SIX

TO COLLECT PHOTOGRAPHS IS TO COLLECT THE WORLD.

Susan Sontag, *On Photography*

If Richard Nickel could not save buildings—if picketing were not enough to interest or arouse Chicago—then at least he could photograph them.

Nickel believed in the power of pictures. Photography gave him a chance to salvage the terra-cotta ornament he could not reach with his long, strong arms. Photography gave him a chance to save whole facades. Richard did not presume that his pictures adequately replaced the structures he watched being demolished; photography was simply one of the few options left when, as he put it, the real estate deals broke and the "bulldozers moved fast."

"The photography and salvaging of ornament is a final preservation measure for the benefit of historians and is in no way a substitute for the whole building," he wrote in 1960 after receiving the commission to photograph the Cable Building. "Architecture is evaluated by form, proportion, placement of parts and spacial qualities. The aesthetic experiencing of a whole building is not possible with photographs or pieces. They are symbols."

Photographing buildings is a matter of interpretation. It comes down to what to show, where to set up the camera, and what moment to isolate. Serious architectural photographers look for the single spot that renders a building most accurately and most beautifully. One foot in any direction may mean that a side wall or a cornice bracket might disappear. As they close in on a building, photographers make it their own. They lead viewers through their pictures by the details they have included. The placement of furniture, a tree, an arcade, or even empty space helps create the right image. Finding the decisive moment—and the decisive location—takes rigorous thought.

Like generations of architectural photographers before him, Nickel used seemingly antiquated view cameras. With swings and tilts and a ground-glass focusing screen, the cumbersome and complex view camera makes up in versatility what it lacks in spontaneity. This determined device extends the vision, producing distortion-free, perfectly focused negatives of exquisite detail.

With the view camera, Nickel performed magic.

By raising or lowering the lens at the front of the camera, Nickel could frame a tall building from top to bottom and still make it appear perfectly upright. His secret was hidden within the accordion-like bellows, which made it possible to change the relationship between the lens at the front of the camera and the film at the back.

Without the flexible bellows, the film holder in the back of the camera tilts as the lens tilts. If the camera is slanted, the subject appears to recede or come forward. Skyscrapers look like they are on the verge of falling and the picture looks distorted.

Nickel could keep perspective correct because he kept the view camera level and kept the film parallel to his subject. The camera made it possible to photograph an entire facade of a building in perfect focus while maintaining perfect verticality.

For most of his career, he used a Sinar view camera that produced 4-by-5-inch negatives (about 13 times larger than the 35mm negative). He shot about 6,000 large negatives of Adler and Sullivan's architecture. Most often he used a 90mm Super Angulon wide-angle lens, but he also used a very sharp process lens, actually made for photographing documents, to take possession of the flat facades.

He often used long exposures—from one-quarter of a second to several seconds—to shoot. The increased light enabled him to close the lens aperture. This increased the area of perfect focus, or "depth of field."

Richard took his less formal photographs—pictures of architectural details and workers demolishing buildings—with a Rolleiflex E2. The Rollei, which he purchased after his military tour of duty in Korea, had the "smoothest, softest, quietest shutter and release imaginable," he wrote, but the camera was never the same after his wife threw it at him during a marital brawl in the 1950s. He later used a Hasselblad medium-format camera, a 35mm Leica, and a Nikkormat FT. The new cameras were much easier to use, but did not produce the same results.

In the late 1960s Richard found that he needed practice once again using the view camera. He wondered if he should discard the new equipment and work classically. "Too bad glass plates went out," he wrote.

Nickel worked for hours in his darkroom, producing sharp, beautifully lighted, and perfectly composed prints. He knew that his photographs had to stay within the realm of reality or they would lose impact. People had to believe his buildings really existed. Like other photographers, in the calm of the darkroom, he studied reality. "You know," he wrote,

> probably, that working in a darkroom makes one muddle-minded. It's dark, quiet, lonely, smelly. . .and you are supposed to make these tonal decisions. . . oh, the big problem, of course, that your eyes keep changing to different light levels. After awhile you don't know what is light or dark or contrasty, or what you want yourself in the print.

Nickel was not much of a success as a commercial photographer. He never took the time to establish himself by preparing a portfolio or résumé, and never knocked on doors to get jobs. When editors at *Forum* magazine wrote him in 1956 with a request to show his work, Nickel responded that he did not have the time.

Instead, he depended on his reputation. He worked for the Chicago landmarks

The Civic Center in Chicago's Loop, 1963–65, by C. F. Murphy Associates and other firms. Nickel documented the construction of this building for several years.

commission and the National Park Service recording dozens of vintage midwestern buildings. He took on small jobs, such as photographing the National Farmers' Bank in Owatonna, Minnesota, for a bank brochure. He was hired by designer Charles Eames several times to photograph Eames's sleek modern furniture and was the first choice of Chicago's two largest architectural firms, C. F. Murphy and Skidmore, Owings and Merrill. He also worked for architects Mies van der Rohe and Harry Weese.

Some architects were leery about hiring Nickel because he was not willing to glamorize their new commissions. Said Weese, "Architectural photography is making purses out of sow's ears, and Richard was too honest to do that kind of work." Glossy, romantic pictures ran counter to the Institute of Design credo. "His photographs stand as a lasting challenge to the falsely dramatic and heavily filtered architectural illustrations that, alas, win solemn citations from the American Institute of Architects," wrote Donald Hoffmann, art and architecture critic of the *Kansas City Star.*

Because of his diverse training at the Institute of Design, Nickel felt comfortable as a general commercial photographer. Only rarely, however, did he have a chance to demonstrate his skill outside of architecture. One of his earliest jobs, photographing poet Carl Sandburg's 1957 visit to Chicago, appeared in the *New York Times Magazine.* He photographed the weddings of several friends in the 1960s and worked as an assistant photographer when John D. Rockefeller IV married Sharon Percy. Richard shot the ceremony from the balcony of the Rockefeller Chapel on the University of Chicago campus and considered it "high class fun."

A few years later, he made money taking portraits. "Since I generally dislike people I'm naturally having a tough time of it, but it's a change," he wrote.

During those years, Nickel charged his commercial clients $100 per day for picture taking and $50 a day for printing. He charged historians $15 for reproductions of pictures from his files and $10 if the photographs were returned in good condition.

As might be expected, Nickel the idealist displayed poor business skills. He spent years collecting even the smallest of his business debts while waiving his fees for people he respected. He objected strenuously about being hurried. When Horizon publisher Ben Raeburn asked Nickel to rush him a batch of old photos for an architecture book, Nickel printed and dispatched them at once, but wrote: "I keep complaining that standards are going down all around me and when I send you a pile like that, I feel I'm just another bum."

It was not the way to encourage business.

Because of the time Nickel spent on his Sullivan work, he never made much of a living from his commercial work. His tax forms indicate that he averaged a $3,500 yearly income from 1960 to 1971. His best year was 1966, when he reported making $9,000. His photographs of architecture received prominent play in architecture magazines such as *Forum, Architectural Record, Progressive Architecture,* and Italy's *Casabella,* and in newspapers, books and general-interest magazines such as *Time.*

By 1964 the majority of Nickel's income came from taking pictures of art work. He was hired frequently by the New York publishing firm of Harry N. Abrams, Inc., to photograph paintings and sculpture in private Chicago-area collections. The pictures, used in coffee-table books, demanded technical skill, but little creative energy.

The year after Nickel died, a retrospective was held at the Art Institute of Chicago. At the time, it was one of the largest photography shows in the museum's 93-year history.

Nickel's dramatic photograph of the half-demolished Garrick proscenium arch, printed as a 40-by-50-inch mural, was the most prominent picture in the A. Montgomery Ward Gallery, but the photo that set the mood was a self-portrait Richard took on the roof of the Republic Building. Standing just above the ornamental cornice, behind a terra-cotta finial, Nickel looked like the defiant captain of a sailing ship.

Along the east wall were quiet, stark, intense photographs of Sullivan's Wainwright Building, Carson Pirie Scott store, Stock Exchange, and Troescher Building; as well as Burnham and Root's Rookery Building and Kansas City Board of Trade. Along the west wall were views of Sullivan's early houses and the Bayard Building in New York City; Wright's Robie House; H. H. Richardson's architecture; and several modern structures. Fifteen more Garrick photographs filled out the show.

The 98 black-and-white prints would have surprised Richard because he had never considered himself a fine artist. In fact, some of the images printed for the show had never been printed by Nickel during his lifetime.

First and foremost, Nickel used his camera to record what he saw. Nickel was a dreamer, but from the start he doubted he could convince Mayor Daley, Chicago, or the nation of the need to save great architecture. So he adopted the role of documentarian, one who gathers as complete a record as possible.

His telephoto lenses inventoried architectural details, from the stencil work of the Auditorium Building to the leafy ornament on Sullivan's last commission, the Krause Music Store. His wide-angle lenses collected the sites, such as the vacant lot on South Michigan Avenue where Adler and Sullivan's Abraham Kuh house had stood long ago. (Nickel used the latter picture to study the marks of adjoining structures so that he could determine the dimensions and roof lines of the demolished Kuh rowhouse.) Nickel's copy lenses recorded the historical pictures he found, as well as newspaper articles, blueprints, architectural renderings, Adler's boyhood school books, and a 1909 auction pamphlet listing Louis Sullivan's household effects. Richard used his cameras casually, like a scholar uses a notepad. He set his found objects and documents down on the floor, held them in place and made a record of what he found.

He also used his camera with great power. His more formal pictures of buildings and ornament were documentary views packed with information. In spite of his love for Sullivan's architecture, Nickel maintained a remarkably objective, restrained stance when taking pictures of Sullivan buildings during the 1950s. Almost all of his shots were straight-on with a long depth of field. The photographs, Nickel wrote photographer Minor White, were simply a "factual report" on Adler and Sullivan's architecture.

Nickel produced drama by fully understanding what he was photographing. He shot the Kehilath Anshe Ma'ariv Synagogue on Chicago's South Side from behind because he wanted to show the force and strength of the design. The building was meant to be constructed of polished red granite, but Sullivan was forced to use rough-cut granite for financial reasons. Thus, Nickel decided to show the idea rather than the result. His photo showed the tall brick back of the church rising well above its neighbors.

"What he looked for, and usually captured, in a building was its essential character—whether it be loftiness, or elegance, or decorative grace, or brandy-and-cigars massiveness, or classical order," wrote M. W. Newman in the *Chicago Daily News*. "He loved the character of light and shadow, the interplay of forms, the city's sombre strength."

He was also unafraid to show how once proud buildings existed—for better or worse—in run-down neighborhoods populated by curious children and Packards with low-hanging mufflers. He showed the dilapidated Albert Sullivan house with a missing bannister, broken skylight, stripped fireplace, and graffiti-smeared walls. He showed the Rothschild rowhouses rotting away in a South Side slum with their cornices stripped and dirty curtains dancing out of the windows in a summer breeze. He showed the city grime that masked the Auditorium Building, the cracked window panes that made the Fanny Kohn residence look haggard, and the battered loading dock that made the Kennedy Bakery seem worn out.

The Max M. Rothschild row houses, designed by Adler and Sullivan in 1883 on Chicago's South Side. The photograph was taken during the mid-1950s. The houses were destroyed in 1976.

Pristine, manipulated, filtered images of the architecture did not serve Nickel's purpose because they were not honest. He was incensed when Hedrich-Blessing, a commercial studio, airbrushed the reflection of Nickel's camera out of his photograph that the firm borrowed.

Nickel was not the Ansel Adams of the American cityscape. Had he stumbled into the Yosemite Valley with a desire to live there forever and share its beauty as did the West Coast photographer, he would have gone beyond picturing the glacial lakes, meadows, forests, gorges, and cliffs. Adams created a beautiful, but melodramatic, National Parks view of the West. Nickel was more matter-of-fact. He would have been more interested in the decaying cow skulls on the desert floor. He delved deeper, portraying his subjects as they often were, pockmarked and scarred and aging. It fit the City on the Make.

Nickel was enough of a craftsman to have mastered any type of photography. He chose a documentary style because he felt it was the clearest way to draw attention to his subject and explain it. For he wanted the buildings—not the medium or himself—to dominate. As he matured, he wanted his photographs to reach and influence the masses, or the "mobocracy," as Frank Lloyd Wright called them. That is why Nickel was more interested in hanging his pictures in the City Hall lobby then in the high-brow Art Institute.

Like Jacob Riis, the 19th-century social reformer who set out to improve living conditions in New York City's slums, or the artists of the Depression-era Farm Security Administration, out to show the value of working-class life, Nickel saw the camera as a tool to make his point. He simply wanted to show that Americans were ignoring, defacing, and destroying the great architecture that surrounded them. Virtually all of his thousands of pictures sing with a humble but strident reminder: "This is what you have."

One of Nickel's photographs shows pedestrians hurrying past the Garrick without noticing the grace of the second-story loggia or the sweep of the tower. Another photo shows the busts of Mozart and Shakespeare eyeing one another in the loggia, deep in shadow behind the rigging of the Garrick marquee and well hidden from the sidewalk below.

In a photo of Aaron Siskind during the mid-fifties, Nickel includes a group of children who surrounded the photographer as he set up his view camera at the Rothschild Flats on the South Side. The kids are fascinated by the man puffing on a cigarette as he prepares to get under the black cloth. They are also fascinated by the dilapidated building that has captured his attention.

Like the paintings of British landscape artist J. M. W. Turner, which made Londoners aware of the romantic beauty of the city's shroud of fog, Nickel's photographs helped people appreciate Chicago's shrouded masterpieces. His photographs revealed a new city—even for people who had lived in Chicago their whole lives.

But the photographs are indeed a private tour. Nickel guides his viewers as if he is standing next to them, pointing out just where to look. Architecture, the most public of art, takes on an intimacy as Nickel directs those who study his work. He offers rewards to those who look carefully: a window washer hangs from the eighth

A window washer at work on Burnham and Root's 1889–91 Monadnock Building at 53 West Jackson Boulevard.

floor of the Monadnock Building's facade, and an array of humorous terra-cotta eagles, gargoyles, griffins, and filigreed pinnacles sit atop the North American Building. Nickel, who labeled the picture "Chicago cheesecake," showed that he had not forgotten the Institute of Design's second-floor-and-above assignment, which made him look up. Like photographer Dorothea Lange, Nickel wanted to use the camera to teach others how to see without a camera.

David Travis, curator of Nickel's Art Institute retrospective, stated, "Nickel's photographs did not turn into the remorseful images of a champion for a lost cause or the angry images of a frustrated crusader. He did not demean his photography to propagandize. His photographs are the proud and clear fragments of a man who followed the fragmentary clues of a genius."

Siskind had enjoined his students to show what set the architecture of Adler and Sullivan apart and to show how all their buildings were part of the "seed germ" that Sullivan spent a lifetime nurturing. Because the architecture was the outgrowth of what Sullivan described as "a harmonious system of thinking," Nickel believed that every pillar and joist was important in tracing the progression of Sullivan's architectural concept. No building was too insignificant to be recorded—from the Euston and Company Linseed and Linoleum Factory to the small garage that was the only remnant of the six-story Knisely Factory.

Siskind, the aesthete, concentrated on showing the beauty of Adler and Sullivan architecture. Nickel, the scholar, was after the profundity of the firm's ideas. The more Richard learned, the more dissatisfied he became with the early

Interior of the National Farmers' Bank in Owatonna from the mid-1950s.

156

photos. So he kept returning to the buildings, rephotographing them as Sullivan envisioned: the Guaranty Building in Buffalo, New York, as—in Sullivan's words—"a proud and soaring thing," the National Farmers' Bank as "a color tone poem." Nickel's juxtaposition of a lone winter tree in front of Sullivan's John Borden house is so obvious it is childlike. He wanted to show Sullivan's organic building theory by demonstrating that the tree did not take away from the house, nor did the house take away from the tree. Although Nickel seldom specified his photographic intent in writing, his notes about the Auditorium Building photographs show that Nickel's primary documentary intent was to explain Sullivan. "I wanted the building, or rather the photographs to convey a feeling of solidity and monumentality," Nickel wrote. "These are the feelings Sullivan wanted to impart."

He photographed buildings at different times of day and in different seasons. Never satisfied with his pictures of the black-stone-slab Ryerson Tomb at Graceland Cemetery on the city's North Side, Nickel returned in winter to contrast it to fallen snow. Now, finally, here was death. He also photographed buildings from all possible angles. He began his portrait of the Dooly Block in Salt Lake City from about a mile away and concluded when he was close enough to show the rough texture of the bright red sandstone base.

There is no question that the tireless stalking made for definitive photographs of Sullivan buildings. He animated the downtown buildings, which Loop real estate developers ignorantly called "dinosaurs," by using the proper combination of camera and lens, by finding the best location from which to shoot, and by choosing the time

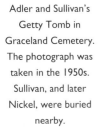

Adler and Sullivan's Getty Tomb in Graceland Cemetery. The photograph was taken in the 1950s. Sullivan, and later Nickel, were buried nearby.

when he could show the buildings in the best light possible, both literally and figuratively. Nickel returned for years to the Loop's Stock Exchange Building and Carson Pirie Scott store and visited most of Sullivan's small midwestern banks over and over again. There was always another building to be recorded or a new way to portray it. The demolition of a downtown St. Louis structure near the Wainwright Building in 1965 was cause enough for Nickel to tote his gear back to Missouri, for the razing afforded the first unobstructed view in decades of the Wainwright's east facade.

The drama of Nickel's prints also resulted from skillful technique. An architect designs a building with mass that stands in space and with surfaces that reflect light. Richard learned how to manipulate mass, space, surface, and light to create renderings as brilliant as their subjects. He photographed Sullivan's exotic, old world Russian Orthodox Church on Chicago's West Side through a picturesque morning mist, and the Getty Tomb in Graceland Cemetery when the rays of the afternoon sun were masked in silhouette by overhanging trees.

Nickel was scrupulous about figuring out the effects of the sun. He carried a homemade chart, developed over several years, telling him the time and season that would show the gritty, old architecture to its best advantage. For close to six months a year there was no direct sunlight on the north face of Chicago buildings, and the harsh winter light created long shadows that made buildings look stark and cold. To avoid that effect, Richard had to plan well in advance.

His favorite time was just before sunset, when the sun's last light created an Edward Hopper purity, pushing dark shadows across the surface of buildings and imparting a luminous quality to the facades. The magic hour, when Nickel could see the sun and its outline, made the all-important details of Sullivan buildings stand out.

One of Nickel's first commercial jobs was to photograph the new Cincinnati library. The pictures appeared in the December 1955 issue of *Progressive Architecture,* but the building's architect, Woodie Garber, apparently was disappointed with the results.

Nickel wrote Garber with a philosophical explanation: "Most architects always find something wrong with the photographs of their buildings mainly because they 'live' their buildings as a myth," Nickel wrote. "Photography deals with reality, and the transfer of a three-dimensional creation to a sheet of paper can never be spectacular."

He was to prove himself wrong. Five years later, after spending months photographing the Garrick Theater, Nickel told Vinci something that must have amounted to a confession: His photographs were as good as, even better than, Sullivan's ornament. Nickel had improved on the Master's work by making—as Aaron Siskind liked to say—photographs that were a new object, complete and self-contained. Nickel had become an artist.

Nickel set out to document Sullivan's glory. But as the buildings he photographed were abused, damaged, and ultimately destroyed, his role evolved into that of a witness. Some of the buildings had already changed by the time he found them. The Barbe residence, built as a four-bedroom mansion for a prominent clothier, had six

Demolition of the facade at the Albert Sullivan residence in 1970. Nickel led a small team of wreckers in saving the entire front section of the house. The pieces are in storage at Southern Illinois University at Edwardsville.

A wrecker demolishes the Babson House's chimney. The house was razed in 1960 to make way for a subdivision.

mailboxes on the front stoop when Richard arrived. The Felsenthal Store, a link between Adler and Sullivan's large commercial buildings and Sullivan's later small banks, had become Jimmie's Lounge, advertising the "Lowest Price in Town for Beer, Wines and Whisky." The Home Building Association in Newark, Ohio, had been remodeled as a jewelry store with a curvy Art Deco entrance. Similarly, the Kimball house was the L'Aiglon French restaurant, the Louis Frank house was the Vandercook College of Music, and the Blumenfeld house was a laundry.

Many of the Sullivan buildings changed before his eyes. His contact sheets show a depressing sequence of decay. The Samuel Stern house, first shown with window shades and a "For Rent" sign during the mid-1950s, is pictured later with broken windows and missing both front door and front railing. The Albert Sullivan house, too, grows old during the 1960s. Gang graffiti covers the limestone front, the cornice and bay windows are stripped, and plywood replaces smashed windows. Nickel shows the chipped mosaic floor tiles and the snow that has blown inside the house. The winter before its demolition, he photographed the beloved house behind a trash bin, leaving no doubt as to his symbolism.

The role of witness must have been a painful one. He drove to the sprawling Babson Estate in Riverside to show the roof stripped off the main houses, the interior gutted, and the windows in the second-floor loggia shattered. He stayed to show the house being flattened and replaced by a sign proclaiming "Choice residential lots for sale." He returned yet again to show paved streets and sewers and finally to show the colonial-style homes that replaced the Babson.

He photographed the three-story Braunstein Store on the North Side, boarded up by the Cleveland Wrecking Company, and the smoldering remains of the

Victoria Hotel in Chicago Heights the morning after it had been destroyed by fire. He photographed the Reuben Rubel house, which looked like it had taken a hand grenade when it was razed, and the Albert Sullivan house, so stripped and picked apart that the camera could see directly through its interior.

At the Garrick, Nickel photographed floors filled with rubble and plaster as well as electrical and telephone wires hanging from the ceiling. He was there on the day when the demolition began and showed a determined man holding a sign that read: "Architectural masterpiece 'Balabankatzed.'"

At the Stock Exchange, Nickel repeated the sequence. He showed the Three Oaks Wrecking Company claiming the building by constructing barricades and scaffolding and the "Building Coming Down 1/2 Off Clearance Sale" signs in the first-floor store windows. This time there was more than one picket, but Nickel focused on a determined man who looked directly at his camera from across LaSalle Street with a sign that read: "STOP."

Once a complete set of photographs had been taken of each Adler and Sullivan structure, Nickel's job as a documentarian was over. He was not required to show what was happening to the buildings, but he felt a responsibility to watch and record the proud Sullivan buildings on death row as they deteriorated and eventually disappeared.

Perhaps saddest of all are Nickel's photographs of the ornate, 80-year-old Adler and Sullivan mansion built for reaper inventor Cyrus Hall McCormick on the North Side. Just before its demolition in 1955, the building was thrown open for a last bizarre event—an artists' gala at which painters were invited to cover the walls. Nickel photographed the interior, once adorned with tapestried chairs, heavy silken draperies, and mahogany beams, now hidden by graffiti. His pictures showed charcoal drawings of ghoulish faces and grotesque bodies floating on the walls.

Buildings were torn down, Nickel believed, because expediency ruled; people wasted and destroyed because nobody cared. This is shown on the faces of the gawkers at photographed demolition sites. Nickel's passersby were always more interested in buildings after the wrecking had begun. They were bored by the subtlety of great architecture; only a wrecking ball made them pay attention.

"In the USA it's money-money-money and therefore, perhaps, face up to the removal of buildings as a fact of life," Richard wrote to architectural historian Paul Sprague during the late 1960s. Sprague had asked Nickel to lecture to college students on the demise of architectural art, but Nickel refused. It would not prove worthwhile, he said. "It's a new age. . .and by the time the kids with new values grow up, everything good and decent will have been wiped out by the shysters, hucksters, and money grubbers. I suggest instead the production of a short film, the most cutting, sarcastic production imaginable to show what a bunch of clods and gangsters and twaddlers run this town."

Like Sullivan, Nickel knew that most or all of Sullivan's buildings would eventually be demolished. Money built the buildings and money would destroy them. It's only the idea that counts, Sullivan had said. The architect resorted to writing in order to keep the seed germ alive; Nickel resorted to photography.

Ever since the camera and photographic techniques were created, photographers have been fascinated with the landscape of buildings.

The inventor of one early photographic technique, Joseph Nicephore Niepce, aimed his experimental device at the roofs and barns of the French countryside, at the walls of his studio, and at the city of Paris during the late 1820s to make heliographs, the world's first photographs. He entered into a brief but fruitless partnership with Louis-Jacques-Mandé Daguerre. Heliographs did not lead to the commercial success sought by Daguerre, who later astounded the world in 1839 with the announcement that he had found a way to freeze and fix an image. One of the first "daguerreotypes" he exhibited was a view of Notre Dame Cathedral.

The ingenious Daguerre was able to produce an image on a sensitized copper sheet covered by a thin layer of polished silver—a "mirror with a memory." The image was highly detailed. Because of the long exposure time required, the first daguerreotypists were limited to portraits, landscapes, and architecture. Portraits were difficult because subjects had to sit perfectly still. Landscapes were difficult because even the gentlest sway of wind or water reduced the sharpness of the final result.

Meanwhile, British scholar William Henry Fox Talbot was developing his own method of photography. Talbot made the first photographic "negative" when he pointed his matchbook-size camera toward the latticed window of his home in 1835. It was the first of many pictures of his estate.

Talbot formally proclaimed his discovery three weeks after Daguerre's own announcement. A few years later, Talbot found that his negative could be developed and transformed into a positive on a sheet of sensitized paper. Although the impressionistic "talbotypes," or "calotypes," could not match daguerreotypes in detail, Talbot's process was simpler, cheaper, and less cumbersome. More important, the negatives could be used to make duplicates. When Talbot published *The Pencil of Nature*, the first book of photographs, he opened with views of Queens College in Cambridge and the boulevards of Paris.

Only a few weeks after Daguerre's announcement, a French journalist predicted that the camera would be of particular value because it would be more accurate than even the most painstaking architectural etchings or paintings. "Travelers may perhaps soon be able to procure M. Daguerre's apparatus, and bring back views of the finest monuments and most beautiful scenery of the whole world. They will see how far the pencil and brush are from the truth."

That is exactly what happened. By late 1839 a French photographer sailed to London and returned with daguerreotypes of British architecture. The work was hailed as wonderfully beautiful. Soon after, a French publisher hired daguerreotypists to roam Europe and the United States. They brought back 1,200 views.

But it was the British who used the camera to conquer the world, at least photographically. It took only a few decades for Talbot and his followers to systematically document what lay virgin to the camera's eye. During the early 1840s they took photographs of virtually all the great monuments of Europe. The Rev. Calvert Jones made pictures of Rome, Florence, Naples, Malta, and Sicily on a grand tour in 1845–46. The Rev. George Bridges, first to photograph the Acropolis from Museum Hill, took 1,700 negatives on his trips. Francis Frith, the first successful commercial architectural photographer, laid claim to Egypt and the Holy Land during the 1850s, and John Thompson ventured into Ceylon, Cambodia, Malaysia, and China in the following two decades. During those early years, photographers were judged more on content than technique. Capturing a new site was tantamount to bagging a prized animal.

The French used the camera to capture the nation's glorious past. In 1851 the French Historical Monuments Commission hired an elite group of photographers to record the grandeur of Gothic architecture. One of the most influential French photographers was Charles Negre, who made two pictures of every building. Negre first showed his subject conventionally from the middle level so that scale and dimensions would be accurately recorded. Then he would do something unprecedented. He took another view that portrayed what the building meant to him.

The photography of buildings remained an academic and artistic pursuit until the 1850s, when the invention of stereography—three-dimensional photographs—put architectural photos on the parlor tables in all of the most proper Victorian homes. The London Stereoscopic Company, established in 1854, sold more than one million views during its first decade. By the 1860s the firm employed 1,000 photographers to document the wonders of the world. Stereographs, the TV of the late 1800s, made the Grand Tour affordable to all.

"All of us have seen the Alps and know Chamonix and the Mer de Glace by heart," wrote a British columnist about stereographs, "though we have never braved the horrors of the Channel. The pyramids of Egypt would fail to astonish the most ingenuous of British schoolboys. We have crossed the Andes, ascended Tenerife, entered Japan, done Niagara, and the Thousand Isles."

As in Europe, the first American camera operators photographed buildings. Samuel F. B. Morse, inventor of the electric telegraph, carried a description of Daguerre's process from Paris to the United States in 1839 and made his first daguerreotype later that year. It was a view of a Unitarian church from his New York University laboratory. The earliest surviving U.S. daguerreotype, dated October 16, 1839, was taken of the Philadelphia Arsenal and Central High School by Joseph Saxon. Within a year, Edward Everett Hale, author of *The Man Without a Country,* took daguerreotypes and calotypes of Boston's South Congressional Church and Harvard Hall.

Until the outbreak of the Civil War, however, the vast majority of photography in the United States consisted of portraiture. Matthew Brady, who gained distinction for his studio's daguerreotype portraits of illustrious Americans, began the nation's grand documentary tradition when he sent a corps of employees, armed with cameras and portable darkrooms, to bring back Civil War images. His photographers could not record action because of the limitations of the recent "wet-collodion" process, which involved preparing negative images on glass plates using wet solutions. So they took scenes showing the effects of battles, mostly pictures of corpses and scarred architecture. As General William T. Sherman's troops marched through Georgia on the Union's trek to the sea, photographers such as George N. Barnard trained their lenses on the battered depots, flour mills, and other Confederate buildings to create unforgettable photos.

After the Union's victory, many of the war-trained camera operators joined the railroad and geological expeditions to document America's great march west. This was where the action was. The mountains and plains—untouched, unexplored and unrecorded—comprised a visual utopia for photographers. William Henry Jackson, one of many whose camera became an adjunct to the nation's "manifest destiny," took astounding views of northwestern Wyoming that helped convince Congress to designate Yellowstone as the nation's first national park.

At the other end of the country, the landscape of New York City—with its formal Georgians, graceful Federals, austere Greek Revivals, and brownstone Italianates—was being largely ignored by photographers. As late as 1900 photo critic Sadakichi Hartmann complained that few people considered the city worth photographing. "I am well aware that much is lacking here which makes European cities so interesting and inspiring to the sightseer and artist," he wrote in "A Plea for the Picturesqueness of New York" in *Camera Notes*.

Within a few years, Alfred Stieglitz and other New York City–based photographers known as the "Photo Secessionists" took the first serious look at the modern American city. Their abstract vision was far more painterly than documentary. Alvin Langdon Coburn manipulated cityscapes, aiming his camera down the sides of buildings, causing vertical lines to converge and creating an unsettling feeling. Paul Strand portrayed the city's overwhelming nature by showing people walking past the huge, black, "rather sinister" windows of Wall Street's Morgan Guaranty Trust Building. Edward Steichen showed the city's elegance with his 1904 picture of the wedge-shaped Flatiron Building. The photo of the building's 285-foot shaft in the soft light of dusk became a classic. It was considered fine art, and architectural photography had come of age.

Richard Nickel's photographic heritage included more than architectural photographers. He also belonged to a family of "concerned photographers," an odd bunch of varying ability but equal determination who spent much of their lives using a camera to understand and portray the world.

Adam Clark Vroman, a Pasadena, California, bookstore owner, spent more than a decade photographing Indians in the Southwest after watching a Hopi snake dance in 1895. He wanted to show evidence of the Indian civilization before it was destroyed. Koyo Okada photographed Japan's Mount Fuji 150,000 times. His goal was to capture beauty, and after 40 years he said he had not yet exhausted his subject. Darius Kinsey photographed generations of loggers in the Pacific Northwest from 1890 to 1940.

More akin to Nickel were Frederick H. Evans and Jean-Eugène-August Atget, turn-of-the-century contemporaries who spent decades making fleeting images of the past. Evans specialized in England's great Gothic churches, producing moody, deep-shadowed prints on platinum paper that are among the most striking architectural photographs ever taken. Atget concentrated on Paris, taking simple, misty morning views of "everything artistic and picturesque" from the rag pickers to the Versailles monuments.

Nickel's photographic ancestry dated back directly to László Moholy-Nagy, whose ideas about the power of the camera first made Nickel aware of its potential. Moholy-Nagy believed that the camera was the machine age's greatest gift. A camera could record the place, look, value, cost, detail, quantity, quality, size, feel, shape, height, and width of whatever it was pointed at. The camera, he wrote, is "correct." It is a special tool for the artist in search of truth because it can make a true image, free from interpretation and distortion. By showing every pore and every wrinkle, and by recording every detail, photographs have great power to teach people, he wrote. Because photographs can be mass-produced, they can affect thousands or even millions of people.

Moholy-Nagy believed that photographers have a special responsibility. Photographers, he insisted, must understand the power of the camera and its potential to drive at the truth. His school gave Nickel a mission. Harry Callahan and Aaron Siskind tended Moholy-Nagy's flame at the Institute of Design after the founder's death. Just as Moholy-Nagy had believed, Callahan and Siskind insisted that art, like science, demanded a life of devotion. One picture always followed another for the serious photographer.

Nickel's photographs are certainly not metaphorical or experimental, as were Callahan's, nor do they intrigue as do Siskind's prints. But Richard learned the meaning of art from them, and lived the devoted life of an artist.

Because Nickel wanted to communicate all that a building had to offer, he fought the impulse to indulge himself. His pictures are sparse, direct, and self-effacing.

"When people are looking at my pictures of Sullivan architecture, I prefer to be completely left out as the maker or interpreter, and I don't care whether this is creative photography or not, just so they get the essence of the building," he wrote Minor White. "But I suppose 'I' or any other photographer creeps in no matter how hard he tries not to."

Only occasionally did Nickel creep into his photographs to make an artistic statement. Here and there he used chipped walls, cracked pieces of terra cotta, fire escapes, exhaust fans, window frames, or moldings to make abstract designs and Siskind-like collages on film. He studied the reflection of rainwater on the tarred roof of the Levi Rosenfeld Store and Flats building, and took disorienting views of the exterior iron bracing system of the Wirt Dexter building more for aesthetic reasons. Yet by accepting the responsibility to document, Nickel knew he must suppress his artistic urge.

Siskind never fully understood his student, who matured rapidly following his graduation from the Institute of Design. When asked whether Nickel would be classified a "great photographer," Siskind replied years after Nickel's death that Richard was too restrictive on himself and too concerned about describing the work of someone else.

"In order to be somebody great, you must project an idea," Siskind said. "Richard's idea was limited by the idea in the object rather than the idea in his head."

John Szarkowski, photography curator of the Museum of Modern Art whose photographic quest of Sullivan during the early 1950s helped him better understand Nickel's purpose, knew that Richard was not limited by the subject he chose. "You might think that the subject is the buildings of Louis Sullivan, and that is of course one way of putting it," Szarkowski wrote, "but that way of putting it is so broad that it encompasses at least a million ideas."

Nickel's interest went beyond architecture. He was more than a humble servant of Louis Sullivan. Nickel was caught in the eternal fight between fadism and classicism, between what the "masses" felt was old and worn out and what he considered truly stately, elegant, and useful. Nickel was fighting for art.

"When a single masterpiece is struck down, the act is attributed to a madman," Frederick Sommer would say at Nickel's memorial service. "But when the coherence of an entire society is vandalized, the destruction is viewed with proud arrogance as evidence of progress. The single destructive act comes as a shock, but anonymous insanity is unseen and unfelt. When forests fall, or millions die in ravaged landscapes, too few will see that this also is madness."

By returning to wrecking sites, Nickel was doing more than nuts-and-bolts documentary work. Like Eugène Atget, who showed the streets of Paris, and Lewis Hine, who photographed the construction of the Empire State Building, Nickel was encompassing far more than mortar and stone. By their insistence on returning to the scene, the three photographers were both examining change and looking at the society that produces such change. Where Atget sensed the dying spirit of Parisian culture, for instance, Nickel perceived a dying idea. Hine's photographs are a celebration of man and machines, whereas Nickel took a more critical view. Hine's "skyboys" have been replaced by Nickel's wreckers; Hine's cranes have been

The arched entrance of H. H. Richardson's 1886–87 Glessner House on Chicago's South Side. The photograph was taken during the late 1960s.

replaced by Nickel's bulldozers. Hine saw the Empire State as a reflection of those who were building it. Nickel saw the Garrick as a reflection of those who were destroying it.

Early 1966 was particularly busy for Nickel as more Adler and Sullivan residences came down. In March three adjoining Max M. Rothschild houses near the Illinois Institute of Technology campus burned down. Nickel did not have a chance to make floor plans or photograph the interior because, in his words, the "IIT jerks" never bothered to tell him about the fire. Later that month the 1883 mansion built for Charles P. Kimball just north of the Loop was razed. Nickel paid the wreckers to help him remove columns, capitals, and ironwork. He salvaged the material for Southern Illinois University, which paid the expenses.

Nickel wanted to see his downstate collection grow as more Sullivan buildings were destroyed. He spoke at the dedication of the collection in 1966, and two years later he was officially hired to continue his salvage work.

At the same time, Richard was disappointed about how the ornament was displayed on the Edwardsville campus. He wrote Jack Randall that the pieces were too spread out and displayed with no logic. Some of the pieces had been cleaned despite Nickel's notes saying that dirt gave the pieces character.

"All my ornament did go to SIU and confidentially Randall hasn't done a very imaginative job in installing it," Nickel wrote in 1966. "He values the wrong pieces often, makes basic mistakes, etc. However, I'm probably unfair because I do regret letting it go out of Chicago!"

Nickel realized the university did not have the money or space for a museum-type display, but the collection played on his mind, even if his obsession with it had lost its intensity somewhat. "Being so far away, I find I am kind of divorced from it," he wrote years later. "As far as my personal involvement, it might as well not exist. I fly in or drive in once in awhile. The real bugaboo is, of course, money. I have learned a supreme lesson from this. Money affects your good judgment like nothing else in the world."

Keeping Nickel busiest was his work to save the vacant John J. Glessner House. The blackened, stone mansion south of the Loop at Prairie Avenue and 18th Street was the last surviving building designed in Chicago by H. H. Richardson. With a sweeping entrance arch that has become a symbol of the city's bold architecture, the Glessner House was put up for sale in early 1965.

Soon after seeing that the house was vacant, Nickel wrote to influential people in the architecture and art communities asking them to convince Mayor Daley of the building's value. "I think it is important for responsible persons to go on record so that the City cannot plead ignorance," Nickel wrote. His letters to the daily newspapers criticized the inaction of the Chicago Commission on Architectural Landmarks. Nickel had hoped that the city would take the lead in saving the Glessner House. Instead, he found the lead being taken by the Chicago School of Architecture Foundation, a new preservation group that enlisted his help. Most of those who attended the organization's first meeting had never been involved in a landmarks fight, Nickel wrote, but many of the original members had backgrounds in real estate and law.

The first thing needed was $35,000 to buy the house. That turned out easier than it seemed. New York architect Philip Johnson agreed to give $10,000 if his grant was matched by Chicago architects. Johnson's donation embarrassed Chicago architects into giving, and within a couple of weeks the new group had raised $41,000.

The Glessner was special to Nickel. Richardson, whose Marshall Field Warehouse building served as a model for Adler and Sullivan's Auditorium Building, had been an important mentor to all of the great Chicago architects during the last three decades of the 19th century. The house, which looked more like a fort than a home, was large enough to be significant but small enough to be manageable. Nickel saw the Glessner—as rugged and geometrically perfect as any Richardson East Coast masterpiece—as a practical experiment that could prove, or disprove, his ideas about preservation. This was a building that actually could be saved.

Nickel's first concern after the house was purchased was to make it presentable to the public. Its last tenants, the owners of a graphic arts company, had marred the interior by installing conduits along the woodwork and fluorescent lights on the ceiling, and by constructing partitions for darkrooms. Structurally the house was in good condition, but not mechanically. Nickel considered living there to supervise the volunteer effort, but decided to simply join the workers and help on weekends. It took several years of hard work to clean up the debris and rehabilitate the house, but Nickel enjoyed the effort.

Richard returned to Boston to teach three sections of basic photography at Harvard University in the summer of 1966. His friend Len Gittleman told Nickel he could probably get permanent work there after the summer and Nickel seriously considered the idea. Early in the summer, he wrote friends back in Chicago that it

Richard Nickel in his first boat, *Vato.*

was good to be out of the "molotov cocktail, multiple murder type of town." However, he eventually decided this would be his last summer at Harvard. In early August he wrote that he did not like teaching the basic courses because his students had such a superficial interest in photography that they found the box camera too complicated.

Once again, Richard spent much of his time at Cambridge tracking down Sullivan. He used Boston city records to translate Sullivan's birthplace to its modern-day address. Disheartened that no appropriate plaque stood in front of the house at 22 South Bennett Street, he wrote several letters to Boston city officials and to local architects' groups. He found the List farm, where Sullivan's beloved grandparents had taken care of him for several idyllic summers in nearby Wakefield, and he found the neighboring Cowdrey Farm, where young Louis had watched his first sunrise "chilled and spellbound" standing beneath a great ash tree. This was where Sullivan first fell in love with nature. Nickel's only disappointment was that he could not find the ash tree. "It must be long dead," he wrote friend Paul Sprague, to whom he sent leaves from a nearby tree.

That summer Nickel joined the Harvard Yacht Club. For $12 he took sailing lessons on the Charles River near the Massachusetts Institute of Technology. By then sailing had become an important part of his life. He had purchased one-half interest in a 14-foot, Finnish-built sloop named *Vato* in 1964 and learned to sail in a burrow pit near the northwest suburban expressways. He spent more time the first years removing paint from the hull bottom and varnishing the boat than sailing it. He added a small oak plate to hold the running light and a battery, and installed a seat so that children could straddle the bow and let their feet drag in the water. When he was finished, *Vato* looked like a piece of furniture. He wrote:

> *Everyone said not to bother with removing bottom paint (that's the American way: "why bother?" tear it down, pollute, the public be damned). But I have made it into an honest monochromatic integral boat. Mahogany hull and Persian red keel. And she doesn't leak, the keel is completely rigid. It was all worthwhile even for a season or two. Wood boats will never return and I am glad to have had the misery and pleasure of one.*

Pretty to look at, *Vato* was a backbreaker both in and out of the water. Richard, however, had little trouble hauling the wooden boat. By now he was expert at pulleys and rollers, and he could singlehandedly lift the boat out of Lake Michigan and attach it onto the trailer. With no lead in the keel, the unballasted *Vato* was difficult to handle at sea. Nickel and partner Lee Timonen had to shift their weight and hike out over the rail frequently to keep the boat upright. Richard, who compared *Vato* to sailing a peanut shell, loved it.

Boating was an aesthetic experience for Richard. He loved the simplicity, design, and workmanship of boats, including the fact that every nook and cranny was put to use. Nickel was a man of passion in search of truth and beauty as he foraged through a slag heap next to a fallen building or as he sailed beneath a billowing spinnaker on Lake Michigan. In the late 1960s he wrote that he was not interested in whether a boat sails fast, but that every line looks right in and out of the water. He loved the feel of the sail and the idea that he skimmed along the lake on the power of the wind.

Power boaters, or "stink-potters," as he called them, were the scourge of the lake for Richard. He assailed a friend for selling a sailboat and buying a power boat as showing "an unmistakable sign of confused values." He wrote, "God made the wind, but corporations like GE (Shell, Standard, etc.) made the damned gas, which should be left underground."

Richard sailed to renew his inner strength. He liked the feeling of being alone and free. He would sail far enough away so that he could see, but not hear, the city. From there, he could appreciate the beauty of Chicago, so calm in its silence. It was like the feeling he got in 1967 when a 27-inch blizzard fell on the city. "The city is stopped dead under the snow," he wrote. "It's wonderful."

The best time to sail, he wrote, was the late afternoon, "when all the power boaters go home to get slicked up for Saturday night dates," or at night when the 30- or 40-footers were tied up and he could see the John Hancock Center sparkling in the distance. He loved sailing because he was a romantic. He loved the beauty of boats and the lake for the same reasons he loved the free-spirit Sullivan.

Although Richard enjoyed sailing alone, he often invited guests. Sailing was an interest he could share with others. He was the true captain of his ship. He told his guests to be on time and gave them detailed instructions on what kind of shoes and clothes to wear and what food to bring. Once on the lake, he made all the decisions. Nickel destroyed at least one friendship when he sailed into heavy winds instead of returning to shore with a guest. Other relationships were strained when he kept the boat out in the late evening.

Besides sailing the *Vato,* Nickel was a regular on a 30-foot sailboat owned by Alfred and Natalie Levy. The Levys, who produced industrial and advertising films, were more than 10 years older than Richard and sailed with him almost every week starting in the mid-1960s. They were a good foil because they were outside the architectural community and because they enjoyed arguing with him. No matter what they discussed—the Garrick (Alfred called it a "rat-infested fire trap"), politics ("Dick was cynical about local government," said Natalie), work ("We thought we were doing him a favor when we threw him a commercial job," said Natalie, "because he was so modest"), anything but religion ("I thought he was an agnostic," said Alfred)—the verbal sparring ended as a battle between the Levys' pragmatism and Nickel's idealism. Sometimes Nickel would bring a book he was reading, and they would argue about it for hours. Sometimes they would sit on the boat for half an hour or so and say nothing, the true test of friendship.

Richard confided in the Levys, telling them that his parents did not understand him and viewed him as an oddball. Because Stanley and Agnes could not relate to his cause, they wanted Richard to stop the "rabble-rousing" and get a job, a wife, children, and a house. The real problem, Richard told the Levys, was that his mother loved him too much, and he knew he was incapable of returning her love.

Nickel, who wore an open-necked shirt and sweater on board, would dress informally but well when he joined the Levys in Burnham Harbor just east of the

Chicago as seen from Nickel's boat *Garden City* as it sits at anchor in Burnham Harbor. The photograph was taken around 1971.

Loop. He often brought women as guests, but they were only friends, and usually they sailed only once. The only two women who ever accompanied Richard more than once were Georgie Anne Geyer, the reporter, and Phyllis Lambert, the daughter of Seagram's owner Edgar Bronfman, who was working as an architect in Mies van der Rohe's office. Both Natalie and Alfred concluded that Richard was simply too shy to establish long-term relationships with women.

"I remember how relieved he was to find out in the late '60s that his wife had remarried," Alfred said. "'I just got a letter that my ex is married,' he told us. This was the first time we knew he had ever been married. He felt he had spoiled her chances. He felt she would be soured on marriage forever."

Richard told the Levys he had been too young and immature when he married Adrienne. He took all of the blame for the divorce. "He was a perfectionist and must have been hard to live with," Alfred said. "If you served him mashed potatoes that were too soupy, he might let you know."

The Chicago sailing crowd is a tight-knit community during the short season from mid-May to mid-October. Like golfers at country clubs, most sailors know their harbor mates after a couple of years. Well-to-do, but not necessarily rich, city sailors share a common love for the sea more than a love for the buck. For day trips, most sailors head to where the wind is most comfortable. If it's blowing from the north, most sail straight into the lake. If it's from the east or west, they head straight north. Lake Michigan has no islands and its ports are far apart, so many sailors race each other.

The Levys taught Richard how to sail their big boat out of the mile-long harbor, around McCormick Place, and into the lake. He did not know sail trim as well as some, but had instinctive feeling at the helm. Natalie sensed that Nickel enjoyed danger, but she always felt Richard had great respect for boats.

In the summer of 1967, Nickel worked as a crew member on architect Harry Weese's fiberglass sailboat in the annual race from Chicago to Mackinac Island, Michigan. The nine-man crew scraped the hull of the craft and feathered the propeller prior to the race, and worked hard under the direction of a retired navy man. Five days after the start of the race, when the 41-foot sloop crossed under the Mackinac Bridge to three long blasts of an airhorn, Weese and the crew thought they had won. The fact was that the signal meant that Weese's *Bounty* was the last to finish and the parties could begin.

Although he never raced again, Nickel loved sailing fast and facing dangers in the seas. He was not a careful sailor. Just a few weeks after he bought the *Vato*, he persuaded a friend to sail into the lake with no motor in reserve. Richard wanted to depend on his own skill. Miles from the shore, the boat was becalmed. They paddled for seven or eight hours before being towed in by a motor boat.

As he became more experienced at sea, Nickel took more chances. After reading Joshua Slocum's book *Sailing Alone Around the World,* Richard modified his boat to look like Slocum's *Spray* and took every opportunity to go out on the lake in bad storms. He wrote that he loved going against a 15- to 20-knot wind because he felt he was facing God. The rougher the water, the more ecstatic Nickel became. Dogmatic, belligerent, and steely, Nickel thought himself infallible on the lake, bouncing off the seats with joy in three- or four-foot waves despite the fact that he could hardly swim. He didn't want to control nature, just outsmart it.

In 1969 he renamed *Vato*. He chose the name *Rhoda,* Greek for "rose," because the boat was small and very sweet. It was also the name of the evil little girl in the movie "The Bad Seed." He wrote: "And my boat is an evil little girl, when I'm at the helm. Ho hum."

Nickel also loved to write letters. Although most of his typed correspondence concerned architecture, hundreds of other letters defined Nickel's daily thoughts—his likes and dislikes—in a stream-of-conscience diary form. If necessary, he might use the telephone, but for most of his adult life he communicated by letter—sometimes writing several a day: notes to confirm appointments, to rail against City Hall, or to comment on an adventure or grievance. "I expose myself at every turn. But, what the hell," he once wrote. Letters, often written late at night while listening to Bruckner or Bartok in the company of 12-year-old Johnnie Walker Black Label Scotch, were lasting. Just to be sure, Nickel kept carbon copies filed carefully in folders. The one marked "RN as kvetsch" had grown fat over the years.

"Have met a girl who lives across the street from Aaron for whom I'd give almost anything—but I have nothing to give," he wrote a friend in 1963. "Let that be a lesson to you."

Several years later Richard wrote that his former wife, Adrienne, had asked him to join her on a skiing trip to Grenoble, France. "It is nice to be wanted once in awhile," he wrote. "Not too often though. She had her chance and that's that."

After selling his car in 1964, he wrote: "All my friends are annoyed at me for not getting a VW, but it's too late now. I've gone and gotten a Chevelle with Powerglide (I can hear you groaning)." After a trip to Montreal with Phyllis Lambert in 1968, he wrote: "We flew down in a private jet. . .575 mph with tail winds. Oh, to be rich and have the means to buy all the important buildings."

That year Nickel considered purchasing a house at 2121 North Leavitt Street near his old Logan Square neighborhood on the Northwest Side. "It's problematic what it will be like to go from a cool-superficial suburb to an old-world type neighborhood," he wrote. "I'm unable to judge how I might react over a period of time. I'm in a good position now, but once I buy I'm stuck. At the same time, since I reject most "modernism" (the pill and thalidomide, faster and noisier jets, smoking, speed, etc.; all kinds of superficiality and pretention) I suppose Leavitt is where I should make my stand."

Nickel also wrote often about the passing scene, from roasted peanuts ("Ah Sears, boiling peanuts and pimply-faced housewives with their curlers and dirty faced kids in tow") to roasted coffee ("Some people still insist on baking coffee grounds because they received those God-damned GE and Sunbeam pots at their wedding I suppose").

He was for gun control ("We have a suburban policeman in our family and the idiot came to Thanksgiving dinner with gun on hip!") and against supersonic planes ("We have enough damned abstract technological projects to pay for. We also have enough half-empty airplanes crisscrossing the country and defacing the sky with white exhaust streaks").

Nickel also lodged dozens of formal letters of complaint. When his bank began offering the new Scenic Americana series of checks, Richard wrote bank officials: "The landscape is being defaced and polluted at breakneck speed. . .and so I suppose the scenery on what means most to us (money) is all that is left, ugh, to create an illusion that all is well? No, I'm sorry to say this is a cheap establishment gimmick. Like the tropical sports shirts Americans wear to Europe, checks show our obscene taste. Next you'll be putting 'Mother' and 'Jesus' on the checks."

When he purchased a new car, he complained to the U.S. Department of Health, Education, and Welfare about the fact that cigarette lighters are standard equipment. "I don't smoke and I hate the odor of cigarette smoke and so I don't associate with people who smoke or even attend functions where the air will be smoke laden. Yet, when I go to buy a car, I am forced to pay for cigarette lighters. That's unfair. I'd much rather have safety belts."

Several weeks later Nickel received a response from a government official who noted, "The point you made is certainly a fair and just one; we are surprised nobody has thought of it before."

The most revealing letters were Nickel's self-observations. "People say rightly of me that I'm too fussy, but if you're not analytic over everything, then soon enough you're a slob, and anything goes," he wrote. "How you eat, look, walk, think, dress, vote, smell, sail, etc."

In another letter he wrote: "Here's the truth that I am convinced of. Jimmy to Helena in 'Look Back in Anger' by John Osborne. 'And if you can't bear the thought of messing up your nice, clean soul, you'd better give up the whole idea of life, and become a saint. Because you'll never make it as a human being. It's either this world or the next.'"

There was a postscript. "I'd like there to be a next but. . ."

By the late 1960s Nickel had developed a distinct philosophy, a moral code that extended to all parts of his life. It was based on the ideas of Soren Kierkegaard, a 19th-century Danish philosopher and one of the founders of the existentialist movement. Nickel said that the greatest gift he had ever received was when his friend Frederick Sommer introduced him to Kierkegaard's writing. "It's taken me 10 years to come to SK," Nickel wrote, "and if my life accomplishes nothing, at least I have appreciated and adored SK, which I am certain is something."

Although Nickel encountered Kierkegaard's books years after Nickel set off on his single-minded pursuit, the philosopher's writing, particularly the books *Edifying Discourses* and *Purity of Heart Is the Will to One Thing,* comforted Nickel by helping him justify his life. Kierkegaard's ideas confirmed that Nickel's passion was not misplaced and that his mission was worthwhile. Kierkegaard believed that the only way to make life meaningful was to search for "personal truth," defined as the concrete set of beliefs at the center of one's existence. These ideas—small or large in scope, religious or worldly in context—must be defined by each individual.

Nickel's personal truth was the value of Sullivan's architecture. It was what he organized his days and his life around. Like someone fighting for a home or a loved one, he struggled for his truth come hell or high water. Richard came to realize that basing a life on personal truth, taking Kierkegaard's "leap of faith," set him on a higher plane. No matter how much vitality and devotion he had to offer, Nickel knew there was not a moment to look down or fall back, and not a moment to question. The automatic pilot was off and he knew that he must take each uncharted step with care.

"The majority of mankind is lazy-minded, incurious, absorbed in vanities, and tepid in emotions," Nickel wrote in 1970. "Yeah, when you say passion they think of bed." By then, Nickel felt like an outsider in his own world. We live in a "docile society ruled by fear of garbage non-pickup," he wrote, in an "age without passion." Kierkegaard had broken his marriage engagement because he wanted to

Adler and Sullivan's 1892 Meyer Building in Chicago's Loop during the 1950s.

devote his life to writing. Reading this helped Nickel finally come to terms with his divorce. "I feel very cleansed," he wrote years after the breakup. "It's like the slate is clean and I can lead a truly SK life now."

Nickel rejected religion because he was spurned by the Catholic church after his divorce and because he felt he did not need it. Although religious emotions lingered, he wrote, "It is too late because I know that religion can only be super-religion, and takes everything. I am too selfish now." Kierkegaard showed him that he was free to choose his own way. "Everybody else compromises to hell, at least somewhere, in their marriage, or work, spending half their life doing something they hate," Nickel wrote.

The philosopher wrote: "The thing is to find a truth that is true for me, to find the idea for which I can live or die."

Tim Samuelson was as close to a protégé as Richard had. Like Nickel, Samuelson was a self-taught expert on Chicago architecture, particularly on Sullivan's work. With a broad, flat nose, thin lips, and baby teeth, Tim had Nickel's ascetic, raw look. Tall and slim, he had also developed Nickel's strength.

Samuelson looked upon Nickel as a celebrity and as a teacher. Richard taught Tim how to salvage and care for large pieces of terra cotta, stone, and ironwork, and how to keep tabs on what Sullivan buildings might be demolished next. Since their first meeting in 1968, Samuelson accompanied Nickel on the rounds he made to check the three dozen Sullivan buildings that then remained in the city. Richard often picked Tim up around nine in the morning so that they could drive past all of Sullivan's houses and stores. In the early afternoon they would stop at Sauer's Restaurant, a converted garage on East 23rd Street, to eat charcoal-broiled hamburgers on round dark rye. Nothing else on the menu, Nickel told Tim, was any good.

Back in the 1950s when the Sullivan vigil had begun, it had taken Nickel all day to make the rounds. As time went by, Nickel started eating lunch earlier.

The buildings were razed in a predictable pattern. Nickel and Samuelson first checked the oldest Sullivan buildings, the private homes built in the 1880s. They were generally in the worst condition. If a building was still inhabited, it was safe—at least for awhile. If a building was vacant, it was an indication that it was about to be demolished.

That meant Nickel and Samuelson had to watch more carefully, checking every two weeks instead of every two months. It usually wasn't long before shattered and unboarded windows told them that the building would soon come down. Metal scrappers most often ravaged the houses first, stripping trim for scrap. Richard and Tim followed, with WD-40 to loosen metal and tools to turn iron bolts, cut metal or woodwork, and pry loose Sullivan's distinctive ornament.

Next on the list was the 1892 Meyer Building, a seven-story Adler and Sullivan loft building at 307 West Van Buren Street. Demolition of the Meyer, which took up almost a quarter of a west Loop block, came as a surprise to Richard. He had no hint of its fate until he chanced upon the building in January 1968 as the scaffolding was being erected.

The Meyer had been one of the original 38 landmarks designated by the city in 1959 and was one of Adler and Sullivan's finest. It was a building of power and character that could be felt by anyone who took the time to pause in front of it. Here was a building as horizontal as the Wainwright and Garrick buildings were vertical. Here was a brick edifice as beautiful as the terra-cotta–swathed Carson Pirie Scott store. Here was a bearing-wall structure as light as the most modern steel-frame skyscrapers of the age.

This was where Adler and Sullivan, perhaps with the help of Frank Lloyd Wright, had met what might have seemed like an impossible architectural challenge: to build an inexpensive factory that was at once utilitarian, so that garment workers on the upper floors had enough light for their needlework; and beautiful, so that wholesale buyers were attracted to the lower-floor showrooms.

The architects chose the bearing-wall type of construction to cut costs. By pairing the windows and separating them with thin, cast-iron columns, the firm liberated the pyramid-like heaviness of the bearing wall and opened up the structure. Once again, they created something new under the sun. And they didn't stop there. To give the building grace and to express its new form, Sullivan created four corner terra-cotta medallions that bubbled over with energy. The energy flowed right into thin bands of horizontal terra-cotta ribbon that swept across the exterior walls and defined each floor.

One of the four terra-cotta medallions that Nickel coveted from the Meyer Building.

Nickel knew the Meyer Building well and loved it. He had photographed it in 1959 for his research and again in 1960 for the Historic American Buildings Survey. He did not formally protest the demolition because he knew it was too late to save the building.

Right from the start, Nickel encountered problems at the Meyer. Two days after he noticed the scaffolding, he returned to take photographs, but was rebuffed by a wrecker who yelled: "Take your goddamned pictures from the street." During the following weeks, he twice wrote officials at the Harvey Wrecking Company requesting to photograph the building interior and make measured drawings. He also asked permission to remove several fire escape grilles and mentioned Southern Illinois University's interest in saving ornament from the building. To his consternation, he received no reply.

"For the first time in my 10–15 years, a wrecking company certainly has me off balance," he wrote Jack Randall at the university. "My state of mind is that I'd just as soon never go back to that site, they've been so completely difficult. And I've not acted smart alec, or proud, or anything. . .and I've gone out of my way to get officials' ok."

He expressed similar sentiments to Ben Raeburn. "Have learned from this experience to keep a better watch on the buildings and environment, and do all the work on still-standing buildings first."

For days, Nickel considered sneaking onto the wrecking site and taking the fire escape grilles from the fourth floor. He was worried about the night watchman.

"Normally, I'd take the chance but as you recall I've already been in jail for trespassing (FLW house) and second time might not be so nice," he wrote Randall. A few days later, Nickel did steal the grilles. He also snuck in at night to make measured drawings.

What Nickel really wanted, however, was too heavy to walk away with at night. He wanted to acquire the square terra-cotta medallions and the cast-iron columns for the Southern Illinois University collection. Knowing that the wreckers feared a demolition injunction or bad publicity, Nickel arranged for the university's president, Delyte Morris, to contact the Arthur Rubloff Company. The Rubloff firm, which managed the building, promised the university that it would be offered ornament, but Nickel remained skeptical. As the months passed, he continued to be treated badly by Bill Beard, the Harvey wrecking foreman whom Nickel described as being "smilingly sadistic."

The final blow came when the Chicago School of Architecture Foundation and the architectural firm of Perkins and Will both put in money bids for the columns. "Ah, the old days are gone forever," Nickel wrote.

But, I have decided one thing, I'll never again let some ornament prevent me from making a fuss about a landmark being demolished. Because we'd get the ornament in any case (assuming the building would go, and they always go!). But meantime, put on a show of strength. When you act weak, they treat you as a weakling and step all over you. Anyway, why let some jerks do that?

The following day Richard was literally laughed off the site by the wreckers. Although he never described the incident in writing, the effect was long lasting. "I could barely sleep last night, thinking of being made the fool by such stupid people as Harvey's gang," he wrote Randall. "Rubloff-Harvey-Goldberg-Beard-Crane Inc." were out to jinx him personally, he wrote. "There is simply too much going wrong. Things like this just don't happen. Two possibilities. 1. I'm going crazy? 2. Someone at Rubloff recalled my Garrick trouble making and now they are getting even." Nickel again criticized himself for acting too weak. "I deserve this abuse. . .but I sure don't like it."

Nickel was at an all-time low. "It's a worn-out routine," he wrote. The experience at the Meyer had been humiliating and miserable. At one point, as he and others put in bids for ornament, Nickel asked himself, "What are we doing?" He wrote: "We don't protest the demolition of an official city landmark, but scramble like idiots for the pieces. So I feel I've compromised my principles, beliefs and intelligence to accommodate Jack with that ornament."

Southern Illinois eventually received one of the medallions, despite Richard's fear that the university's piece would be "accidentally smashed." The other ornament Nickel pulled out of the rubble—fire-escape treads, window sills, column capitals, and terra-cotta panels—had almost no meaning, he wrote, because they were out of context.

A few weeks later Richard was quoted in the *Chicago Tribune* as saying: "There is a dangerous trend today, that people who want to save old buildings are kooky. Fifty years ago when people warned about saving the lake, they may have been thought as kooky, but here we are."

Nickel's personal life, too, was deteriorating. In mid-1966 he had received a $7,500 grant to finish the Adler and Sullivan book from the Chicago-based Graham Foundation for Advanced Studies in the Fine Arts. On his application, Richard wrote that his past problems had been the result of "inexperience and immaturity, lack of confidence, hopes for perfection." He predicted that he could finish the book in 18 to 24 months of full-time work. "I think I have learned the lesson of not overextending myself, and that I have sufficient self-discipline to hold to a schedule."

It was not to be. Richard had expected to start work right after his return from Harvard in the late summer of 1966, but he stalled, telling friends he was tired of the book. He called it a "cultural obligation" and expressed—for the first time— a lack of interest in new Sullivan leads. To his friend Charles Gregerson, who told Nickel about the possibility of a Sullivan commission in Kalamazoo, Michigan, Nickel replied, "I don't care about that stuff anymore." In 1967 Nickel wrote: "I'm so full of Sullivan, Sullivan, Sullivan that sometimes I feel homosexual. And despite that, I agree he is God but wonder about all the disciples and saints and the holy ideas of the Chicago School."

The project was about to take over Nickel's life again, but this time he was rebelling. He wrote his friend and architectural historian Paul Sprague in an unsent letter: "Siskind urged me to bite a live rampaging steer and my teeth are too weak, but not so weak they'd fall out and knock me on my seat. Madness. Steers. Oh, God, never show this to a psychiatrist or it will all be out."

When Richard traveled to New York City in early 1967, he did not have the courage to see Raeburn at Horizon Press. Instead he wrote him in May that he was seriously considering abandoning the project. He wrote that Sprague was more capable to do the work, but concluded: "I'd like to take one final crack at writing the text for the architecture book, and if the going is rough and I see it is impossible to equal Paul's writing, then perhaps we can work together. He has been very patient with me." Nickel ended by saying that he had no regrets about not finishing except for disappointing Raeburn, Siskind, and the people who gave him money. He said the earlier book would have been an embarrassment. "My standards are higher than ever, for good or worse. I don't exactly believe that nothing is better than something—well, almost."

Nickel devoted more time to writing, but was still mired in self-doubt. Determined to find out what made Sullivan tick, Nickel was nearly paralyzed when he thought about the finished product. He wrote Raeburn in late 1967: "I'm still carrying my cross and not making much headway. What a mess. I did stop most of my everyday work for awhile but then I let it overcome me again. Perhaps the best thing would be to lock up all the cameras and the darkroom for the period required to get the writing done."

His failure to get on with the book strained his relationship with Aaron Siskind. Nickel was embarrassed about his own writing shortcomings and angry with Siskind. Although he never confronted his mentor, Richard wrote often that he considered the failure to be Aaron's responsibility, too. "I think he's a bad counselor," Richard wrote. "He saddled me with this project, which my own serious approach turned into the cross of my life. There are many things I resent now, for example his not getting me to go to Yale or Harvard for art history, instead of holding me down at IIT. I don't know what I'm doing the last 15 years as a result."

Nickel was supposed to receive three payments of $2,500 each as a fellow of the Graham Foundation. He was supposed to make three interim reports that detailed progress on the book, but he never sent any reports. In 1969 foundation director John Entenza called Nickel and requested that he return the first two payments, which totaled $5,000. Nickel agreed over the phone, but wrote Entenza later that he had spent some of the money to get floor plans prepared.

"The day we discussed the matter, I was docile and agreeable, and how else could I properly act?" Nickel wrote. "There didn't seem to be any choice. But that evening I realized that returning the money would be disastrous, in so many ways." Nickel asked to start work again, and promised to report in a few months. He returned $2,500 in hopes that it would eventually be paid back along with the final payment.

In order to devote full attention to the book, Nickel slowly withdrew from the preservation movement. Soon after he received his Graham Foundation grant, Nickel wrote architect Wilbert Hasbrouck that he planned to stop attending meetings of the Chicago School of Architecture Foundation.

If I have any "stuff" left it will go into my Adler and Sullivan book, and after that I kind of hope I never have to deal with architects or buildings again. I'm now interested in my own profession both in terms of making money and doing some personal work, and in music, sailing, literature. . .in about that order. And if I have to do photography of some specific interest then I'd as soon photo boats. Except, alas, they ain't art.

Meanwhile, a new city landmarks ordinance was being pushed forward. Nickel had little to do with the creation of the new law, but he took an active role in gathering support for the ordinance in 1968. "I really think it's time to put pressure on City Hall over the landmark legislation and I think the way is a long and steady barrage of letters from concerned persons and institutions," he wrote his old Garrick partner Thomas Stauffer, the man behind the new law.

Nickel wrote three or four letters a night. Once again, he helped orchestrate an effective preservationist initiative.

The City Council voted 44-0 to pass the ordinance creating the new Chicago Commission on Historical and Architectural Landmarks. For the first time in city history, landmark preservation had a firm legal basis. Daley appointed the new commission on April 17, 1968, and on May 10 the members held their first meeting.

However, when the Chicago School of Architecture Foundation refused to take a stand for the Meyer Building, Nickel once again considered quitting the organization. He wrote in March 1968 that the group was controlled by "fuddy-duddy AIA types" who worry about money and security. "I think I am doing everyone a disservice by lingering on at CSAF. It's not that I don't care about Glessner House, or about the foundation (although I've questioned its value or need since the beginning), it's mainly personal: 1. I work best alone, and 2. I don't care one hoot about administration and operation."

He finally quit in May, writing that he was also stopping all his work as a commercial photographer in order to finish the book.

"This means I will be asking questions and help of other people instead of being asked and helping," Nickel wrote. "I prefer not even to think of Glessner House during this period (some people can do several things at once but I can't; my book will take superhuman effort to get the perfection I demand) so I wish to resign from the board."

It was also during these years that Nickel started thinking about death. Several incidents—the death of John Vinci's father, the apparent suicides of two friends, and an accident that sent his father to the hospital—may have triggered the thoughts.

A few days after Vinci's father died in 1968, Richard wrote: "Better to be wiped out totally, instantly, all alone, no one knowing." After the suicides, he wrote: "I think I'll leave this lovely life like old Willis, or old Slocum, just set out one day and gamble it away." After a car fell on top of Nickel's father, Richard wrote: "So like Dylan Thomas says, Do not go gentle into that good night, he almost left us doing what he apparently loves to do, messing around with undersides of cars. Ho hum. And I'm my father's son."

Richard, who jacked up the car and rushed his father to the hospital, closely observed the people in the emergency room—a screaming child with a burned face and shoulder and a man dying from emphysema. His father's injuries turned out to be minor. Wrote Richard: "Life is so fragile, and death is a simple fact there. All so fascinating."

Like Sullivan, who saw the sea as a symbol of the infinite, Richard thought often about death when he was out on his boat. In 1967 he wrote that 50-mile-per-hour gales did not stop him. "What's the alternative? I'll tell you: to die slowly in bed with cancer and then have your 'friends' ape all around your corpse and finally have a party after you're under."

Death, powerful as it is, did not have to end a life's work, Nickel wrote. Mies van der Rohe's death in 1969 did not severely affect Nickel. "He was such a force, death barely matters," Nickel wrote friend A. James Speyer. Once again, all that mattered was the idea.

Richard soon adopted an important new character trait: the Kierkegaard role of sufferer. Nickel realized that his infinite passion was bounded by his life and by his times. "To you, it's sunlight and pleasure and to me it's challenge, variation, range, etc.," Nickel wrote his friend Lee Timonen. In another letter to Timonen, Nickel wrote:

Anyone who lives in this world and doesn't wish to die is sick-sick-sick. There's so much wrong, and so much going wrong, and we have so little power to do anything about it, that anybody who takes the situation seriously can only wish to die.

The only saving virtue of life today is all the space achievements, and the mastery that these guys have, landing on the moon and sending back choice photos, floating around 200 miles up, etc. I gladly pay taxes to see this continue. But everything down here is a mess.

Kierkegaard's description of a poet in *Either/Or* fit Nickel's view of himself as a photographer.

A poet is an unhappy being whose heart is torn by secret sufferings, but whose lips are so strangely formed that when the signs and cries escape them, they sound like beautiful music. . .And men crowd around the poet and say to him, "Sing for us soon again"; that is as much as to say, "May new sufferings torment your soul, but may your lips be formed as before; for the cries would only frighten us, but the music is delicious."

Nickel came to understand that the more he suffered, the greater was his work. The more buildings were destroyed, the more precious and sweet were his photographs.

As the 1960s came to a close, Nickel sought a life of his own. Having restored his sailboat, *Vato,* he spent much of 1968—at age 40—again looking for a house to purchase. He wanted to strike out, away from his parents, to find a place where he could try out his own architectural ideas. "If I do find a building I think I'll keep the whereabouts secret and not get a phone," he wrote. "OR, maybe to hell with it all. I'll just buy a bigger boat and sail the hell away from all this."

Nickel's father, Stanley, watches as workers begin installing a new sidewalk in front of Richard's storefront apartment at 1810 West Cortland Street in 1969.

Adler and Sullivan's 1881–82 Revell Building in Chicago's Loop. Photographed by Nickel in the 1950s, the building was torn down in 1968.

Of course, because the house had to be perfect, Richard's search had by now stretched over several years. In 1968 he considered "rehabbing" an abandoned three-story firehouse at 158 West Erie Street just north of the Loop, or moving into John Vinci's North Side two-flat at 3152 North Cambridge Street. Later in 1968 he came close to buying a house at 2121 North Leavitt Street in the old Northwest Side neighborhood where he had grown up. There, he wrote, he could grow old watching processions and funerals at nearby St. Hedwig's Church and listening to bells ring every night and Sunday morning. He would not go to church with the regulars, he wrote, but would invite the nuns over for portrait sessions. "I suppose Leavitt is where I should make my stand," Nickel wrote, but he never followed through.

For a while, Nickel stopped looking in the city because he felt Chicago was "one big slum." In the end, however, he bought a house at 1810 West Cortland Street, about three miles northwest of the Loop in the city's East Humboldt Park neighborhood. Nickel paid $7,500 in February 1969 for the storefront bakery building with a two-bedroom apartment on the second floor. It was far from any friends or family. Because it was a return to his Polish roots, Nickel called it his "Polish palazzo."

Richard could have moved right in after the owner, Lottie Jankiewicz, closed the bakery. But Richard thought of the Cortland storefront as more of an "aesthetic experience" or "architectural enterprise" than a place to live. He loved the house's elegant front elevation, its simple floor plan and its history dating back to 1889, when it had been known as Grimm's Bakery. He enjoyed sitting on the front steps admiring the pretty Puerto Rican, black, and Polish girls of the neighborhood and the great dome of St. Mary of the Angels Church across the street. The Renaissance-style Polish basilica had been built in a style similar to Michelangelo's dome of St. Peter's Cathedral. But what Nickel enjoyed most was the squadron of nine-foot angels that looked down from the church upon his new home.

Nickel planned to retain the first-floor layout. The bakery in the rear would be converted into a kitchen, utility room, and photo work room. The store up front would become a living room, music room, and library. The two second-floor bedrooms were connected by a bathroom and kitchen. He gutted the kitchen to make another bathroom. Now he had two self-contained upstairs units. He considered renting out the back bedroom, but decided instead to build one big apartment that would include "the Sullivan manuscript room, where I would grind out those essays, and a bed to collapse on." Because he didn't want to be rushed, he set no deadlines. He spent 1969 cleaning out the remains from the bakery, repairing his front sidewalks and laying a new sewer line. He spent 1970 clearing out his backyard, taking apart—brick by brick—the huge old bakery oven behind the house and planting a honey locust tree. Now, like a suburbanite, he could look out his back window at a tree.

Everything needed attention and everything took time. When neighborhood kids walked on his still-wet new sidewalk, Nickel repaved it and stood guard outside one long December night. Everything needed to be perfect. "With boats, buildings, books, B's (Bruckner, Beethoven, etc.) going, I get very little really done," Richard wrote. It took him days just to find the right hardware. All this, he said, "for a modest building in a bourgeois neighborhood."

Nickel loved the Cortland Street store. He slept there occasionally, but continued living with his parents in Park Ridge.

Inexorably, however, he was drawn back to the buildings. "Every morning I wake up I think Revell-Revell, but at the same time I have a block against going to Adler and Sullivan demolition sites," he wrote during the last days of the six-story Revell store in October 1968. The loft structure, at the northeast corner of Wabash Avenue and Adams Street, had been Adler and Sullivan's largest before receiving the commission for the Auditorium Building in 1889. It was layered with cast-iron and stone ornament. Richard managed to fill a truck with the best pieces during the summer of 1968 for the Southern Illinois collection, but he hesitated to return to make serious photographs. Nickel's "totally traumatic" experience at the Meyer Building the previous January had left him "super defeated" at the Revell. "And the Revell goes unrecorded by RN," he wrote. "I'm just so tired of seeing Adler and Sullivan works defaced, demolished. I've witnessed it and been involved (plans, salvage photos) so, so long. I'm at the end of the road."

And there was a new factor: Nickel now found himself in competition for the ornament. Demolitions even of undistinguished Adler and Sullivan commissions, such as the Herman Braunstein store and flats on the Near North Side, now attracted a crowd of collectors. One was Jack Ringer, a real estate operator who coveted the ornament for its resale value.

"It's different now than it was 10 years ago," Nickel wrote in 1968. "Like the Meyer site, every night there are kids from the various architectural offices scrounging around along with Ringer and others (the Near North apartment dwellers who live in bland low-ceilinged rooms) cutting in. I hate to struggle with people over this stuff. A new generation is involved, and I prefer to leave it to them. Let them collect it out of ignorance or blind enthusiasm, or money, or whatever. Nix." Most of Nickel's time during the first several months of 1970 was spent salvaging the Albert Sullivan house. This was the two-story home at 4575 South Lake Park Avenue that Nickel seriously considered buying for himself in 1963. Since then, the house had been converted into a neighborhood community center for boys in the surrounding black ghetto. Nickel kept an eye on the house, and grudgingly grew to respect the woman, Janice Greer, who created the Lake Park Project. But, he wrote, the house had "gone to pot" under her "reign of liberalism." The interior was in shambles, damaged by fire and a leaking roof. All that was left was the plaster decoration in the ceiling of the entrance hall and the room's mosaic floor. In 1970 Greer closed the doors of the Lake Park House, leaving a trashed, weather-scarred hulk.

Even in this condition, the house was exceptional. Perhaps because he had built it for his mother, Sullivan had enriched it with some of his most beautiful ornamental designs. The wrought-iron front door, the first-floor limestone lunette and window columns, and the second-story leaded-glass windows and copper window bay were grand works of decorative art that played off a simple stone facade. The copper had long been stripped off the building and most of the stone was covered by graffiti, but Nickel could not bear to see it end in a heap of rubble. In 1963 he had written, "The whole facade is so perfect it should be saved and reconstructed some place, but ideally we should find a solution to save the building." In 1970 he felt the same way.

After learning that the house was virtually abandoned, Nickel wrote officials at Southern Illinois University in Edwardsville that they should consider purchasing the house and wrecking it for the arched lunette alone. The lintel was the last link to Sullivan's work at the Chicago's World Fair of 1893. Its design had been repeated in plaster and used on his fabled Transportation Building.

"I hardly think the house is worth saving. . .or else I'd hesitate to proceed with ornament salvage," Nickel wrote Harry Hilberry, who had taken over as architectural coordinator at the university and was overseeing the Sullivan ornament collection. The house, in the "toughest and most hopeless ghetto area in Chicago," was likely to be condemned and wrecked soon, Nickel wrote. It was important to take action now. Richard had learned from his experiences at the Meyer Building in 1968 not to wait. "Things have changed since the Garrick," he wrote. "Now lots of organizations and individuals consider Sullivan ornament 'Hot stuff.' In the old days it would be a snap but not now. . .too many architecture buffs know and care."

Nickel convinced Hilberry of the Albert Sullivan house's value through a series of letters in late January 1970. The trick was to gain control of the ornament in a manner that did not attract attention. "The problem is how to approach him," Nickel wrote about Richard Greer, the owner of the house. "If I ask about the ornament itself, he will hesitate and wait for the highest bidder. . .if there hasn't been a bidder already. If I ask about buying the house, he will think I'm a kook, or suspect another motive."

What Nickel did was to persuade the Greers that Southern Illinois University would pay for the wrecking in exchange for title to the house. "It's fun carrying on like a capitalist!" Nickel boasted on the day he gave the Greers an SIU check for $2,800.

For once, Richard was in charge of the demolition. "Found everything intact at 4575 today," he wrote on March 11, his first day at the site. "A few cars stopped to creeping and people (white) gazed out. . . .Few took the trouble to get out: such is the depth of interest, or is it that they are so afraid of Negroes?"

Yet predictably, what began as a project to save the building's best pieces of ornament soon grew out of hand. Not just content with taking out the lunette, Nickel began removing the entire assembly of stone slabs around the doorway, numbering every piece so that it could be reconstructed.

About three weeks later, Nickel wrote Hilberry that he and his brother, Donald, were working to remove the final material. Donald was a pharmacist who lived in the Chicago suburb of Schaumburg at the time. Although they had gone their separate ways over the years, Nickel and his brother had maintained their family loyalty.

"This all turned out differently than I expected," Richard wrote of the work. With the help of two wreckers, the brothers salvaged much of the front facade. Eventually, Richard and Donald were working 16-hour days by themselves. The work was exhausting and so dangerous that Richard refused to let anybody help them. With only a hydraulic jack and dollies, the job appeared to be far beyond their capacity. But they persevered, lifting 500-pound pieces of limestone by brute force. They worked until their shoulders were raw with the skin peeling off. At the end of one work day, Donald looked at Richard as they sat in a nearby park and said: "We can't go home. We can't drive. We can't lift our arms."

Richard was so methodical that only once did Donald even question him.

"How can you do this day after day?" he finally asked his brother.

Richard replied simply that the house was beautiful.

The brothers ended up saving the entire section of stone cladding surrounding the front door, the ornamental columns of the first-floor window and parts of the carved decoration of the porch. They received $3,000 from SIU. "There's nobody in the world who knows what effort was involved. . .except perhaps my brother," Nickel wrote Hilberry in June.

The following year, Nickel repaid his brother by helping him move from the Chicago suburbs to a 144-acre farm in Plainfield, Wisconsin, with his wife, Harriet, and their teenage daughters, Susan and Nancy. Leaving the city had been Donald's dream ever since the boys had vacationed on their relatives' farm in Michigan. Donald had seen a newspaper ad for the farm and bought it. Richard wrote that Donald wanted to raise cattle and avoid humans.

By the 1970s Nickel's interest in sailing had turned into a passion. He chartered a 40-foot yacht for two weeks of sailing in the Virgin Islands in 1969. "Let me warn you, friend," he wrote Paul Sprague, "that the sail is more deadly than the woman, the whiskey bottle, music, Sullivan, etc."

Warm-water sailing in the steady winds of the Virgin Islands is a dream vacation for Chicago sailors. But the trip—with Jack Randall and three of his friends—turned into a nightmare with Nickel at the helm. One of the shipmates, John Casey, wrote what he intended to be a humorous account of the adventure. But the humor is snuffed out by the anger he felt toward Nickel, whom he described as looking "every other inch a captain."

The group met at Kennedy Airport in New York City and flew together to St. Croix on January 12. Nickel, who had made most of the arrangements, was chosen to be captain. Randall, the only other crew member with sailing experience, was the navigator. Casey, 53, vice president of marketing for a pharmaceutical company, was the cook. The other two shipmates, engineers by training, were general helpmates.

They left on the Cal-40 *Freelance* two days later. Casey's journal of the following week is filled with accounts of Nickel's recklessness. On January 15 the boat passed at full speed through a narrow, rock-filled passage between St. Thomas Island and a small island.

Nickel's mentors— photographers Frederick Sommer (foreground) and Aaron Siskind—aboard *Garden City* around 1970. Sommer's wife, Frances, is in the background.

Having successfully escaped disaster on Current Rock, the captain ordered us toward the next navigational hazard, Brothers Rock, and then before we reached these, spotted an even more threatening hazard and yelled, "There's a better one," and had us head straight for Blunder Rock. I asked the navigator in a whisper whether he thought our captain had a suicidal complex.

Although it rained the following day, the bad weather only challenged Nickel. "The captain sees seeds of opportunity in every disaster," Casey wrote, "and when the radio reported a sailboat with six men crashed on some reefs near Puerto Rico, he was invigorated enough to get up."

After refusing to buy a map of the Roadtown harbor, Nickel made several runs toward it in order to dock and pick up supplies on January 17. First he ran aground, but hoisted the main sail to break loose. On a later attempt, Richard—whom Casey described as having a "complete aversion to caution"—hit a dinghy directly. The two people aboard were not injured and Nickel tried again. By the fourth attempt, people on the dock scattered in panic as Richard sailed in.

After picking up supplies, Nickel ordered the ship to raise sail. "As we came around the far point of the island into the open Caribbean," Casey wrote,

We were met by a sight I shall never forget. Terrifying is my word for it, but this is a personal observation, since the captain merely seemed pleased. Just as I gaspingly asked how big the waves were, the ship heeled, and I asked where the life jackets were. The swells were 10 feet or more, the navigator told me, and the life jackets were in the stern storage compartment. I didn't feel reassured, since he asked for a life jacket, too. With life jackets buckled, I held on with both hands. The captain, who was standing on the deck, yelled to put up the jib. As I muttered I would kill him if he did, the rest of the crew advised against it. After a half hour of suicidal sailing, even the captain had enough, and we came around and returned to the leeward shore of Peter Island and finally anchored in a quiet cove.

That was enough for Casey, who told Nickel he was going to spend the final days of the trip on the island.

"The captain's eyes narrowed as he asked if it was my intention of jumping ship," Casey wrote. "Trusting in the captain's good nature, I admitted to the possibility of spending several nights ashore. It was a miscalculation. Captains haven't changed since the days of Captain Bligh, in fact things have gotten worse."

As he rowed to shore, Nickel yelled, "Nobody jumps a ship of mine!" and "What is your Social Security number?"

Almost out of range, Nickel shouted, "These are no idle threats!"

The following year Richard bought for $7,000 a 26-foot El Capitan sailing boat manufactured by Chris Craft. The boat depleted Nickel's savings from the Southern Illinois University cache. He had second thoughts, but wrote, "Might as well get a little excitement out of the sky and water and sails."

The simple boat, designed by the firm of Sparkman Stephens, had a rich, warm green hull and white deck. The greens and reds of the hatches and other mahogany surfaces reminded Richard of the colors Sullivan had used in his small-town banks. The tiny Seagull outboard motor reminded Richard of the toy steam engines he had played with as a boy. The boat could take six people out comfortably for day-sailing or could sleep four in its modest cabin. More important, it had a 300-square-foot sail, compared to *Rhoda*'s 85-foot sail. "Marvelous. Scary!" Nickel wrote.

Richard spent more than a year in search of the right boat. "I do like the boat as an object. Maybe I should start collecting boats!" he joked. He wanted a monochromatic, spartan boat with a simple interior. Paying for continuous picture windows, crowned foredecks, boutique toilets, and extra plush was like paying for ugliness, he wrote. He wanted something that was not too fast, not too safe, and not too roomy. He liked the confinement of a small boat because it was like going into a sloped roof attic. Boats were for sailing; they were not meant to be luxury condominium cruisers.

"When you board a boat the idea is a totally new experience, and the more different you can make it, the more pleasure it gives," he wrote. "Bare feet, eating on the fly, carrying body waste around (or using a bucket), going to sleep at 9 and waking with the immense light is all part of it. To hell with all the safety features, radios, etc."

Nickel and his father spent several days in Milwaukee buying the boat, swabbing it down, waxing the hull, oiling the teak rail, and installing a toilet. He sailed it back to Chicago in the midst of severe weather warnings.

"I've named her *Garden City* after all the idealists of early Chicago art history, and after Chicago's unrealized potential," Richard wrote a friend. To another friend, Richard wrote that the name, which harked back to the city's motto, *Urbs in Horto,* was "dull, but then so am I. Naturally this is after the hull color and the fact that I care about the city and parks, etc." To his mother, Richard wrote that he had chosen the name because "I figure since I'm always sailing in or around or past the city, I should acknowledge it. Also, there's a slim chance that someone in the Park District will appreciate that name. . .and they will award me the harbor of my choice. Clever college boy, huh mother?"

Demonstrators mill around
the entrance of the Stock
Exchange Building in 1971.

It's a joint where the bulls and foxes live well and the lambs wind up head-down
from the hook.

Nelson Algren on Chicago in *Chicago: City on the Make*

With three taps of his gavel, Chicago Stock Exchange President William B. Walker closed the final session at the exchange's Dearborn Street location on April 30, 1894. The joyous mood of the morning dampened as noon approached and the final bell sounded. "A cheer for the old home," one trader shouted, prompting a last accolade. Then there was quiet. Within moments the old hall was deserted.

The mood lifted again as the traders and their guests took lunch, bought boutonnieres and traveled the few blocks through the Loop to their new home. At 1 p.m. banners were gently dropped from the second-floor window, the U.S. flag was unfurled 172 feet above, and Rosenbecker's Orchestra took up the "Washington Post March." The new Chicago Stock Exchange Building was open.

Newspapers hailed the structure at the southwest corner of LaSalle and Washington streets as the "model office building of the world." From the marble restaurant in the basement, through the stairways and corridors trimmed in mahogany and red oak, to the 400 offices with hot and cold running water, the formidable structure represented the most sophisticated mix to date of Adler's and Sullivan's individual and collaborative abilities.

Construction began May 1, 1893, and continued often day and night. It was here that Adler pioneered the use of caissons for commercial buildings. On the west side, deep wells were dug to bedrock and filled with concrete so that the shocks from piledrivers would not disturb the working presses of the neighboring Chicago Herald Building. It was here that Adler once again performed a miracle—supporting the 10 upper floors of the building on only four columns in the wide-open expanse of the great Trading Hall.

Sullivan's touch was everywhere. The focal point of the Stock Exchange was the LaSalle Street entrance, a terra-cotta arch that stood 40 feet wide and 30 feet tall and was one of Sullivan's most graceful works. The exterior of the building was also clad in an intricately detailed skin of terra cotta. Above the ground-floor storefronts was a two-story band of arches that framed the Trading Room to the south and a banking room to the north and suggested the distinct functions of each room. On the upper stories, tier after tier of identical offices was enclosed by an undulating skin of projecting bays and flat wall surfaces.

The key to the nine-story office section was Sullivan's attempt to entice the maximum amount of sunlight into the offices. In the Garrick the architect had experimented with "setbacks," diminishing the mass of the building on its upper floors. Now he experimented with windows, pairing the large plate-glass "Chicago windows" with bay windows on the LaSalle and Washington street sides and carving out two large light courts in the back. "There is not a dark or undesirable office in the building," wrote *The Economist* in 1894.

The building was topped by a horizontal colonnade of free-standing columns and a windowless attic concealed behind the projecting cornice. Like many mercantile buildings of the age, the Stock Exchange was about strength and power. Sullivan did not build an updated version of a medieval fortress. He created might by using modern materials and a new design.

The Stock Exchange Building was financed by Ferdinand W. Peck, a major Adler and Sullivan client who had also built the Auditorium Building. It took eight months to build and cost $1,131,555, well below estimates because the Financial Panic of 1893 drove down the price of labor. Nickel found the first reports on the building in the January 7, 1893, *Economist,* which stated that Peck and his family had secured an option on an 80-by-100-foot piece of property and combined it in 1892 with their own 100-by-100-foot piece. The Pecks first received a permit to construct a 12-story store and office building, but later received a permit for a 13-story building on the combined 180-by-100-foot property. "So you see," Nickel wrote, "they were planning a building on that corner anyway and probably being shrewd guys decided to get the adjoining property for a more monumental building and then get the Chicago Stock Exchange in as tenants to dignify the building."

That is exactly what happened.

In the spring of 1892, exchange officials contacted the Pecks about finding a trading hall. The exchange had moved seven times in its first 10 years. Boom times during the 1880s and the World's Columbian Exposition brought wild success to the traders, and now they wanted a large, permanent home. The Pecks provided a trading hall rent free for 15 years in the hope that it would lure much of the financial community up LaSalle Street.

The district was an important part of Chicago and of the United States. The rough-and-tough cowboy heroes of the Midwest were being replaced with even rougher and tougher capitalists. The Babbits built railroads, mined gold, cornered wheat markets, and speculated on hog bellies as they gathered wealth. Chicago was becoming a great city, perhaps on its way to becoming the greatest. "Here, midmost in the land, beat the Heart of the Nation, whence inevitably must come its immeasurable power, its infinite, infinite, inexhaustible vitality," wrote Frank Norris in his novel *The Pit.* "Here, of all her cities, throbbed the true life—the true power and spirit of America; gigantic, crude with the crudity of youth, disdaining rivalry; sane and healthy and vigorous; brutal in its ambition, arrogant in the new-found knowledge of its giant strength, prodigal of its wealth, infinite in its desires."

Long-stemmed roses and carnations were placed on the rostrum on that last day in April 1894 when the Trading Room opened. The president's desk was surrounded by a pink and crimson flower badge and the visitor's gallery was packed by ladies in bright spring costumes. The first thing that must have struck those who entered the room was the use of colors—Sullivan's colors. Reds, olive greens, golds, and yellows—57 shades in all—covered the walls, columns, and ceilings in six major patterns that were both as simple and as complex as a chambered nautilus. At first glance, the kaleidoscopic patterns seemed to be based on geometry as circles and ovals, squares and diamonds changed shape and danced with each other. On second glance, the patterns seemed based on nature itself as weblike patterns expanded and retracted in the background. Or was it the foreground?

"Forms emerge from forms, and others arise or descend from these," Sullivan wrote in his *Kindergarten Chats.* "All are related, interwoven, intermeshed, interconnected, interblended. They exosmose and endosmose. They sway and swirl and mix and drift interminably. They shape, they reform, they dissipate. They respond, correspond, attract, repel, coalesce, disappear, reappear, merge and emerge: slowly or swiftly, gently or with cataclysmic force."

The newspaper critics, who uniformly hailed the room, had difficulty describing it. Most pegged the work to the exotic Middle East. One said it was "thoroughly Moresque in design. . .with the color genius of the Japanese." It was neither. It was the original work of architect Sullivan and master decorator Louis J. Millet, a Sullivan friend from the Ecole des Beaux-Arts who worked on several Adler and Sullivan interiors.

The Trading Room was a place where great economic forces came together, and Sullivan wanted to transfer that idea in architecture. At the Garrick Theater, he hid all the trusswork that held up the suspended ceiling of the theater. In the Trading Room, Sullivan showed how the beams carried the load. Each of the two trusses held 1,200 tons—or the weight of 12 locomotives, as a *Chicago Evening Journal* reporter marveled. Sullivan opened up the top of the room to create a recessed, coffered ceiling that expressed the beams. He did not expose the beams, but covered them in a suspended skin of stenciled plaster. Each part of the trusswork—the main ceiling beams and the cross sections—had a different function, so Sullivan decorated them with different stencilwork.

He also showed off the architectural triumph of the room by focusing attention on the four columns that held up the great space. He covered the columns in scagliola, a plaster surface that gives the appearance of marble, and topped each one with gilded plaster crowns.

Instead of installing a huge chandelier in the center of the ceiling, Sullivan drew in natural light through an innovative series of prismatic glass. The light then filtered through art glass panels that rimmed the room. He supplemented the light with carbon-filament bulbs, but the main effect—the mix of the pastoral world with the mercantile world—could not be missed. Author Norris wrote about the nearby Board of Trade: "There in the centre of the Nation, in the heart's heart of the affairs of men, reared and rumbled the Pit." How different would be the Trading Room.

Built to last, the Stock Exchange was lovingly maintained by an army of electricians, carpenters, and day workers who mopped the corridors, cleaned the washrooms, and shined the windows; and by a night crew of Polish cleaning women who kept up the building as if it were their own. The McCormick Estates, which owned the building from 1906 to 1958, lavished the Stock Exchange with maintenance money even during the Depression. The policy created a loyal group of tenants who could afford to move to more modern buildings, but chose to stay. Judson F. Stone, manager of the estates and board chairman of International Harvester, worked out of the building and demanded that it be in perfect condition. He was not very charitable about the building's shortcomings. If he had to wait more than 30 seconds for an elevator, he wanted to know why.

Structurally, there was little wrong with the building. The floor in the southwest corner sloped slightly, but was fixable. The iron supports holding the huge cornice needed to be replaced. The building's biggest problem was its antique floor plan. The offices were small, and there was only one toilet per floor. By the late 1960s the exterior of the building needed a good cleaning. Faced with buff-color terra cotta, city soot had taken control of the building long ago. It had taken on a black, ominous look.

For better or worse, little changed at the Stock Exchange. The lobby floor and the original second-floor elevator screens were replaced in 1921. Sudler and Company purchased the building from the McCormick Estates in 1958, painting the hallway wood trim and replacing the hydraulic elevators around 1960 with high-speed automatic elevators. City ordinances required that the remaining Sullivan-designed elevator screens be removed when the elevators were replaced.

Outside, the first-floor storefronts changed as new stores took over. On the upper floors, some of the Chicago windows were replaced by sash windows and damaged terra cotta was replaced. The most significant change to the exterior was the new entrance that the architecture firm of Brenner Danforth Rockwell designed to replace the original entrance beneath the LaSalle Street arch. This was the 1964 project that Nickel had protested—and lost.

The major interior changes involved the Trading Room. In 1908, following the end of the 15-year rent-free lease, the Chicago Stock Exchange moved out of the Trading Room to the Rookery Building down LaSalle Street. Later that year, the room was converted into the Foreman Brothers Bank. The bank remained there until 1928. When it left, the main floor was converted into small rental offices. Unable to rent the space during the early years of the Depression, the owners drew boundaries for an indoor tennis court, and the space was used for recreation by employees of the McCormick Estates. It may have been the only marble tennis court in the world. Owners of a new health club tried to rent the space for a swimming pool and theater, but the plan was rejected. During the following decades, a false ceiling was added to the room so that air conditioning and lights could be added. The room was divided and subdivided to create small offices. All of Sullivan's ornament was covered and the room virtually disappeared.

In 1959 Larry Ackley, longtime manager of the building, gave young Nickel a tour of the space above the false ceiling. Here were the scagliola columns and the gilded column capitals, the art glass windows and stencilwork. It was a tour that Nickel would never forget.

Soon after the new Commission on Chicago Historical and Architectural Landmarks was established in 1968, news spread that Jupiter Corporation had purchased the Stock Exchange Building. "If you tell anybody I told you this I'll deny it," commission member Joseph Benson told David Norris, the young architect who had helped Nickel and Vinci salvage the Garrick Theater. "They're going to tear down the Stock Exchange."

Norris called Nickel. "The feeling was, 'Oh no, not again,'" recalled Norris years later. "A lot of us thought 'What's the use?'"

Jupiter was owned by real estate developers Jerrold Wexler and Edward W. Ross, who had made their money and reputation by building the 40-story Outer Drive East apartments along Lake Michigan east of the Loop. The building was a monetary bonanza but an aesthetic disaster. In 1968 Wexler and Ross paid $3.3 million to purchase the development rights for the Stock Exchange Building property. They did not buy the land, but bought a 99-year lease with the intent of tearing down the building and constructing a taller and larger building. They also bought the development rights to an adjacent piece of property to the west, creating a 160-by-180-foot parcel ripe for development.

After the Stock Exchange changed hands, building manager Ackley raised the rents in the hope of convincing the new owners that the building was a good investment as it stood. Ackley was successful in bringing in more money, but the developers were not interested. Wexler was an aggressive operator, not willing to sit on property that could be "improved." Ross said efforts to save the building were "a lot of garbage." The building was mechanically outdated and violated building codes. "We had two choices, spend a fortune remodeling it with no assurance people wanted this type of building, or tear it down to build a modern building," he said.

Wexler and Ross went ahead with plans to demolish the building. When the landmark issue was raised, Ross said he called the city's top architecture firms—Skidmore, Owings, and Merrill and C. F. Murphy—and was told by partners at both firms that although the building was not one of Sullivan's best, it would still raise preservationist hackles if plans were pushed forward to demolish it. Wexler and Ross were ready for a fight, but it was a fight they preferred to avoid. "As much as possible, I like to avoid trouble," said Wexler years later. "I don't like my name on other people's lips."

In April 1969 Wexler and Ross were approached by a group of businessmen interested in buying the Stock Exchange. Ross told them that the building was subject to a landmark fight and quoted a selling price much higher than his purchase price. The businessmen, who called their group the "30 North LaSalle Partnership," agreed to purchase a one-year option in November 1969. They wanted a year to purchase enough land adjacent to the Stock Exchange so that they could build a 50-

story "super skyscraper." The agreement stipulated that the group would buy the Stock Exchange development rights for $6.3 million if the building were not declared a landmark.

The new partners smelled gold. They were convinced that the demand for downtown office space, particularly along LaSalle Street, would guarantee success. The partners had visions of buying half or even all of the block, and then putting up a building with at least 20,000 square feet of office space per floor. That was what the law and accounting firms wanted, and no building in the Loop had offered that kind of space.

The partners—mortgage bankers Nathan H. Boehm and Donald J. Moloney, attorneys William J. Friedman and Harold E. Friedman (no relationship), and real estate executives Melvin R. Luster and Jerome Whiston—were not concerned about the possible landmark fight. They had great clout. Whiston, for instance, was the only surviving son of Chicago School Board president Frank Whiston, one of Mayor Daley's closest friends. If worse came to worst and the Stock Exchange were declared a landmark, the partners figured that the city would be forced to buy their property for the price they had paid.

Thus, as they started buying land near the Stock Exchange, the 30 North LaSalle Partnership had little to lose and fortunes to gain. Like any developer trying to assemble a big land parcel, the partners were forced to pay inflated prices—up to twice as high as the land was normally worth—to purchase the property they wanted. They bought the development rights of the adjacent 60-by-180-foot lot to the west of the Stock Exchange for $430,000, then bought the development rights and the land of another adjacent lot—this one 40 by 180 feet—for $1,052,000. The partners offered $1,250,000 for one more adjoining 40-by-180-foot parcel, but the Musicians' Union refused to sell.

By now the Stock Exchange Building was doomed. The city could never compensate the new owners for these prices. The old building could never bring in enough rental income to make it profitable on this inflated piece of property. Big business had built the Stock Exchange and big business had destroyed it.

Meanwhile, the new landmarks commission slowly began the process of choosing the first buildings to be legally protected. In January 1969 Nickel and other members of the commission's advisory committee recommended that the Stock Exchange be chosen along with the Auditorium Building, Carson Pirie Scott store, Glessner House, Monadnock Building, Robie House, and the Rookery. In September the commission voted to hold public hearings on all seven buildings.

"A fine fight is promising to save what is left of the Old Stock Exchange building at 30 N. LaSalle (Adler and Sullivan, 1894)," Nickel wrote in November. "The building has been sold, as we understand, and much of the rich distinctive ornament has been stripped out."

He was not overly optimistic. He knew the fight would be a critical test of the 1968 landmarks ordinance. "Everyone is getting worked up for a big emotional jag over 30 N. and of course it's unrealistic since Hizzoner couldn't give a damn, and this is capitalistic democracy," Nickel wrote later in the year. "What might carry the day is the general momentum toward clean air, rivers, general beauty—an opposition to the war, segregation, etc."

Richard wanted to stay out of the Stock Exchange fight. By the late 1960s Nickel sensed the start of a new wave of destruction. He was fed up and cynical. He knew too well from the Garrick battle how the city operated. He thought a new fight was a hopeless waste of time because not enough people cared. For too long he had played the role of the holy fool, the entertaining court jester. Let them have their way, he thought, let the jerks have their way and that's that. Fighting was a hopeless waste of time. They would tear down the city anyway.

But he was drawn back to the fight. "Sitting in the darkroom grinding out routine prints, I got to thinking what we, the concerned few, would do if the City says nix and decides against saving the Stock Exchange," Nickel wrote March 16, 1970, to M. W. Newman of the *Chicago Daily News*. "I think we ought to make a stink. . .perhaps we shouldn't wait to do so since the decision seems inevitable to me."

Nickel was too busy during the early months of the Stock Exchange fight to join. He spent the first several months of 1970 salvaging the Albert Sullivan house. In April, when the job was finished, he rushed to Florida for a couple of days to drive his parents home. His father, Stanley, had suffered an eye problem that did not prove to be serious. Later that month Nickel carted ornament in a U-Haul truck to New York's Metropolitan Museum of Art for the exhibit "The Rise of American Architecture."

The new boat and commercial work also kept him busy. In addition to architecture, he photographed artwork—such as a Giacometti sculpture and *Saturday Evening Post* covers. After driving to Dwight, Illinois, to photograph Frank Lloyd Wright's First National Bank, Nickel wrote, "I find everyone is in a hurry. They

Nickel after a hard day of salvaging in 1968. He took this self-portrait after work at the demolition site of Adler and Sullivan's 1884 Louis E. Frank residence on Chicago's South Side.

don't ask can I do it well only how fast." After spending four days photographing the Springfield Executive Mansion, he wrote that he had ground out a set of 42 16-by-20-inch matte prints because officials could not decide which photos they liked. Then the governor's secretary called him for three more sets. He wrote: "It's a living, but. . . ." Nickel was so busy he could hardly keep up with the disappearance of Adler and Sullivan buildings, missing the demolition of the 1884 Anna McCormick residence at 1715 South Michigan Avenue. In late August Nickel was able to salvage only the final remains of the 1884 F. A. Kennedy Bakery, later known as the Pettibone Company Warehouse, on Desplaines Street just west of the Loop. "It's dark and stinking inside due to all the bums," he wrote. "They're harmless but you find them in every corner of every floor, either asleep or just leaning against a wall."

And the martyr's self-doubting continued. In another letter, Nickel wrote:

I look forward to the day when I never have to enter a wet, charred, smoky building again. Hah, Pettibone Co. which last occupied the building (bakery) told me they left photos and blueprints in a vault there, which had been left locked and vandals busted the handle off. So I broke through the wall (16") but didn't find much inside. They were mistaken. Just some small real estate plans, useless, and no photos. The story of my life, struggling over nothing.

Eight major witnesses, mostly college professors and architects, testified in favor of the Stock Exchange at two public hearings before the new landmarks commission in February 1970. Nickel attended the hearings, photographing or tape recording them for the commission. He did not testify, and wrote after the February 12 meeting: "I can't remember ever having so much fun. I imagined all the profs were on trial themselves!"

Richard Bennett, president of the Chicago chapter of the American Institute of Architects, set up the defense of the building by arguing the importance of saving the past in general. "The best evidence of the need people feel for contact with history are the thousands of airplanes that go all summer long taking our citizens to get the feel of old cultures," he said. "Our culture isn't old, but it is ours, and some day if we keep it, it will be old and of equal value."

Paul Sprague focused on the building itself. "The Old Stock Exchange set the stage for everything that will come," he said. "Here we are in modern Florence. Here we are willing to destroy a heritage as vital as this with insufficient reflection. Here we have something which is not simply local and parochial. What we have is something which people of Illinois and the Midwest and the United States are justly proud of, which all mankind will look back to in the future as the origins in the architectural work of their own time. This is the beginning."

Thomas Stauffer apologized for his nervous stutter and then rang out a moving argument that a mature city should cherish its cultural heritage and spend money for the preservation and restoration of great architecture. "We will hear a great deal about progress," he said. "Progress does not consist of starting over at every sunrise. Progress consists of the accumulation of achievements. This building is a great achievement, not only historically but as a present living work of art. Progress, truly understood, will find a way to preserve this and other achievements."

The arguments for the building were countered by the LaSalle Partnership. "In a nutshell, no private interests can afford to maintain the present structure on the present site," said Earl A. Talbot, attorney for the partnership. He told of the partners' plan to build a $45 million building and said the city would have to pay $15 million to acquire the Stock Exchange and the surrounding land. "The Stock Exchange has outlived its usefulness," Talbot declared.

The other witnesses called to speak against the Stock Exchange argued that the building was obsolete and that the financial district needed a large modern building. They detailed the complicated financial arrangement that had been set in motion three years previously, and discussed the tax advantages of a new tall building.

George R. Bailey, the building manager who described himself as "one of the villains of the Garrick case," took another opportunity to speak out against Sullivan architecture. During the Garrick hearing, Bailey had declared that "keeping the Garrick is like keeping an elephant for a pet—very expensive." Ten years later, he said of the Stock Exchange: "You know, keeping a 13-story office building is like keeping an elephant for a house pet; I mean, it's a big thing." Later, he compared the Stock Exchange to a once-beautiful chorus girl at age 75. "I would think you would want to get rid of her and just keep a picture of her when she was young and beautiful."

Perhaps the most damaging testimony were the words of Sullivan himself, read by a little-known Chicago architect named Irving Moses who volunteered to take the stand. He read from Sullivan's *Kindergarten Chats*.

And decay proceeds as inevitably as growth, function is declined, structures disintegrate, differentiation is blurred, the fabric dissolves, life disappears, death appears, time engulfed. The eternal life falls.

Out of oblivion into oblivion, so goes the drama of creative things.

The landmarks commission, however, voted on February 24 that the Stock Exchange Building was worthy of landmark status. The recommendation was submitted to the City Council, which passed it back to the Committee on Cultural and Economic Development. The committee held a public hearing on April 30 and voted 5-1 on June 30 against the designation. Committee members estimated it would cost $12 million to condemn the building, another $3 million to install air conditioning, $113,000 to restore the first-floor exterior, $233,000 to clean and replace the Washington Street facade, and $360,000 to restore the Trading Room. "The basic consideration in designating a Chicago landmark is whether the esthetic values outweigh total cost," said Alderman Edwin Fifielski, head of the committee. "The City of Chicago cannot afford the luxury of a building as a landmark that, though it may be treasured for historic value and architectural originality, is too far deteriorated to warrant the cost of rehabilitation."

The City Council voted 38-5 not to declare the Stock Exchange a landmark. The National Trust for Historic Preservation called it "black Monday."

Title to the Stock Exchange Building finally passed to the 30 North LaSalle Partnership on January 29, 1971. On that same day, the partners issued eviction notices. The tenants were told to leave the building by April 30. Demolition plans were announced for late spring.

The new owners, who had already raised $7 million in mortgages to purchase the property, began raising more money to build. It was difficult finding a mortgage investor because the partners did not have a major tenant for the building. They didn't think they needed a lead tenant because the location was so ideal. After weeks of searching, the partners received a letter of intent for $50 million in long-term financing from the Metropolitan Life Insurance Company of America. Met Life also put up an extra $4 million in equity. In April the partners formed a joint venture with Tishman Realty and Construction Company, which had built Chicago's giant John Hancock Center. Tishman, one of the nation's major developers of large commercial buildings, agreed to oversee the demolition of the old building as well as the construction, leasing, and management of the new one. In return, Tishman received 30 percent of the ownership. The Dallas architectural firm of Thomas E. Stanley was hired to design the new building after the Chicago firm of C. F. Murphy refused the commission. The Murphy firm did not want to be part of the destruction of the Stock Exchange.

The developers did not feel like villains. "We were not out to destroy greatness," said Jerome Whiston years later. "We checked and found the Old Stock Exchange was one of the least important Adler and Sullivan buildings. We felt as if we were against a small group of vocal academics." William J. Friedman—whose grandfather Leopold Schlesinger had hired Adler and Sullivan to build the Loop department store later known as the Carson Pirie Scott store, and whose father, Oscar Friedman, had hired Frank Lloyd Wright to build Midway Gardens—snarled at the suggestion that he was a philistine. "The building was an old clunker, run down, not maintained, the elevators were barely operating," he said. "The grillwork, doorknobs and keyholes were artistic, and the partners agreed to save them." Friedman, who as a boy had wanted to be a streetcar conductor until he found out he couldn't keep the nickels, said he saw the Stock Exchange as an "extremely lucrative tax deal." Ironically, Nickel had contacted him by letter and phone in 1959 to discuss the Adler and Sullivan residence built for Leopold Schlesinger. Friedman was cordial and directed Richard to his mother, who had grown up in the South Side home.

The partners thought that the issue of landmark status was dead after the City Council vote, but several architects and attorneys made subsequent proposals to keep the building alive. In September 1970 the Art Institute presented an exhibit of Nickel photographs, as well as drawings and architectural fragments from the building, in an attempt to spark interest.

To the surprise of many, the city landmarks commission voted 8-0 in February

1971 to reopen the landmark process. Two days later, the city building commissioner ordered his staff not to issue a wrecking permit. The primary reason for the vote was a proposal by John J. Costonis, an attorney, and Jared Shlaes, a real estate consultant, that seemed to offer a solution. They suggested compensating the developers by transferring the "air rights" above the Stock Exchange Building to another downtown site. The Stock Exchange land was zoned for a building up to 45 stories. Under the plan, the city would offer the landowners the right to develop an extra 45 stories at another location, or even sell the air rights to another developer if the Stock Exchange were maintained as a landmark. The development-rights transfer plan was endorsed by three of the four daily newspapers.

Ada Louise Huxtable, the *New York Times* architecture critic, summarized the proposals and wrote: "Chicago is. . .choosing what kind of a city it wishes to be. It will either default, or show its legendary drive and shrewdness by finding answers. They will be answers for what passes, in these uncertain times, as civilization, and much of the civilized world is watching."

Wrote the *Chicago Sun-Times*, "This new proposal moves the issue from the hand-wringing and tsk-tsking stage to the specifics."

Richard Friedman, Daley's Republican opponent in the spring mayoral election, came out in favor of finding money to save the Stock Exchange. He accused Daley of promoting "high-rise giantism" and said the city should seriously consider the development-rights transfer plan to save Loop landmarks.

Nickel was convinced that the Stock Exchange's future was in the hands of Mayor Daley, who had a clear view of the building from his City Hall office.

"Perhaps we should all forget 30 N. and work for Friedman," wrote Nickel. "That's the key to the matter. Dumping Daley." Richard switched his voter registration to Chicago, and spent several weeks going door-to-door in his East Humboldt Park precinct to solicit support for Friedman. On election day Nickel worked as a Republican poll watcher. The women election judges, he wrote, spent their time talking about sex or baseball instead of housing, education, or expressways. Friedman lost. Nickel managed to drum up only 60 votes to Daley's 250 in the precinct as Daley was swept to his fourth term.

"It was a rewarding experience because while I before deplored Daley abstractly, I now have first-hand experience of the machine in operation," Nickel wrote. "Not about downtown money-making but how he uses the simple people. They are so very easy to seduce. . . .They are timid and fearful for what little they do have might be lost. This all has roots in the machine system. In which people are taken care of by their grown-up daddies, Hizzoner and the aldermen, and precinct workers."

Daley loved the city; he loved growth and progress, too. True, he had absolute power over city government, and he could have squashed any attempt to save the building by the landmarks commission. But he could also have saved the building by himself. In March Daley went so far as to appoint a committee to find a way to save the Stock Exchange. Then he ordered that no wrecking permit be issued until he received the committee report.

With an upcoming election, Daley felt he needed to do the right thing. He was torn, according to Earl Bush, a top aide. He enjoyed his role as a cultural leader, quietly supporting the Chicago Symphony Orchestra and Lyric Opera of Chicago and bringing the Picasso statue to his new Civic Center. But, said Bush, "Daley couldn't see how the city could afford to buy the Stock Exchange. He felt if he taxed people on things they didn't care about, he would have a problem."

Nickel believed Daley had the power to save the Stock Exchange with one phone call, because to live in Chicago is to believe in clout. Daley could have easily convinced his hand-picked Public Building Commission to float bonds and purchase the building for office space. The city was spending more than $1 million a year in office rental space, and the Stock Exchange could have been used as an annex to nearby City Hall.

But Daley owed allegiance to the developers, four of whom were friends. He was a builders' mayor, loyal to those who were putting Chicago back on the map. Daley met privately about once a week with William J. Friedman and the partners. He told them to be patient. Just as during the 1960s Garrick fight, Daley may have wanted to see the political battle over the Stock Exchange play out before he took sides.

Leading the renewed fight to save the Stock Exchange Building was a new organization called the Landmarks Preservation Council. Its leader, a young attorney named Richard Miller, combined legal maneuvering, public relations, and threats to keep the building alive. The council, formed in February 1971, helped Stock Exchange tenants file a lawsuit to resist eviction, introduced a City Council ordinance to designate the building a landmark, sent telegrams and letters to City Hall, bought full-page newspaper ads, gathered 3,000 petition signatures and hired a mini-skirted 19-year-old model, who was declared "Miss Chicago Landmarks," to pass out Save the Old Stock Exchange buttons.

Miller's vigor matched Nickel's. The attorney demanded meetings with both Daley and developer Jerome Whiston. On April 14, the anniversary of Sullivan's birth, Miller held a gravesite observance at Graceland Cemetery on Chicago's North Side. It was a publicity stunt, and Miller asked Nickel to lead the ceremony. Nickel encouraged Miller's effort, but resisted any involvement beyond becoming a member of the council. He often went to Sullivan's grave on the April anniversary, but this time said he had had a belly-full. "Some people love a good fight," Nickel told Miller the night before. "I hate it."

As usual, he could not stay away. About 20 people attended the ceremony. At the last minute, Nickel showed up, too. He placed a wreath bearing three red roses—for the Stock Exchange, Auditorium, and Carson buildings—on Sullivan's granite marker. "Let these three roses stand as mute supplicants for positive action by the city of Chicago to preserve just three major masterpieces of Sullivan's work," intoned Miller. The ceremony was covered by one of the daily newspapers and placed on the obituary page.

There were moments during the next six months when it seemed that all was lost in the battle to save the Stock Exchange. And there were moments when it seemed that the building would be saved after all.

In late April disgruntled tenants took a substantial amount of ornament from the halls and stairways. Dozens of copper-plated, cast-iron balusters—one of Sullivan's most distinctive designs—were unbolted and ripped out from the stairs, as were brass hand rails and wall ornament. In May one of the remaining tenants won a court order requiring the partners to restore full service while the tenants' lawsuit against the eviction notices was alive. Partner Friedman suggested shutting off water and heat to the tenants. But the building managers settled on refusing to mop floors, empty waste baskets, or provide tissue paper in public washrooms. The tenants won the tissue battle, but lost the war. At another court hearing, they agreed to leave the building in June.

The landmarks commission voted unanimously on May 28 to recommend, once again, that the Stock Exchange Building be designated a city landmark. The reasons for the vote was a proposal by prominent Chicago architect Harry Weese that showed how the Stock Exchange could be linked to a tall office tower. Weese suggested that the old building be used as an elaborate entrance and annex to the new building. He proposed converting the Stock Exchange courtyard into a grand atrium foyer leading to a bank of elevators in the new building. The Adler and Sullivan building, which would be restored and connected to the modern building at every floor, would be considered a "plaza" in zoning terms, thus making it possible to build a 47-story building on the adjoining parcels to the west.

On July 1 the committee appointed by Daley to find a way to save the Stock Exchange recommended that Chicago buy the building and adjacent land for resale to a developer who would follow Weese's plan. The committee estimated that the city would pay up to $18 million for the building and land, but would recoup most of its investment when a private developer was found. Daley endorsed the idea, and told the committee to find a developer by August 11.

The day before the deadline, the development firm of Romanek-Golub and Company agreed to take on the project. Marvin Romanek promised to present a detailed plan in 60 to 90 days showing how the firm would develop the project. The *Chicago Daily News* described the proposal as a "last-hour breakthrough." Wrote reporter M. W. Newman: "The offer appeared to be the long-sought rescue commitment needed to save the famous 77-year-old building from razing. And it came, apparently, in the nick of time."

Oscar D'Angelo, a member of the committee, said he had approached Romanek and Eugene Golub because they were friends and because they had just rehabilitated the Old International Harvester Building on Michigan Avenue. The partners had created a thriving firm in a matter of a few years, and they were hungry to establish a good reputation. "You tell me or the mayor directly what it takes to do the project," D'Angelo told them.

D'Angelo, a street-smart attorney who cared a great deal about the building, left for vacation convinced he had saved the Stock Exchange.

Nickel kept busy in 1971. During January he took care of his mother, who was suffering from hardening of the arteries. Agnes was hospitalized for two weeks. Richard's aunt Marie Nickel passed away later that month. Richard prepared a photo tribute for her funeral and spent weeks serving as the executor of her will.

Once again, Richard was preoccupied with death and aging. He made out his own legal will and, after visiting a convalescent home, wrote:

> *Now here's where people should visit before they have their babies. Of course, I wonder if people who have babies ever think at all? You look at these broken down heaps of people, and at the mean–looking attendants, and you have to wonder if you dare to introduce anybody into this "banquet." I can't imagine myself when the end is near thinking "Oh, it was wonderful, it was worthwhile." What would I have to accomplish to think it was wonderful or worthwhile?*

Later in the year, Richard lamented over the "diminished work" of a friend, the abstract expressionist sculptor Theodore Roszak. Nickel had admired Roszak's work since the late 1950s and had sent him fan letters over the years. In September Nickel accepted Roszak's invitation to his new show in New York. The quality of the art saddened Richard. "We all grow old and hopeless," he wrote. Soon after, boat designer Bill Tripp was killed in a car crash. To Richard, Tripp was the Mies van der Rohe of boat design, a man who brought simplicity to the sea. "Ah, the world gets weaker and weaker, dumber and dumber," Nickel wrote. "The good people get knocked off, the good buildings get smashed, the lofty values wither."

Richard spent much of his time rebuilding the rear wall of his Cortland Street house. The wall needed to be modified after Nickel dismantled the bakery oven in

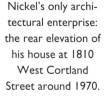

Nickel's only architectural enterprise: the rear elevation of his house at 1810 West Cortland Street around 1970.

1970, leaving a large hole. With John Vinci, Nickel designed a new rear elevation with tall semi-arched windows, glass doors, and a deck in the back. It was his first design work, and he loved it. Then he worked as a "lackey," building the new wall with Vinci's brothers, who were masonry contractors. The job went slowly. In February he wrote that he was too tired, dirty, and depressed to think about the art of building. The effort was also driving him bankrupt. "What a lesson," he wrote. "And yet, I derive immense esthetic satisfaction out of taking a wreck and improving it." He was also having recurrent nightmares—his first since returning from Korea. He dreamed that the house was broken into and defiled while he was trying to bring it to "some sort of perfection."

Nickel made about $4,300 in 1971 from his photo work. In January he wrote that he had a lot of disgruntled customers; in February, that "Life and work are crushing in on me!!"; in March, that "I've never found it so difficult to get work out before. Getting old, and Daley's machine is wearing me out I guess."

The Adler and Sullivan book lived on, but in a dormant state. Editor Ben Raeburn wrote Richard a warm, chatty letter in August after Nickel sent him a list of photographers to whom he wanted to send the finished product. "Now all we need to do is publish the 'Complete Works of Adler and Sullivan,'" wrote Raeburn. "Ready? Devoutly hope so."

During the summer, Richard met a young man researching the Chicago architect William Le Baron Jenney. The researcher seemed to be on a mission, Richard wrote, just like he used to be. Richard still took his projects seriously, but he no longer took himself seriously. "Yes, it's possible, definitely possible, that I may yet come through with the Adler and Sullivan book or 1810 Cortland. . .but both involve more work and problems and idealism etc. than I ever, ever anticipated," he wrote. "And in both cases I lack the real ability to resolve them alone." In another letter, Nickel wrote Raeburn: "This doesn't mean that I have given up. But like Louis, I am a realist. The boys wouldn't be interested in the Complete Documentation anyway."

Work at his Grimm's Bakery house was grim. "I didn't anticipate the time involvement, my lack of energy, rising labor costs (they're absurd, almost as absurd as life itself), etc.," he wrote in November. "I'd pull out except I'm really happy with the struggle. . .I'll fight the Goddamned system to the bitter end like Dylan Thomas' poem 'Do Not Go Gentle.'" The building and the sailboat took up too much time, he wrote, "but, better to have owned it and given it up than to never have launched a decent yacht. Right?"

Once again, sailing was Nickel's salvation. "Nothing like swimming off a beautiful yacht (ahem) at anchor a few miles offshore, on a hot sunny weekday, with just the whir of traffic audible, the only clue that all the slobs are working and there you are living it up," he wrote in 1971. For the first time, Richard found a sailing companion, a woman named Carol Sutter. However, in November, he lamented: "The one gal who did sail with me regularly finally depressed me. . .an innocent 9-to-5er, with nothing to live for but the everyday pleasures." In another letter, Richard wrote that she was too preoccupied with her apartment. "So I phased her out in true Kierkegaardian fashion. She was so docile, so lifeless." Their

relationship would take a surprising turn later, however.

In early autumn Nickel had *Garden City* lifted out of the water for winter storage. "Fantastic to see it flying through the sky on a construction crane," he wrote as the boat was swung onto a cradle. "Very dramatic."

Then came the bad news. Marvin Romanek, the "white knight" developer who had told reporters in July that saving the Stock Exchange Building was "feasible in all respects," announced on September 27 that his firm was no longer interested in the project. He offered no explanation.

Decades later, Romanek-Golub's role remains unclear. The two partners refuse to discuss the matter. Architect Harry Weese, who worked with the firm in studying an alternative plan, suspected from the start that the two partners had little interest in saving the Stock Exchange. "They were bad mouthing the building terribly," he said. Attorney Oscar D'Angelo, who suggested the firm to the mayor's committee, said he was shocked by the late withdrawal. Romanek and Golub never hinted they were considering withdrawing until the September letter, D'Angelo said.

Developer William J. Friedman suspects Romanek-Golub's offer to study the site was a ploy to delay construction of his new skyscraper. Romanek-Golub was the leasing agent for a 38-story office building under construction two blocks away at 180 North LaSalle. Friedman thinks Romanek and Golub wanted to slow down the 30 North LaSalle building so that they would get their building on the rental market first.

"They just had more clout," Friedman said.

The delay caused Metropolitan Life to withdraw its $50 million in financing and $4 million in equity. The 30 North LaSalle Partners eventually secured a $49 million mortgage from the Prudential Insurance Company of America.

City officials issued a permit to demolish the building on October 1. The permit gave Three Oaks Wrecking Company permission to begin interior demolition and a minimum of exterior work on the roof and back wall until the scaffolding outside the building was installed.

Richard Miller and his Landmarks Preservation Council spent the following two weeks feverishly trying to halt the wreckers. The organization filed petitions

Protesters gather in front of the Stock Exchange Building as the scaffolding is installed in October 1971.

and lawsuits in the state Supreme Court and the Cook County Circuit Court and organized a fund-raising campaign (which netted $5,200) to save the Stock Exchange. The *New York Times* described it as a "12th-hour effort."

Demonstrators marched in front of the building on October 6. *Chicago Sun-Times* reporter Rob Cuscaden wrote that the "mixture of suit-and-tie types, housewives, and students and their signs looked depressingly familiar to persons who remembered the forlorn efforts to save Sullivan's equally famous Garrick Theater a decade ago: 'Save our Architectural Heritage,' etc. They may well have been the same signs."

Nickel helped organize a protest on October 8, the 100th anniversary of the Great Chicago Fire. Although he had spent the previous day hanging placards in the Loop, only 25 people showed up. "So perhaps it boils down to our getting what we deserve. . .the same reason the environment has gone to hell over the years," he wrote.

Later that Friday, attorney Frederick Cohn held his wedding in Nevers Restaurant and Lounge on the first floor of the Stock Exchange. The restaurant had been shut to the public the day before, so Cohn, a former tenant of the building, stood outside to direct his guests past the "Closed" signs. "If one should get married, he should hold his wedding in a lovely place," he told a reporter.

Nickel took part in one final demonstration on October 15. By then he had become caught up in the fight and was churning out protest letters as passionate as any he had ever written. "Alas, I find I'm so full of venom against the Chicago government, the establishment, and even capitalistic democracy, that all my drafts are unusable," he wrote to Skidmore, Owings, and Merrill partner William Hartmann.

It's ridiculous. We have a department of interior, we have a landmarks commission locally, and isn't it the responsibility of a mayor of a city to be concerned for our spiritual welfare as well as physical? Why aren't these agencies responsive, and why must individual citizens have to fight for everything?

It shatters me that matters concerning the landmarks continue, and we tear down these obvious, obvious, works of art! In my total depression—and I'm not the only one who is gravely depressed over this terrible development—I mixed a double Scotch and viewed "Civilization" on TV. It made my blood boil, as the saying goes, that our Mayor can be so lacking in imagination, sympathy, and especially the wisdom to take advice.

Nickel spread the blame beyond Daley.

I charge the cultural elite of Chicago with the doom of Chicago School buildings. They rape the city for private fortunes in order to enjoy private art in the suburbs. It's sickening! Worst of all, in an age of reality and enlightenment, it's so uncultured, so ignorant. In particular, how can the architectural profession shy away from this? In a city of slums, why must the quality buildings be doomed? . . .You can't convince me there are no alternatives.

Later that year, 120 Dutch architects and city planners stood in front of the Stock Exchange Building and murmured the word *schande*. They had come to Chicago to study the city's great architecture and were met by the scaffolded Adler and Sullivan building. The word meant "shame."

Now began the second battle over the Stock Exchange: the fight for ornament.

In mid-October the Metropolitan Museum of Art announced that it wanted to acquire the building's entrance arch. Director Thomas P. F. Hoving, who previously had moved an original Egyptian tomb to New York, now planned to disassemble the facade of Sullivan's skyscraper and reinstall it as a working entrance in the courtyard of the new American Wing. Museum officials had coveted the arch for more than a year and had written letters to the Chicago landmarks commission since February detailing their interest if the building were demolished.

They never received a reply, but the Metropolitan's imprimatur made Stock Exchange Building ornament hot property. Chicago officials met with the 30 North LaSalle partners several times in late October and announced that the partners would reconstruct the entrance arch in the city, donate ornament to the Art Institute of Chicago and to the University of Illinois, and pay for a photographic record of the building. This was, in effect, the price paid for the demolition permit.

Nickel applied for the job to photograph the building. He proposed to produce a book similar to his demolition books on the Cable and Republic buildings. "I recommend we do a thorough job of esthetic recording," he wrote, describing how he would photograph the exterior shell from top to bottom, as well as the Trading Room and the interior from the cornice support system, typical offices, corridors, and elevators to the basement. He would also provide demolition photos and scaled photos for future reconstruction work. In a brusque manner, Nickel wrote "$10,000" at the bottom of the letter.

Richard was recommended for the job, but not pushed. Partner William J. Friedman was surprised by the proposed cost, and suggested the fee be cut in half. Nickel refused. In mid-November Friedman hired photographer Orlando Cabanban.

"I really goofed on the Stock Exchange work for Tishman," Nickel later wrote.

> *I wanted to do it, not for them but for myself, and yet I didn't handle the bid intelligently or realistically. The original $10,000 bid was obviously too high even for a sympathetic client. . .and Friedman couldn't give one damn about my intents. And even when reduced, I was unrealistic. The result is that I may do the work anyway but not get paid. A real dope. Too emotionally involved, non thinking, non business.*

The Art Institute had no formal plans for the ornament, but wanted to save as much as possible from the Trading Room. Architect John Vinci convinced the institute that there were treasures left in the room, and was hired to supervise demolition of the room and salvage ornament. Vinci asked Nickel to help.

Vinci, whom Nickel introduced by saying "It rhymes with da Vinci," was by now Nickel's second self. Nickel depended on Vinci's knowledge and training as an architect to support his intuitive feelings about buildings. Vinci, in turn, benefited from Nickel's innate appreciation of buildings. As an architect, Vinci was taught to first visualize a building as a collection of nuts and bolts—much as a doctor is taught to view the body as muscles and bones. Nickel, who saw a building like a sculptor would view a body, taught Vinci how to grasp the essence and meaning of architecture.

In 1961 Vinci had been Nickel's sidekick and apprentice as they had worked together stripping plaster from the walls of the Garrick Theater Building as it was demolished. At the Stock Exchange, Vinci hired Nickel to help dismantle the Trading Room. It was a role reversal that did not go unnoticed by the two.

Since their salvaging days in the 1950s, they had fought and fallen in and out of friendship. For years the two had argued about Vinci's hippie clothes and friends, the Vietnam war, politics. Both from close-knit Catholic families, Vinci became a greasy-haired, bandanna-wearing anti-war activist. He set up obstacles in his friendships, demanding others to overlook his appearance, his friends, and his enormous dog, and instead judge his inner self. Nickel, who voted for Goldwater and Nixon, considered himself a "liberal conservative."

Yet no matter how much they differed or how often they argued, Nickel and Vinci never parted company because they maintained the same feeling about architecture and the same rage against what was happening to the city. They had grown dependent on each other to vent their anger and appreciation. Nickel was quiet; Vinci spoke his mind. Nickel never had Vinci's organizational skills; Vinci never had Nickel's patience. They worked well together. Richard griped when John smashed and bashed plaster in the Garrick Theater with a hammer, or yanked stencil canvas from the ceiling of the Trading Room, but Richard knew that the "spastic madman" would take it down without a crease or a pucker.

"As you know, John and you and I are bound by the Garrick and Sullivan," Nickel wrote David Norris in 1971, "and I suppose that will endure all other threats, fancies, dirty diapers and senility and whatever may come along."

By his own admission, Vinci was a scrounger, a manipulator, and an operator. He had a way of winning people's confidence and convincing them to do the right thing. The son of an immigrant building contractor, Vinci was the first in his South Side family of four sisters and two brothers to go to college. He was the only member of the freshman class at the Illinois Institute of Technology who said "dese" and "dose" and "dem." It did not take long for Vinci to make an impression. His imaginative, if somewhat primitive, drawings gained the notice of his teachers, and his resourcefulness gained the attention of his classmates.

As a sophomore architecture student, Vinci trucked his father's scaffolds and forms to the campus and built—by hand and alone—a six-foot platform for Duke Ellington's band at a school dance. Ellington and his band made quite a sight performing the night away in the famed Crown Hall building on the IIT campus. Even

Mies van der Rohe, director of the school, was impressed. He sat in a Barcelona chair like a child, listening to the fabulous sound and watching the colored lights reflect off his building.

Vinci spent five years moving around the glass-enclosed one-room schoolhouse that was Crown Hall. He worked until midnight, when his father picked him up for the short ride home. Often, Vinci would watch Nickel—the older Institute of Design student—take photographs of student architectural models. The word was out, even then, that Nickel could make architecture come alive.

Vinci spent years during the 1960s working for the Chicago firm of Brenner Danforth Rockwell, then started his own practice with Lawrence Kenny, an IIT friend. Perhaps more importantly, he traveled the world, grounding himself in art and literature and developing an architectural vision of his own. He also became something of a prankster. It was hard to know whether Vinci was serious or joking. To many, his mischievousness belied the seriousness of his commitment to art. But not to Nickel.

Work on the Trading Room began on November 8. The room—100 feet long, 75 feet wide, and 30 feet tall—was cold and dark. The ceiling was dirty and peeling. Many of the stenciled canvases had fallen off or been ripped off for souvenirs. Dirt from decades of neglect had piled so high that mice or rats had carved paths through it. It took a great leap of the imagination to see the beauty here. Even the gilded capitals looked like cheap plaster. But Vinci and Nickel knew the true beauty of this huge and foreboding place. "I think it is sort of like a holy room," said Nickel after the work began. "The more you are in here the more you are in awe of it."

During the first three weeks, Vinci, Nickel, and two other helpers—Vinci's friends Pat Fitzgerald and Alan Moreland—took down the partitions and false ceiling, unblocked the windows, opened the former visitors gallery, and cleaned up the room so it was as close to its original condition as possible. On November 15 the original ceiling was unveiled for the first time since the Depression. Now, with the gold-leafed column capitals, leaded art glass, and carbon filament lamps showing, the room looked like it had when it was first built. Nickel spent days taking composite photos, while Vinci began coding each part of the room. Sometime during those first weeks, Vinci and Nickel formed a grand plan to save the room.

"Why do we just save pieces? Why don't we save the whole room?" Nickel asked Vinci during the first weeks of work.

"Well Richard, that's kind of impossible," Vinci replied.

They decided to have Richard photograph the room so that they would have a record if it were ever reconstructed.

David Hanks, assistant curator of American decorative arts at the Art Institute, thought Nickel and Vinci's suggestion to reconstruct the Trading Room was "harebrained." Hanks believed that the Trading Room was a work of art as important as any work at the art museum, and he believed that the ornament salvaged from the building meant little unless it was set in architectural context. But the museum had only haphazardly collected architectural material and had no money for such an undertaking.

That did not stop Vinci and Nickel from going ahead with their plan. As Vinci said years later, "Things always have a way of working themselves out."

The work is a "torturous grind," Nickel wrote on November 21. He was suffering from a cold and was so covered by soot and dirt that he was hard to recognize. He and the other three workers were unwelcome guests when they showed up at a downtown restaurant every day for lunch. After work, he had to undress outside his Park Ridge home and take two showers. Although Nickel never believed the Trading Room would stand again, he pressed on.

The work was also dangerous. Some of the Trading Room skylights were exposed to the upper floors and had cracked when objects had crashed through from upstairs during demolition. Even a soda can made a huge dent in the Trading Room floor when it dropped from the upper floors through the skylights.

Richard worked seven to nine hours almost every day in the Trading Room from early November until the end of January, earning $10 an hour. Even though Vinci was in control, he did not give orders to Richard. As at the Garrick, they worked as a team: John on the scaffold pulling down the stenciled canvas and cutting off plaster while Richard photographed each section. The canvas was cleaned, vacuumed, rolled on a cylinder, and wrapped in drop cloths. Richard drove the salvaged material to the Art Institute. "It was quite a scene," recalled Pat Fitzgerald.

"We would pull into the back dock, where they were used to receiving priceless paintings. We were filthy, hauling in the plaster and junk. There was a lot of head scratching among the security guards, even wonder whether we belonged. But after awhile, they were amused by us."

Richard was careful to be a helper, not the leader. He deferred to Vinci several times when a documentary filmmaker showed them at work. The work was "Vinci's folly," Nickel later wrote. They were simply struggling to finish it "like the idiots we are and forever will be." Nickel grew tired of the filthy job and wrote several letters of resignation to Vinci. The letters were ignored, so Nickel kept working.

They persevered. As at the Garrick, Nickel and Vinci roamed the building during its final days. "The wreckers, at first, treated us with great hostility, but after the pressures were off they gave us free rein," wrote Vinci in *Image* magazine in September 1972. "The Riccio Brothers of Three Oaks Wrecking Co. allowed us to go to the top of the building and photograph the demolition. Soon we were everywhere, photographing, exploring and recording."

Nickel wrote on November 21, "Now that I get to see the building every day, I appreciate it more than ever and wish I had fought more over it. . .although I have no illusions anymore."

In the same letter, Nickel thanked Richard Miller for his campaign to save the Stock Exchange. Nickel said he could not participate in Miller's Landmarks Preservation Council financially or psychologically. "My income is so low and my expenses so high, from years of concern and charity, that art has simply become too costly. . .Ah. . .maybe just depressed from working in dirt and cold day after day in the doomed building."

Vinci and his crew next dismantled the art-glass skylight panels that rimmed the Trading Room ceiling. The glass panels were not distinguished, and many were damaged or missing, but Vinci and Nickel needed the glass if the room were ever to be rebuilt.

Unbolting the heavy cast-iron mullions that held the glass in place was the most challenging part of the salvage effort because the flat-head bolts were sunken and covered by putty and a layer of paint. They also were frozen by the winter weather. Finding the bolts was difficult enough while balancing 30 feet above the floor on a scaffold. The crew eventually learned they could unscrew most of the bolts more easily by soaking them in an oily solution. The heavy mullions were lowered by a block-and-tackle. The crew then devised a crating operation, constructing cardboard frames for each piece of glass and each mullion.

In late November the work was stopped by Larry Riccio, head of Three Oaks Wrecking. Riccio claimed that the 85 art-glass windows and mullions that Vinci's crew removed belonged to the wrecking company. He demanded $40,000 from the Art Institute.

Nickel sympathized with Riccio. The four brothers who ran Three Oaks had tried to humiliate Vinci and the crew at first. But Nickel and the Riccios had developed a good relationship. Nickel knew that William J. Friedman and the 30 North LaSalle partners had forced Three Oaks into giving up much of the building ornament, and now the wreckers were standing firm against the Art Institute. Nickel had no love lost for the Art Institute after the museum had left his Garrick ornament outside for years.

"If it's such a glorious system, this free enterprise, then why is everyone with a higher cultural sense so shocked when a guy like Riccio goes by the book," Nickel wrote Vinci. "Where's the truth? All this wishy-washy double standard. Who are these lofty institutions that deserve sympathy? I'd rather see some grubbing dagos come out on top than the Art Institute, because I know too many truths about the institute and other institutions."

The art museum made a tentative agreement to purchase the windows and by mid-December museum officials were making serious plans to reconstruct the Trading Room in the Art Institute's new wing. Vinci and his crew removed 200 skylight panels and 400 cast-iron mullions.

By December the cold was making work even more difficult. Water—used to hose down debris from the upper floors—was showering down on the Trading Room. The water froze in puddles, which Nickel and the others skated upon. The weak winter sun could not penetrate LaSalle Street, so even when the temperature rose above freezing, the floor and the room remained frozen. On December 27 Nickel wrote that he was a "physical wreck." The work was supposed to be

The last days of the Trading Room in Adler and Sullivan's Chicago Stock Exchange Building. The room had been stripped apart for its eventual reconstruction when this photograph was taken in 1972.

finished by January 1, but Vinci got a month's extension. Richard again tried to quit, but Vinci convinced him that the job would be completed soon.

The Riccios stopped the salvage work again on January 9. They refused to let Vinci and the crew work until they had a final agreement with the Art Institute on the purchase price of Trading Room material. The wrecking company was pressed to pay salaries and needed a quick money fix.

Nickel intervened. "Although I've never been convinced of the determination or sincerity of the Art Institute and Skidmore Owings and Merrill to reconstruct the Trading Room, it surely is a meaningful and heroic project," Nickel wrote the Riccios.

Too unique, too stupendous, really, for the common mentality of Chicago! Don't you agree that the Trading Room, if it had not been obscured by the lowered ceiling, might have been a primary factor in seeing the building more broadly appreciated and finally saved from demolition?

So now we are at an impasse in the negotiations, and even the fragile hope that the room will be reconstructed is fading. I am frankly on your side in the situation, within reason. I think the Art Institute should overlook the early deal, sympathize with any arm twisting you might have gotten early, and face up to the value of the total amount of decorative materials they are receiving.

Richard suggested that the Riccios offer a firm price.

The move worked. On January 17 the Art Institute board voted to purchase the skylight glass for $30,000, and work began again.

Vinci and Nickel had started their work in the Trading Room by being extremely careful. At first they were much more methodical there than they had been in the Garrick Theater. But in the final days, the effort was much like the Garrick days as they worked frantically, taking plaster column capitals, marble, long strips of stenciled canvas, lighting fixtures, window sashes, and ventilating grilles. Now Vinci and Nickel were looking for flourishes, anything that hinted at hidden stencilwork beneath layers of paint. Using a carbide saw and wire cutter, they ripped through metal lath and removed whole sections of wall.

Finally, the foursome could think of nothing more to take. By the end of the month, the tiny room at the Art Institute was full and the budget was virtually exhausted. It was getting colder and more dangerous to work. The gallery, which overlooked the trading room, was open at the top and the wreckers were starting to demolish the back wall of the Trading Room. By now, they could see out of the room. By the time they left, on January 31, the place was again a mess.

Life returned to normal as the Trading Room job ended. In late January Nickel wrote that he had listened to his record player for the first time in months. In February he spent time with his father as Stanley recovered from more surgery.

Adler and Sullivan's Max M. Rothschild Building at 210 West Monroe Street. With the help of wreckers, Nickel salvaged four of the structure's cast-iron panels just beneath the roof in 1972.

Richard also finished work as executor of his aunt's small estate, a job he described as "a massive complicated headache."

It was time to think about his future—and about sailing. His two nautical desires were to purchase a giant spinnaker for *Garden City* and to sell *Vato*. The spinnaker was impractical. It would cost $285 for the sail and $200 to $300 for hardware, and could be used only in ideal winds. But, oh, how symbolic!

"The spirituality of 539 square feet flying over *Garden City,* what is that worth on a summer day offshore of Chicago, the city of 'Where's mine?'" he wrote to Paul Sprague on January 28. "There's very little joy left in life when one knows all the ugly truths. The yacht is a singular solace, like a bottle of booze."

The sale of *Vato*—his tiny, prized first sailboat—was symbolic, too. In 1971 Nickel started advertising that the boat was "reluctantly for sale." He described the mahogany lapstrake hull, the laminated oak ribs, and pine keel in detail, but got no response.

"It serves as a symbol to me that the world is full of clods, who don't appreciate nothing—from the Stock Exchange down to a small boat," he wrote in early 1972. Nickel eventually found "Mr. Right-Deserving," a Chicago man who appreciated the boat and paid $1,400 for it.

Again the old doubts returned. In January he wistfully wrote: "I'm thinking of going into some non-esthetic field, where I can work for self-satisfaction and not get involved in this crum bum society. For two cents I'd throw everything I own away (except records and selected books), move into a trailer at Klimek's boat yard, dilly dally the days away and never come back to Chicago."

Nickel returned to photography as most of his days in 1972 were spent salvaging his career. In January he took photographs of Stockyards Gate as well as the Rookery, Old Colony, Manhattan, and Reliance buildings for the landmarks commission.

In February Richard turned down an offer to work two or three weeks in Philadelphia photographing 40 Frank Furness buildings. Furness was the first major architect for whom Sullivan worked and Sullivan's earliest important influence. The Victorian master, Sullivan wrote, struck him "like a flower by the roadside." Richard rejected the offer, calling the $200 a day a "low money proposition. . . .I'm getting tired of being the patsy for everyone who wants favors or historical material, and then when the commercial jobs come along they call on Cabanban, or Turner or Hedrich." Instead, he produced exhibits of architectural photos for the Milwaukee Arts Center and Illinois State Museum.

On January 31, the last day of work in the Trading Room, scaffolding began going up around Adler and Sullivan's 1880 Max M. Rothschild Building. The five-story store at 210 West Monroe Street was the oldest existing building designed by the firm. Sullivan had framed the upstairs windows with an ornate cast-iron front. Up until this time, architects had used cast iron to look like stone. Sullivan—the builder—painted the cast iron a light gray to show how it differed from the huge stone piers, and exposed the flanges and bolts to show how the material worked. Then Sullivan—the poet—expressed what the structure was all about. He transformed the building into a flower with rigid piers that tapered as they rose and burst into ornament at the top. It was here that Sullivan codified many of his ideas about material and ornament.

Nickel, flush with the success of saving the Trading Room, convinced the Art Institute to consider taking the Rothschild's entire fifth-floor facade, windows and all. But the stone piers proved to be too heavy and the plan impractical. Richard did manage to arrange for Southern Illinois University, the Art Institute, and Glessner House officials to purchase four of the building's 12 cast-iron cornice panels. The other eight panels were scrapped. With the permission of Butch Mandel, the National Wrecking Company foreman, Nickel and Tim Samuelson picked up two cornice panels and several small fragments from the scrap pile. It was the heaviest material they had ever salvaged by themselves and almost ruined the station wagon owned by Nickel's father. Helped by another man, they carted the pieces to Nickel's house at 1810 Cortland and split the booty. Now that he had property, Richard wrote, he would probably start to hoard again.

He also wanted to save a window bay from William Le Baron Jenney's seven-story Leiter I building, also slated for demolition. "Hah, hah, every year we keep asking to save larger elements, and maybe finally we will ask for the whole building and they will submit," he wrote in February 1972.

Jenney's building, at the northwest corner of Wells and Monroe streets, was one of the world's first glass box structures. Built in the 1870s and 1880s, the building stood tall on a primitive metal frame. Nickel was impressed by its open glass area and saddened that the landmarks commission had not fought for it. "Right now all I could want is a trip to the Virgin Islands to forget all this architectural madness," he wrote.

Of course, Nickel could not leave. He spent most of his time salvaging four flights of stairs from the interior of the Stock Exchange Building for the new American Wing of the Metropolitan Museum of Art. Each flight of two straight runs was purchased for $5,000. Richard was paid $500 to photograph and number the stairs and supervise the removal. The first shipment of two flights was left outside the Stock Exchange in a pile. Several pieces were broken or exposed to the weather by the wreckers. Richard's paint markings were washed away in the rain. "I'm afraid, too, that they're not treating it as kindly as they might," Nickel wrote Metropolitan curator Morrison Heckscher. "They seem to just give the labor instructions and turn around and return to the trailer. Four brothers, what a mess."

The final shipment fared no better. Several of the iron stair pieces were once again piled outside and were broken by falling terra cotta. Nickel was called to the site February 21 to inventory the pieces before they were shipped to New York. He wrote Heckscher: "I couldn't even keep a reasonable accounting of what was going aboard, there were so many interruptions, so much confusion and on the whole it was like dealing with a bunch of dummies." The following day, Nickel wrote: "We are dealing with some greedy incompetents in these wreckers."

Since March 1971, when they had won a bid to demolish the Stock Exchange, the project had been a nightmare for Larry, Gus, Joe, and John Riccio, the four brothers who owned and operated Three Oaks Wrecking. They had built their company by getting contracts from the city during the 1950s to raze South Side houses to make way for the Dan Ryan Expressway. By the 1970s, the brothers had enough equipment, employees, and insurance to compete for downtown jobs and boast on their business cards: "We wreck anything in the Universe. Not yet equipped for Outer Space."

At the Stock Exchange the Riccios were caught between the preservationists, who demanded that Three Oaks not be issued a wrecking permit, and the building owners, who pushed the firm to complete the job in 130 working days. Months of delay caused Three Oaks to suffer huge costs. The firm was portrayed in newspapers as the villain of the long fight.

The Stock Exchange, which Three Oaks agreed to raze along with the adjacent 11-story Civic Center Hotel for $337,500, presented new challenges for the firm because it was in the heart of the busy financial district and because its floors were especially brittle. What might sound like an advantage to a wrecker was actually a disadvantage, because the fragile floors made the wrecking hard to control.

Three Oaks also had to work around Vinci's crew and around the *Law Bulletin*, a newspaper that was allowed keep its basement office open until January 1972.

"When demolition proceedings started, we were obligated to keep them [*Law Bulletin*] dry," said Larry Riccio.

> *So we had to take out the entire fourth floor, all the partitions and clean it and put a roof on it to keep the moisture and weather out, the dust and what have you. From there. . .after we had done that, we proceeded up to the top, built a chute to carry the rubbish from the top to the bottom above the fourth floor. Prior to that, scaffolding and sidewalk sheds were put out. From there, we went to the top and removed the penthouse and the roof by hand. It was lowered down through the chute and whatever objects we wanted to save though the elevators. And then, the procedure repeats itself floor-by-floor on down.*

Chicago officials do not allow the use of explosives to raze buildings. Until the *Law Bulletin* closed in January, much of the demolition work was by hand. The wreckers used breaking bars and sledgehammers to slam the interior walls and small tractors to push away the debris. Burners used torches to cut the steel frame and the rods that supported the clay tile floors. Although much of the debris was initially dropped off the rear of the building into the courtyard, on December 28, 1971, city inspectors formally warned Three Oaks to stop the dangerous practice. "All debris must be dropped through enclosed chutes," the inspectors wrote.

The work was slow. The upper floors were wrecked with the help of a 9,000-pound "frost ball," which was dropped onto a floor until the floor gave way and fell one floor below. A building this size could have been wrecked in three months, but Three Oaks spent much of November and December removing and accumulating ornament. The Riccios came to think of the Stock Exchange as a golden goose. They had tied up money and manpower for months while waiting for the demolition permit, and now they wanted a return on their investment. They ended up selling $38,505 of material at a makeshift store at the site. Mail slots went for $250, door knobs for $150. Railings and window pulls went for less. "The Stock Exchange is the scandal and tragedy of our time, except nobody will know it," wrote Nickel about Three Oaks's control of the ornament. "It's like an iron curtain across the place, by 3 Oaks Wrecking. They 'own' that building and don't let no civic or intellectual cry babies shove them around."

With Vinci and his crew finally out of the building in February, an extra large crane was brought in so that the lower four floors could be wrecked by heavy machinery. In the front of the building—along the LaSalle and Washington streets side—the wrecking looked orderly, floor by floor. But in the back, the huge rubble piles hinted at the disorganization.

Nickel was careful to keep on the Riccios' good side because he wanted access and ornament from the building. He advised them about the value of artifacts and gave them photographs for free. Yet as a veteran of wrecking sites, he knew that the company was having serious problems. When a piece of terra cotta dropped 12 stories onto the Three Oaks trailer, Nickel wrote: "This is not a competent company."

Then, in early March, 100 feet of metal scaffolding used by the wreckers blew

A contact sheet showing Nickel and his fiancée, Carol Ruth Sutter, in 1972.

off the east facade of the building's ninth floor onto LaSalle Street during the morning rush hour. The scaffolding, wood, bricks, and tarpaulin showered down on passersby, injuring eight people and damaging two cars. Nickel, the complete documentarian, rushed to the scene to photograph the damage. Three Oaks made the front page of all four daily newspapers. The wreckers denied any wrongdoing, but it was yet another incident that caused delay.

In March 1972, the 43-year-old Nickel fell in love with 32-year-old Carol Sutter. They had met at a Lyric Opera rehearsal in the late 1960s, sailed together several times in the early 1970s, and frequently corresponded by letter for several years. It was not until that early March, when she accompanied Richard on a trip to Milwaukee, that their relationship blossomed.

Richard was ripe for romance. His former wife, Adrienne, had remarried and Richard felt comfortable with Carol. Siskind believed that Carol helped Richard solve years of sexual frustration. "He never said anything specifically about his problems with women until he sent me a postcard about Carol," Siskind said. Siskind psychoanalyzed that Nickel had spent years wrestling with an "emotional conflict" he felt toward women. "He had so little passion for women, he must have wondered whether he was a homosexual."

Shy Nickel obviously had a difficult time meeting and establishing meaningful relationships with women. His marriage to his first love, Adrienne, had turned sour quickly. Richard wrote he had become disenchanted with sex by age 23. During the 1960s, he wrote that he usually dated only the "wishy-washy and scarety-cats," perhaps out of fear of falling in love again. Nickel said that he was similar to his heroes—Sullivan, Kierkegaard, and Bruckner—because they, too, had failed relationships. Nickel talked and wrote often about women, but he convinced himself he did not have the time for long-term romance.

They were an unlikely couple for a whirlwind love affair. Carol shared Richard's enthusiasm for art, but did not share his passion. To Carol, fine art was something to be studied, understood, and appreciated. She was a meticulous, organized, disciplined woman who figured out what she wanted and went after it. For years, she had focused her attention on her career. When Richard walked into her life, she shifted her focus.

Quiet, intelligent, and serious, Carol grew up in Grosse Pointe Farms, Michigan. Her father ran an insurance office and her mother worked as an elementary school teacher. Carol had been engaged once before, and had become deeply saddened when her marriage plans dissolved. She developed a mental toughness from the experience that defined her life. Like Richard, Carol was a crusader. But her crusades directly involved people. Since her years at Elmhurst College in suburban Chicago, Carol had wanted to counsel people. For a time she had considered becoming a minister, but eventually shifted to social work. Now she worked as the supervising social worker at Lutheran General Hospital in Park Ridge, serving as a liaison between physicians and patients. Even off work, Carol talked to people like an analyst, drawing them out so that she could help. She was a force.

Carol, described by Richard as "delicate," had a pretty, ready smile and

Wreckers remove a stair "stringer," or side panel. This is one of the items Nickel wanted to take on his final return to the Stock Exchange Building.

slender figure. She wore her auburn hair, which had earned her the childhood nickname "Rusty," in a flip, the style of the day. Her fair skin and elfin features made her look almost like Nickel's sister.

"While there's no doubt of my deep feeling for Carol, what helped it along was the Old Stock Exchange experience, the futility of rehabbing 1810 alone, of owning the boat alone and begging for guests, and seeing my parents deteriorate with age, etc.," Nickel wrote in late March. "All very depressing, so I either had to finally settle on a companion or get rid of all this crap."

Nickel proposed to Carol in mid-March and she accepted. They planned a small wedding on June 10. It was the same day Richard had married Adrienne, but he never told her.

He liked almost everything about Carol, except her Scandinavian furniture. "I'd go through almost any ridiculous social routine to please her through the marriage-wedding planning," Nickel wrote in late March. "However, she does appreciate me as an individual and knows that forcing me into changes could only bode bad."

Carol was open-minded, receptive, and eager to take on Richard's interests. "She's crazy about me and I figured the least I could do was reciprocate," Nickel wrote. In another letter he wrote: "Just to show you what a jewel she is, she thinks we ought to create the condition that I would finally finish my Adler and Sullivan manuscript." At night she even let him read Kierkegaard to her.

Late that month, Nickel took Carol to an antiques show to buy an engagement ring. Carol toyed between a simple gold ring for $150 and a grander ring with a large blue stone for $375. The decision, he wrote, was strictly hers because he planned to spend $600 for the new spinnaker and gear. "It was a matter of did you want to impress your friends with glitter, or unimpress them with your subtlety and fineness," Nickel wrote his cousin Adeline Helwig on March 27. Carol chose the simpler one.

Richard was a different person now. "I'd do anything, make any changes, to please her, make her happy," he wrote. "Aughhh!" His friend Lee Timonen said he smiled all the time now. His accountant, Robert McGowan, said Richard talked about love as if he were a 20-year-old. To Tim Samuelson, Richard wrote: "I'm afraid our days of adventuring, salvaging, avoiding the cops, etc. in the cause of Sullivan will soon terminate. For me anyway."

Richard told only certain people about his marriage plans. "My parents don't believe it," he wrote. "They thought I was a lost cause."

How fast life was changing. Richard and Carol planned to live in her high-rise Lake Shore Drive apartment for the first few months after their wedding while they started on a crash program to finish rehabilitating his Cortland Street building.

"Those will be busy but happy months ahead," Nickel wrote in uncharacteristically ebullient prose. Richard promised Carol that the Stock Exchange would be the last demolished building he would enter.

On March 21, 1972, Carol wrote him: "They say that yesterday was the first day of spring but you and I know that this year spring came early. It is our *beautiful* secret."

At the end of March, Richard met her parents in Michigan. Before the trip, Richard and Carol discussed what he should wear. Finally, Richard told Carol that it was more important for her family to accept him than for him to please them.

The weekend was a success. Richard wrote on April 3:

I enjoyed meeting your family, and working on the kitchen team, and going to church, and meeting people whom I can't remember and being accepted (they do accept me don't they???) into the fold.

The flight back was soupy, especially over Lake Michigan and we saw ground very low over the steel mills of S. Chicago. Then a swift ride along the shore and a smooth landing at Meigs. . . . Wonderful to see the Meigs-McCormick relationship from the air. Oh, if only there could have been a yacht down there at the end of the airstrip, to give me some idea of how we look!

Nickel's world now included Carol. It was "our" *Garden City* and "our" book now. Along with his architectural notes, Richard now carried a sheet of paper with all of Carol's clothes sizes.

"Just like all the delay and the 'chance' of your coming to me, I'm happy to let things fall in place as they may," Richard concluded the April 3 letter.

Carol wrote back:

I called last night to be sure you landed smoothly—didn't want to go along not knowing really for sure. I'm just full of little love trivia—the impressions of having your things still here, a piece of hair left in the bathroom which I inadvertently sent down the drain.—But the nicest love trivia is that I slept in your bed. Maybe that's why I slept so long and sound.

One thing tho—I never recall dreaming when you are with me—but last night I dreamt a number of dreams about the two of us—can't recall them much now but they were pleasant times together—my loving companion.

I'm very proud of you and very, very happy and it's strange you being so far away, my captain.

Nickel kept returning to the Stock Exchange Building. He went to negotiate with the Riccios over ornament for Southern Illinois University. And he went to take ornament for himself.

At least twice, Richard raided the Stock Exchange in secret. One night he sneaked into the building to take an abandoned desk. After lowering it from the Trading Room window, Nickel ran back into the building and walked down with a huge cast-iron stairway newel post strapped on his back.

Nickel also came back just to be in the building.

"Dick had asked me several times to come over to the building and I didn't want to," wrote friend Robert Kostka. "I didn't feel any danger, but felt that it was a pretty depressing thing to see. Dick said he felt it was like sitting with a dying friend."

Larry Riccio said he instructed his foreman not to let anyone on the site except for employees and those with permission. But by April, Richard was a familiar face.

The Riccios deny that Richard was allowed to take anything.

"He was given permission to take nothing," said John Riccio, the general office manager. "Everything he took out of the building was actual thievery."

However, Nickel's letters indicate he made several agreements with the Riccios. For example, he wrote Tim Samuelson on February 22: "I didn't have a chance to tell you also that when I was momentarily alone with Joe, he suggested that if I wanted anything for myself, to speak up. I replied that of everything, I like the small screens but that I wasn't sure he would want to give one up."

On March 20 Richard wrote Harry Hilberry at Southern Illinois University:

My own relationship with him [Joe Riccio] is so cordial and [imbued] with mutual feelings and understanding, that I don't think he would treat us badly.

He also told me that if I would do the labor, I could remove a second-floor window lintel. I will do that free for SIU, if I can do it in a day or two. Not the whole lintel, though, perhaps a third or fifth of one but enough to make visual sense. Demo is momentarily stopped because of a scaffolding collapse (did you hear about it?) but he said I could do that work once things proceeded.

The lintel was the horizontal panel of ornamental terra cotta separating the second- and third-story windows on the LaSalle Street side. The section Nickel wanted was about four feet tall and six to seven feet wide. He decided he would try to sneak out some other pieces of ornament—a stair stringer, the iron panel supporting steps, for Southern Illinois University, and stainless steel for his darkroom—when he went to get the lintel panel.

On April 12 Richard and Tim Samuelson stopped first at the Three Oaks yard on the South Side to pick up a terra-cotta column from the 13th floor of the Stock Exchange, then at the National Wrecking yard to pick up cast-iron ornament from the Rothschild Building. Both pieces would be shipped to Southern Illinois University. Richard was easing Samuelson into his apprentice role. Only 19 years old, Samuelson already knew almost as much about Sullivan as Nickel, who told Hilberry that he wanted Samuelson to continue the ornament collection at SIU. Richard was protective of Tim, keeping him away from dangerous work and warning him repeatedly about the dangers of demolition sites.

A few weeks earlier, Richard had made a list of Tim's ornament that Tim had stored at the Cortland Street building.

"You'll need this if anything happens to me," he told Samuelson.

"Don't talk that way; it gives me the creeps," Tim told Richard. Tim left the car without taking the list, but Richard mailed it the following day.

Rubble spills onto the
Trading Room floor.
Weight from rubble
may have collapsed the
structure and been
one of the causes of
Nickel's accidental
death in April 1972.

Richard also wanted Tim to learn from his mistakes.

"Sorry to trap you into that 3 Oaks-Vinci loading-unloading routine today," he wrote Samuelson after long delays in shipping the Stock Exchange stairs to the Metropolitan Museum of Art in February. "However it's good you should experience as early as possible how people take advantage of one's time if you let them!"

On April 12 Richard told Tim he needed help the following day at the Stock Exchange.

"If we don't get that lintel panel soon, they're going to wreck it," Nickel said. He also told Samuelson about his plan to sneak out the stair stringer and other items.

Richard expressed no doubt that he would be allowed onto the site, and said he would ask the Riccios if Samuelson could join him inside. Nickel arranged that Tim would come to the alley next to the building between 1 and 2 p.m. Richard would signal from the Trading Room window if Tim could come onto the site. Richard said he would bring an extra hardhat.

That evening Nickel took a portrait of Robert McGowan, his accountant. McGowan had once asked Richard if he knew a commercial portrait photographer and Richard replied, "You're looking at one." Richard spent two hours at the McGowans' home and returned to Park Ridge late to develop the film. He called John Vinci, whom he had not spoken to in weeks, and left a message asking to borrow salvaging equipment.

Just before going to bed, Richard jotted down a reminder of the items he wanted to take the next day:

Lintel s.s. on first
stringers—table on 2
column facing on 3 behind lintel

The following morning, April 13, his mother baked blueberry muffins. She was hanging clothes on the line outside the Park Ridge home when he came out of the house.

"Mother, mother, you'll be back in the hospital if you keep doing that," Richard said. "When I come back, I'll do it."

She told him what time dinner would be served. Hurrying, Richard waved good-bye.

"I'm going down to the Stock Exchange and have to make a few stops on the way," he said, pushing a muffin into his mouth.

His first stop was at Lutheran General Hospital, where Carol worked. He had hoped to see her for a moment. She was busy, so he left her a note on the envelope with McGowan's prints: "Please try to call Mrs. McGowan once or twice this afternoon to advise you have the pictures and that you will drop these off on the way home. Will you?, or she can come to Lutheran General for them."

Then, in big letters, Richard wrote: "Rushing. Sorry to miss you."

Inside the envelope, he wrote McGowan that the printed portraits were a bit too dark. He tried to keep prints light, he wrote, but they always came out "rich and dark," just the way he liked them.

From there, Nickel drove to Vinci's North Side home to pick up a heavy rope and tackle.

Nicolina Tack, who worked as a companion for Vinci's ailing mother, stopped Richard for a few minutes. She knew him from the Trading Room days when she fixed him breakfast before they headed off to work. "I just heard you are going to get married. I thought you would ask me," she teased.

Richard smiled, and said he was happy. "I think it will work out real nice," he told her.

Richard arrived at the Erie-Franklin parking lot just north of the Loop at noon. He changed into his work clothes and headed to the Stock Exchange Building.

The building was especially dangerous at this point in its demolition. The interior was rotting away. Several of the floors had shifted and even collapsed. Two wreckers had been injured weeks before when they dropped through the floors. One of the wreckers had fallen one story and another two stories but, amazingly, both suffered only cuts and bruises.

By now the floors were completely soaked. Since the start of the job, the men had hosed down rubble at the site to settle dust released in the wrecking. The new Environmental Protection Agency had strict rules about the amount of dust at wrecking sites. City building inspectors had closed one or two other wrecking jobs that winter because of too much dust and they warned Three Oaks several times. John Pruitt, the Three Oaks foreman, said his wreckers ran three hoses of water all day long.

The water, and the holes cut into floors to drain it, weakened the building. Along with snow and rainwater, the hose water sat on the floors and washed away mortar. Eventually, much of the water seeped into the porous clay tile arches inside the floors. During the winter, freezing and thawing further weakened the floors. By spring, the floors were so heavy with water they groaned when walked on.

Larry Riccio said he was not concerned about the condition of the floors because by then most of the wrecking was being done by the crane. "We were allowed to just smash it all in and haul it away, and that is exactly what we were doing," he said. The only time men were used inside the building was to cut and drop steel beams. When the men worked inside, they put planks over the floors for protection.

The structure was also weakened because wreckers used the elevator shafts as rubbish chutes. Larry Riccio said the practice of dropping debris down the shafts was standard. However, heavy equipment operator Ray Beinlich said the wreckers tossed discarded rugs down the shafts. The rugs, which should not have been dropped, clogged the shafts.

The debris accumulated in the shafts and spilled onto the nearby floors. The floors were not strong enough to carry the load and the movement of the rubbish loads may have loosened the connection of nearby steel beams.

Riccio said the shafts were emptied every day. Beinlich disputed that fact in a deposition he gave in 1975.

"See, the one elevator shaft which we were using for a chute was part way plugged up. And it was like an upside down cone," Beinlich said.

"Why was it plugged up?" he was asked by an attorney.

"We weren't using it," Beinlich said. "We didn't bother to clean it out."

That morning, before Nickel arrived at the building, several bays from the lower floors had caved in.

John Pruitt, the wrecking foreman, saw Nickel walking alone in front of the building between 1 and 1:30 p.m. Pruitt said he told Nickel about the morning collapses and that the wreckers were dropping debris from the upper floors. "I told him to get out of here," Pruitt said later. "I went up to the second floor to check it. The last time I saw Nickel was him walking north on LaSalle Street."

Beinlich recalled that he had actually seen Nickel first and told him about the danger. Moments later, Beinlich saw Pruitt walking Nickel off the site.

"We both walked him to the gate together," Beinlich recalled years later. "Pruitt had him in hand. He was angry and told him 'Get the fuck out of here,'" Beinlich said.

"As we watched Nickel walk off the site, I remember telling Pruitt what an idiot he [Nickel] was," Beinlich said. "He was a nice guy, but he wouldn't take no for an answer."

Nickel returned.

He was either in the Trading Room or directly underneath in the first-floor restaurant when a section of the Trading Room floor collapsed. Either a steel beam loosened and crashed onto the floor, or the floor gave way by itself.

Beinlich, who found Nickel's body, is certain that Nickel was in the restaurant looking for material.

"The rubbish had a long way to build up. It didn't have any more walls to knock out," Beinlich said in his deposition.

"It built up more and more, giving more of an explosive force?" he was asked.

"More weight on it," Beinlich said.

"Until it got so much weight it just collapsed?"

"Boom. Yes," he replied.

Nickel had no chance. The floor fell instantly.

Steel makes no sound before it yields.

The Trading Room as it
has been installed at the
Art Institute of Chicago
and as photographed by
Robert Thall.

Richard Stanley Nickel's death was ruled an accident by a coroner's jury. At his family's request, he was buried in Graceland Cemetery, the final resting place of Louis Sullivan, John Wellborn Root, Daniel Burnham, and Ludwig Mies van der Rohe. John Vinci, who handled the arrangements, could have purchased a plot for Nickel next to Sullivan but decided against the idea. Richard was too modest. Vinci and architect Lawrence Kenny designed Nickel's gravestone. Vinci says it is an abstract design, but it is quite reminiscent of the pentaprism, the small structure that sits atop a 35mm camera.

Richard, in a will he made out March 18, 1971, left all of his belongings to his brother, Donald. "I don't believe in cost or show of exposed bodies or embalming or brunches after the burial," Nickel wrote. "NONE OF IT. Any money I leave I prefer be used for some living purpose."

He warned Donald not to underestimate the value of a few favorite pieces of Sullivan ornament that he had kept in his collection. It was not the first note Richard wrote Donald on the subject of death. After receiving his $12,000 check for his ornament collection, Richard wrote: "Should I fall off a building before I get a chance to use it, then it's yours."

Nickel wrote in the will, "I don't have any or many personal close friends (except Sullivan, Kierkegaard, Bruckner, etc.) except John Vinci and Frederick Sommer." He told Donald to consider them.

In 1973 Donald filed a multimillion-dollar lawsuit against Three Oaks Wrecking charging that the company had failed to warn Richard that the building was in an unsafe and dangerous condition. The case was settled out of court in 1979 with

Richard's estate receiving $35,000. After paying expenses and lawyer's fees, Donald ended up with about $18,000.

Garden City, Richard's cherished sailboat, was sold for $4,925 in 1972 to a man who transported it to Madison, Wisconsin. His house at 1810 West Cortland Street was sold for $9,000 in 1972 to sculptor Stanley R. Stan. In 1982 portrait photographer Marc Hauser purchased the building for his studio. St. Mary of the Angels Church, across the street and down the block, has been restored.

After his death Richard was cited for his service by the Chicago chapter of the American Institute of Architects and by the Chicago Association of Commerce and Industry. May 13, 1972, was declared "Richard Nickel Day" in Illinois and the City Council passed a resolution noting with "deep sorrow the tragic death of Richard E. Nickel." His middle name was Stanley.

The day after the body was found, Jacob Burck of the *Chicago Sun-Times* drew a cartoon of a tomb that read:

Richard Nickel
1928–1972
Killed in Action rescuing Chicago architectural treasures

The caption read: "Landmark."

M. W. Newman wrote in the *Daily News* that Nickel's death was more than an accident. "The recovery of his body from the rubble this week marked him as a sacrifice to art, but, even more, a civic offering to the altar of greed." Donald Hoffmann wrote in the *Kansas City Star:* "Now that the concept of architectural preservation is socially chic, and even the government issues preservation postage stamps, it is convenient to forget a man who stood alone."

Years after Nickel's death, Chicago writer Studs Terkel remembered Nickel in his book *Chicago.* "I had met Richard Nickel, oh, maybe a month or so before it happened. The way he talked, oh God, about beauty and past and history and how we must hang on to some things and continuity and all that stuff, I guess you'd have to say he was crazy."

Adler and Sullivan's Trading Room was reconstructed and opened in 1977 at the Art Institute of Chicago. John Vinci fought hard to have the room rebuilt as close as possible to its original state. "I was sick and tired of saving bits and pieces," he said. Vinci and his associate, Lawrence Kenny, relied on Nickel's photographs in putting the room back together. On the day after the room was dedicated, *New York Times* critic Paul Goldberger called the Trading Room one of the finest interiors created before the turn of the century. Along with Edward Hopper's *Nighthawks,* Grant Wood's *American Gothic,* and Georges Seurat's *Sunday Afternoon on the Island of La Grande Jatte,* the Trading Room is one of the art museum's major attractions.

The grand Stock Exchange Building entrance arch was reassembled as a free-standing piece of sculpture outside the Columbus Drive entrance of the Art Institute. In addition, the mosaic staircase landings recovered during the last days of the Garrick were displayed at the museum for many years.

Ornament collected by Nickel and others is now on display in the Art Institute's Henry Crown Gallery. The terra-cotta and cast-iron pieces are mounted on the wall in a permanent exhibit called "Fragments of Chicago's Past." They look like mounted, stuffed heads from a hunting expedition.

The Garrick garage and restaurant, which replaced the Garrick Theater Building in 1962, was itself threatened with demolition during the early 1990s. However, financing fell through for the larger building that was to replace it. The garage, on the north side of Randolph Street between Dearborn and Clark streets, still stands. A metal plaque memorializes the Adler and Sullivan building and recalls Nickel's fight to save it. The plaque reads: "Through the efforts of public spirited Chicagoans, much of the plaster and ornament was saved when the Garrick was demolished in 1961, and distributed to museums, universities, and art centers throughout the nation."

Hundreds of pieces of Adler and Sullivan ornament—from the first fretwork Nickel saved at the Albert Sullivan house during the early 1950s to the Stock Exchange column he saved the day before he died—are on display at Southern Illinois University at Edwardsville. The University Museum also maintains hundreds of pieces, including the entire front facade of the Albert Sullivan house, in storage. University officials hope to build a large museum on the campus near St. Louis that will include the facade, a flight of Stock Exchange Building stairs, and other ornament.

A large part of the second-floor loggia from the Garrick serves as the entrance of Chicago's Second City comedy club at 1608 North Wells Street.

The Stock Exchange stairs that Nickel saved for the Metropolitan Museum of Art are on permanent display in the American Wing of the museum in New York City.

A massive section of terra cotta—60 feet long and 18 feet high—from the top of the Stock Exchange Building was donated to the University of Illinois at Chicago. The material, which includes a corner cornice and columns, has never been reassembled. It has been placed outside a university building just west of the Loop. Much of the material has been stolen or damaged by the weather.

Finally, tons of ornament from Holabird and Roche's Cable and Republic buildings, which Nickel had salvaged in 1960 with city money, were dumped into Lake Michigan after being stored at Navy Pier for several years.

The corporation owned by the partnership that destroyed the Stock Exchange Building never went bankrupt, but two of the partners went bankrupt as individuals. Rising interest rates and a drop in downtown office rental snagged the partners' plans for profit. The corporation filed for protection from creditors in a Chapter 11 reorganization.

Work on the 30 North LaSalle Building, which replaced the Stock Exchange, began in October 1972. At the topping-off ceremony for the 42-story skyscraper in October 1973, Mayor Richard J. Daley declared: "This is another example of the confidence people have in the city of Chicago and its future."

Inland Architect critic Nory Miller described the dark, glass building as "shoddy, cheap and pretentious."

Three Oaks Wrecking Company went out of business in 1973. In May 1972 Joseph Riccio wrote to Art Institute Director Charles C. Cunningham that Nickel's "tragic death" had changed his attitude toward the artifacts. He said his own collection of ornament would remain dormant in his South Side yard until he could find a proper home for it. Most of the company's Stock Exchange material—several truckloads—was either sold to a private dealer in 1990 or donated to Southern Illinois University at Edwardsville.

Only a few Adler and Sullivan buildings have fallen since Nickel's death. Downtown Chicago's Troescher Building was torn down in 1978 and the Springer Block in 1990. The Marengo (Illinois) Schoolhouse was demolished in 1993 to make way for a McDonald's restaurant. The Brunswick-Balke-Collender Factory on the Near North Side and the Aurora Watch Factory in Aurora, Illinois, both were destroyed by separate fires in 1989.

The Troescher Building came down after a valiant fight. Tim Samuelson, Nickel's protégé, salvaged what was left. "It's funny," he said. "For all the interest in buildings and ornament, when the building is coming down I always seem to be there by myself."

At last count, 21 Sullivan buildings remain in the Chicago area and about 20 others stand in the rest of the nation. At least one standing Adler and Sullivan commission, a factory west of the Loop, has been discovered since Nickel's death.

The Complete Architecture of Adler and Sullivan has never been completed, despite a continuing effort by Vinci, Siskind, Samuelson, and Ben Raeburn. Plans remain for it to be published in the future.

John Vinci has become an honored architect. In addition to designing new buildings, he has restored several important buildings in Chicago, including part of Sullivan's Carson Pirie Scott store and Adler and Sullivan's Auditorium Building.

Carol Sutter mourned her fiancé but went on with her life, marrying Thomas H. Eads in 1975 and giving birth to Emily Louise Eads in 1977. Six weeks later, just a few days after she attended the opening of the Trading Room, Carol was killed in an automobile accident. Tom recovered and is raising Emily.

Nickel's parents, Stanley and Agnes, moved to Donald Nickel's farm in Plainfield, Wisconsin. They died several weeks apart in 1985. Donald and Harriet Nickel continued working the farm until 1993. They plan to retire to Florida soon.

Harry Callahan and Aaron Siskind moved from the Institute of Design in Chicago to the Rhode Island School of Design in Providence. They retired during the 1970s. Siskind died in 1991.

Frederick Sommer, who delivered Nickel's eulogy at a 1972 memorial service in the Glessner House, continues work at his home and studio in Prescott, Arizona. "Thinking," said Sommer at age 87 in 1993, "is the most eloquent human work." Callahan, Siskind, and Sommer are all recognized as masters of contemporary art photography.

Thomas Stauffer, who had helped lead the Garrick fight, moved from Chicago to Berkeley, California, during the 1970s. He became the "house guru," an elder respected for his virtue and learning, at Au Coquelet coffeehouse there and died several years later in retirement. "We DO leave footprints on the sands of time, but mostly, no one gives a goddam long after whose they are," he wrote in 1980 recounting his role in the Chicago landmark fight.

Jack Randall, who had stood up for the Garrick Theater and later found a home for Nickel's ornament, was instrumental in saving Adler and Sullivan's Wainwright Building in St. Louis and Sullivan's Guaranty Building in Buffalo, New York. He has completed a book, dedicated to Nickel, about architectural masterpieces around the United States.

Alfred Caldwell, 89 in 1994, continues to teach a popular "Architecture and Civilization" course at the Illinois Institute of Technology.

Tim Samuelson, following in Nickel's footsteps, continues to save ornament from the wrecks of Chicago. He has also been instrumental in the restoration of several buildings, most notably St. Louis's Union Station.

In the late 1970s Samuelson found a large assembly of terra-cotta ornament in the weeds near Adler and Sullivan's old Hammond Library Building. Richard had salvaged the piece a decade before but, unable to take it home, apparently had hauled it into the weeds to keep it secret.

It was Nickel's final gift.

Inever met Richard Nickel. I became aware of his work in a wonderful little guidebook, *Chicago's Famous Buildings,* edited by Arthur Siegel and published by the University of Chicago Press in 1965.

Like Nickel's project, my book began as a college assignment. In 1975 I interviewed University of Illinois law professor John J. Costonis about his effort to save landmark buildings. Costonis told me how a Nickel photograph of the Old Stock Exchange had influenced the way he saw the building. He lamented the fate of the building and the photographer. I became interested in both.

When I returned to Chicago in 1979, I began work on what I thought would be a magazine article on Nickel's life and death. My first interview was with John Vinci, Nickel's best friend and partner.

"If you want to write Richard's story, you'd better look at the notes and letters he left behind," Vinci told me. Little did I realize that meant combing through tens of thousands of documents as well as thousands of photographs. I spent the first several months of my work in Vinci's basement, where much of the material was stored.

When I finally started interviewing Nickel's other friends, I was frequently asked: "Did you know Richard?"

I had to give the question some thought.

The appointment books and extensive records that Nickel left behind gave me an opportunity to figure out just what happened to him over the course of his life. His letters, neatly typed and carbon copied, gave me a sense of what he thought. The photographs and negatives made clear what he saw.

I conducted tape-recorded interviews with more than 100 of Nickel's friends, family, and associates. In addition, I contacted hundreds of other people by phone or letter in order to check information and fill in the gaps. Very few who knew Nickel were surprised by my project. Several times his friends told me they had always wondered when somebody would write a book about him.

Nickel's friends helped me understand my subject as a real person. Most helpful in providing details of his life were Lee and Pat Timonen, David Norris, Jack Randall, Ben Raeburn, Jerry Sinkovec, Irene Siegel, Ben Weese, Rachel Baron

Heimovics, Paul Sprague, Kazimir Karpuszko, Robert Kostka, Carl Condit, Wilbert Hasbrouck, Charles Gregersen, Joseph Benson, Hermann G. Pundt, and Phyllis Lambert. They shared memories and showed me letters I hadn't seen before.

I have traveled the city and the country to track down the architecture that Nickel found so enticing. With the help of Vinci and Tim Samuelson, I have looked at almost every known Louis Sullivan building, attempting to see them through Nickel's eyes.

I have read hundreds of books to better understand art, architecture, and photography. In the end, I relied on first-hand information—autobiographies, statements, and contemporary accounts—to portray historical characters such as Louis Sullivan, László Moholy-Nagy, Aaron Siskind, and Richard J. Daley.

Three short, simple books inspired me the most. Nelson Algren's *Chicago, City on the Make* (New York: Doubleday, 1951) showed me how poetic even the dark side of my city can be. Susan Sontag's *On Photography* (New York: Farrar, Straus & Giroux, 1977) taught me the power of the camera. Tom Wolfe's *From Bauhaus to Our House* (New York: Farrar, Straus & Giroux, 1981) helped me understand the movement that eventually would catapult Nickel into art.

Journalists Ruth Moore Garbe, Jacob Burck, Georgie Anne Geyer, Donald Hoffmann, Studs Terkel, Ada Louise Huxtable, and M. W. Newman helped me place Nickel in perspective. I relied on their work and that of other journalists from Chicago's newspapers, the *Daily News, Sun-Times, Tribune,* and *American* (later known as *Today*). I was also greatly helped by "On the Adler & Sullivan Trail with Tireless Richard Nickel," an article in the June 1969 issue of *Inland Architect* by Norman Mark.

Two other books served as a backbone of my general research. They are Carl W. Condit's *The Chicago School of Architecture: A History of Commercial and Public Building in the Chicago Area, 1875–1925* (Chicago and London: The University of Chicago Press, 1964) and David Lowe's *Lost Chicago* (Boston: Houghton Mifflin, 1975).

CHAPTER 1

To re-create the search for Nickel's body, I talked to every principal involved. I talked to Nickel's friends John Vinci, Tim Samuelson, Robert Furhoff, and Charles Simmonds; his brother, Donald, and his parents, Stanley and Agnes. I talked with Chicago Building Commissioner Joe Fitzgerald; City Architect Jerome Butler; building inspector Patrick Noonan; Richard Miller of the Landmarks Preservation Council; Randall J. Biallas of the city architect's office; Ray Beinlich, who found Nickel's body; and Dr. Robert Greene, who performed the autopsy. I also interviewed firefighter Ted Latas and police officers Kenneth Griesch, Thomas Sweeney, Michael Mulcahy, Edwin McNulty, and Dale Buehler.

I relied on Chicago Police Department records, inquest proceedings, and documents from the wrongful-death lawsuit filed in 1975 against the Three Oaks Wrecking Company. Following the settlement of the case, both the Nickel and

Riccio families gave me permission to study the documents prepared for the case. The information, stored in the law offices of Paul Lurie and J. Richard Stanton, turned out to be a treasure trove for this chapter and Chapter 7.

CHAPTER 2

Donald Nickel and his wife, Harriet, showed me every scrap of information and photographs on the Nickel family. Besides them and Richard's parents, I was also helped by relatives Adeline "Dolly" Helwig, Bernice Bognar, Frances Nickel, Emma Piel, and Mae and Gabe Krupinski. *Polk's Chicago City Directory* (R. L. Polk & Company) helped me track down the addresses of the family after their arrival in Chicago.

Family friend Florence Squeo walked me around Nickel's first neighborhood, took me into his boyhood homes, and showed me the stained-glass windows at St. Cyril and Methodias Church that so influenced him.

Boyhood friends Jack and Tom Cussen, Richard Lapinski, Lewis Bugna, and Harry Nowak told me about the Logan Square neighborhood where Richard grew up.

Adrienne Dembo discussed her marriage to Nickel. I also consulted court divorce records.

The Polish Museum of America Library provided me with information about Polish immigration to Chicago and accounts to describe the Stanislawono community where Richard's ancestors settled.

Nickel's army friends, Roland Rogers "Woody" Schumann and Elmer Riddle, discussed Nickel's service in Occupied Japan. I corresponded with Raymond Hargett, Kyle Lacy, and Curtis Black, Jr., to recount his experiences in Korea. Many of these army buddies provided me with photos and letters.

I was given access to Nickel's army records from the General Archives Division, National Archives and Records Service, in Washington. The Department of the Army provided me with information on Nickel's units.

Most of my information on the Institute of Design comes from interviews with Nathan Lerner, who was in Moholy-Nagy's first Chicago class; E. Raymond Pearson, the institute's informal historian; and institute officials Jay Doblin and John Grimes. Documents and records were also gathered from Institute of Design material found in the special collections at the University Library, University of Illinois at Chicago.

The Institute of Design at the Illinois Institute of Technology provided me with Nickel's academic records.

The most helpful books on Moholy-Nagy were:

Caton, Joseph Harris. *The Utopian Vision of Moholy-Nagy*. Ann Arbor, Mich.: UMI Research Press, 1984.

Kostelanetz, Richard, ed. *Moholy-Nagy*. New York and Washington: Frederick Praeger, 1970.

Moholy-Nagy, László. *Vision in Motion*. Chicago: Paul Theobald, 1947.

——————. *The New Vision: From Material to Architecture. Abstract of an Artist*. Preface by Walter Gropius. New York: Wittenborn & Schultz, 1947.

Moholy-Nagy, Sibyl. *Moholy-Nagy. Experiment in Totality*. Foreword by Walter Gropius. New York: Harper's, 1950.

CHAPTER 3

I relied on Nickel's notes from the Institute of Design to help me piece together his academic years.

I interviewed teachers Aaron Siskind, Harry Callahan, and Alfred Caldwell. I listened to a tape-recorded interview of Siskind and a tape-recorded lecture by Caldwell during the 1950s. I interviewed Institute of Design students Len Gittleman, Art Sinsabaugh, Joe Sterling, Mary Ann Lea, Leon Lewandowski, Lyle Mayer, Ray Metzker, Chuck Reynolds, and Charles Swedlund.

The article "Learning Photography at the Institute of Design," by Siskind and Callahan in *Aperture* 4, No. 4 (1956), detailed their teaching techniques during the early 1950s.

Nickel's "A Photographic Documentation of the Architecture of Adler & Sullivan," an unpublished master's thesis completed at the Illinois Institute of Technology in 1957, explains his early search for Adler and Sullivan buildings. Nickel made detailed records of every Louis Sullivan building, describing his own thoughts on the buildings and registering notes on his photography. The records were used in preparing his unpublished book on Adler and Sullivan architecture. All of the documents were shared by their custodian, John Vinci.

Librarians Nancy Boone, Ruth Schoneman, and Joyce Malden discussed Nickel's early scholarly work. Malden's Municipal Refererence Library was particularly helpful in gathering information about urban renewal in Chicago.

To understand Mayor Daley, I talked with Daley administration officials D. E. Mackelmann, Earl Bush, and Ira J. Bach, as well as Alderman Leon M. Despres and architects William Hartmann and Harry Weese.

Hinman Kealy recalled his trip with Nickel to the East Coast. Ralph Marlowe Line discussed his work as a photographer with Sullivan biographer Hugh Morrison.

Tim Samuelson helped me grasp the essence of Louis Sullivan. Every Sullivan building mentioned in this book was analyzed with the help of Tim's perceptive eye. We visited the buildings in person, except those that no longer exist. Those we visited through photographs.

The most helpful books on Sullivan were:

Millet, Larry. *The Curve of the Arch: The Story of Louis Sullivan's Owatonna Bank.* St. Paul: Minnesota Historical Society Press, 1985.

Morrison, Hugh. *Louis Sullivan: Prophet of Modern Architecture.* New York: W. W. Norton, 1936.

Sullivan, Louis H. *The Autobiography of an Idea.* New York: Dover Publications, 1956.

——————. *Kindergarten Chats and Other Writings.* New York: Wittenborn Schultz, 1947.

——————. *A System of Architectural Ornament According with a Philosophy of Man's Powers.* New York: AIA Press, 1924.

Szarkowski, John. *The Idea of Louis Sullivan.* Minneapolis: University of Minnesota Press, 1956.

Twombly, Robert, ed. *Louis Sullivan: The Public Papers.* Chicago: University of Chicago Press, 1988.

Twombly, Robert. *Louis Sullivan: His Life and Work.* New York: Viking Press, 1986.

Wright, Frank Lloyd. *Genius and the Mobocracy.* New York: Duell, Sloan, and Pearce, 1949.

CHAPTER 4

The Chicago Historical Society's Archives and Manuscripts Department maintains the papers of Thomas Stauffer, Leon M. Despres, and the Chicago Heritage Committee, as well as a few papers by Richard Nickel. These documents helped greatly in chronicling the effort to save the Garrick Theater Building.

David Wallerstein, who decided to tear down the Garrick Theater, and his attorney, Edwin Rothschild, discussed the case against the Garrick. Stauffer and Despres discussed the case for the building. Stauffer also corresponded with me for several years.

I was given access to the files of the Commission on Chicago Historical and Architectural Landmarks, which included most of the testimony given at public hearings and public reaction to the effort to save the building. I looked at hundreds of Western Union telegrams. Nickel tape recorded and transcribed many of the public hearings on the Garrick.

Documents from the lawsuit over the Garrick's fate were made available from the warehouse of the Cook County Circuit Court Clerk.

The Garrick was a complicated building. The accounts that explain it best are Carl Condit's article "The Structural System of Adler and Sullivan's Garrick Theater Building" in *Technology and Culture* 5, no. 4 (fall 1964), and Paul Sprague's article "Adler & Sullivan's Schiller Building" in *The Prairie School Review,* 2, no. 2, Second Quarter (1965).

I also interviewed architects William Horowitz and Arthur Dennis Stevens, who played a role in the Garrick's demise and salvage.

CHAPTER 5

Architects George Sample and Jacques C. Brownson discussed the demolition of the Republic and Cable buildings.

Nickel's photographs of these two buildings are in unpublished books at the Ryerson and Burnham libraries at the Art Institute of Chicago. They are:

"The Republic Building, 209 S. State, Chicago, Ill. Holabird and Roche, architects. A Historical Record." Prepared by Skidmore, Owings & Merrill, 1961.

"Historic American Buildings Survey of the Cable Building. 57 E. Jackson, Chicago, Ill. 1899–. Holabird and Roche, architects." Prepared by Naess & Murphy, 1961.

Architects Daniel Brenner and H. P. Davis Rockwell discussed their renovation of the Old Stock Exchange during the mid-1960s.

Philip Gardner described his arrest with Nickel at Frank Lloyd Wright's Oscar Steffens House.

Jack Randall told me about Nickel's decision to donate his ornament to Southern Illinois University at Edwardsville.

A list of Nickel ornament at the university is contained in the book *Louis H. Sullivan: Architectural Ornament Collection,* Southern Illinois University at Edwardsville (Edwardsville: Southern Illinois University, 1981).

CHAPTER 6

Helping me critique Nickel's work were photographers Harold Allen, Orlando Cabanban, Robert Thall, Frederick Sommer, and Tom Yanul. Also adding criticism were photo historians John Szarkowski, David Travis, Peter Hales, Richard Pare, David Brown, David Brodherson, Tim Barton, and Larry Viskochil.

Travis's Department of Photography at the Art Institute of Chicago maintains a collection of about 100 Nickel photographs, which were printed following his death.

All of Nickel's negatives and contact sheets are in the possession of John Vinci.

John Casey provided the account of Nickel's trip to the Virgin Islands.

Philosopher Samuel J. Todes helped me understand Soren Kierkegaard.

Natalie and Alfred Levy told me sailing stories.

Susan and Wayne Benjamin discussed Nickel's work at the Glessner House and his involvement in the Stock Exchange fight.

The Graham Foundation for Advanced Studies in the Fine Arts opened its files on Nickel.

The most helpful books on photography were:

Gassan, Arnold. *A Chronology of Photography. A Critical Survey on the History of Photography as a Medium of Art.* Athens, Ohio: Handbook, 1972.

Newhall, Beaumont. *The History of Photography: From 1839 to the Present.* New York: Museum of Modern Art, 1982.

CHAPTER 7

As mentioned in Chapter 1, the files concerning the Nickel family's wrongful-death suit were instrumental in piecing together Richard's work at the Stock Exchange Building.

To help understand the transactions that resulted in the demolition of the building, I talked to 30 North LaSalle Partnership members Jerome Whiston and William Friedman and their attorney, Earl A. Talbot. To analyze the deals, I talked to real estate authorities Edward Ross, Larry Ackley, and Jared Shlaes; appraiser John Leydon; architect Jack Hartray; and attorneys Oscar D'Angelo and Allen Hartman. Richard Miller and David Roston of the Landmarks Preservation Council also helped.

Fred Cohn, who was married in the Stock Exchange Building days before it was demolished, shared his wedding memories.

Containing two worthwhile accounts of the Stock Exchange battle are "Chicago's Most Complicated Real Estate Deal," an article by developer Herbert Jacobson, in *Realty and Building* (January 27, 1973), and John J. Costonis's "The Problem: The Vanishing Urban Landmark," in the *Harvard Law Review* 85, no. 3 (January 1972).

To document the legal proceedings, I used the files of the Landmarks Preservation Council and the Commission on Chicago Historical and Architectural Landmarks as well as federal court bankruptcy records of the 30 North LaSalle Partnership and the building inspection files maintained by the City of Chicago.

To understand the salvage work, I talked to wreckers Milt Ruttenberg, Frank Venezia, and David Diny, who served as a representative of the Riccio family. I also talked to Nickel's partners, John Vinci and Pat Fitzgerald. Wayne Boyer, who documented the last days of the Trading Room, shared his film. Morrison H.

Heckscher of The Metropolitan Museum of Art, David Allen Hanks of the Art Institute of Chicago, and collector Ivan Karp discussed the value of what was saved.

Tom Eads, Joyce Keys, and Ruth Sutter helped me write about Nickel's fiancée, Carol Sutter.

Robert McGowan, Nickel's accountant, told me about his client's last photo assignment the night before he died.

I reviewed an extensive correspondence between Nickel and Harry H. Hilberry at Southern Illinois University at Edwardsville. It is kept by the Office of Cultural Arts and University Museums.

Finally, I also relied on John Vinci's *The Trading Room: Louis Sullivan and The Chicago Stock Exchange* (Chicago: Art Institute, 1989).

Major buildings by Adler and Sullivan
(in Chicago unless noted)

1879
CENTRAL MUSIC HALL
Southeast corner of Randolph and State streets
Demolished in 1900.

1880
BORDEN BLOCK BUILDING
Northwest corner of Randolph and Dearborn streets
Demolished in 1917.

GRAND OPERA HOUSE (remodeling)
119 North Clark Street
Demolished in 1958. Nickel photographed the remaining back wall of the building.

JOHN BORDEN RESIDENCE
3949 Lake Park Avenue
Demolished in 1955. Nickel photographed the building.

MAX M. ROTHSCHILD BUILDING
210 West Monroe Street
Demolished in 1972. Nickel photographed the building and salvaged ornament.

1881
LEVI ROSENFELD BUILDING
Southeast corner of Washington Boulevard and Halsted Street
Demolished in 1958. Nickel photographed the building and salvaged ornament.

JEWELERS' BUILDING
15-19 South Wabash Avenue
Still standing. Nickel photographed the building and salvaged ornament during a remodeling.

REVELL BUILDING
Northeast corner of Wabash and Adams streets
Demolished in 1968. Nickel photographed the building and salvaged ornament.

J. M. BRUNSWICK-BALKE–COLLENDER FACTORY
Bounded by Orleans, Huron, Superior and Sedgwick streets
Destroyed by fire in 1989. Nickel photographed the building.

1882
FRANKENTHAL BUILDING
141 South Wells Street
Demolished before 1950.

HAMMOND LIBRARY
44 North Ashland
Demolished in 1963. Nickel photographed the building and salvaged ornament.

MAX M. ROTHSCHILD FLATS
3200 South Prairie Avenue
Demolished in 1978. Nickel photographed the building.

HOOLEY'S THEATER (remodeling)
124 West Randolph Street
Demolished in 1926.

1883

RICHARD KNISELY STORE AND FLATS
2147 West Lake Street
Demolished in 1958. Nickel discovered and photographed the building and salvaged ornament.

MAX M. ROTHSCHILD ROW HOUSES
3201-05 South Indiana Avenue
Demolished in 1976. Nickel photographed the building.

ANN HALSTED HOUSE
440 West Belden Avenue
Still standing. Nickel discovered and photographed the building.

CHARLES P. KIMBALL RESIDENCE AND STABLE
22 East Ontario Street
Demolished in 1964. Nickel discovered and photographed the building and salvaged ornament.

MORRIS SELZ RESIDENCE
1717 South Michigan Avenue
Demolished in 1967. Nickel photographed the building.

REUBEN RUBEL STORE AND FLATS
309 South Clark Street
Demolished before 1950.

F. KAUFMANN & COMPANY STORES AND FLATS
2310-12 North Lincoln Avenue
Still standing. Nickel discovered and photographed the building.

MARENGO SCHOOLHOUSE
Marengo, Illinois
Demolished in 1993. Nickel discovered and photographed the building.

AURORA WATCH COMPANY FACTORY
603 South LaSalle Street, Aurora, Illinois
Destroyed by fire in 1989. Nickel discovered and photographed the building.

SOLOMON BLUMENFELD RESIDENCE
8 West Chicago Avenue
Demolished in 1963. Nickel photographed the building and salvaged ornament.

WRIGHT & LAWTHER OIL AND LEAD MANUFACTURING COMPANY FACTORY
Northeast corner of Beach and Polk streets
Demolished before 1950.

1884

MARTIN BARBE RESIDENCE
3157 South Prairie Avenue
Demolished in 1963. Nickel photographed the building and salvaged ornament.

REUBEN RUBEL RESIDENCE
320 South Ashland Avenue
Demolished in 1958. Nickel discovered and photographed the building and salvaged ornament.

F. A. KENNEDY & COMPANY BAKERY
27-33 North Desplaines Street
Demolished in 1970. Nickel discovered and photographed the building.

ANNA McCORMICK RESIDENCE
1715 South Michigan Avenue
Demolished in 1970. Nickel photographed the building.

MAX M. ROTHSCHILD HOUSES
Southwest corner of Indiana Avenue and 32nd Street
Demolished in 1964. Nickel photographed the buildings and salvaged ornament.

ANN HALSTED ROW HOUSES
1826-28 Lincoln Park West
Still standing. Nickel photographed the building.

ABRAHAM STRAUSS RESIDENCE
3337 South Wabash
Demolished about 1953.

KNISELY FACTORY
551-557 West Monroe Street
Demolished during the late 1950s and early 1960s. Nickel photographed the building.

RYERSON BUILDING
16-20 East Randolph Street
Demolished in 1939.

TROESCHER BUILDING
15-19 South Wacker Drive
Demolished in 1978. Nickel photographed the building.

SCOVILLE BUILDING
619-631 West Washington Boulevard
Demolished in early 1970s. Nickel discovered
and photographed the building.

McVICKER'S THEATER (remodeling and
addition)
25 West Madison Street
Partially demolished before 1922. Nickel
photographed the remaining brick wall of the
building.

LEOPOLD SCHLESINGER RESIDENCE
2805 South Michigan Avenue
Demolished before 1950. Nickel photographed
the remaining fence on the building lot.

LEON AND PAULINE MANNHEIMER
RESIDENCE
2147 North Cleveland Avenue
Still standing. Nickel discovered and
photographed the building.

LOUIS E. FRANK RESIDENCE
3219 South Michigan Boulevard
Demolished in 1968. Nickel discovered and
photographed the building and salvaged ornament.

HERMAN BRAUNSTEIN STORE AND
FLATS
Near the corner of North Milwaukee and
North avenues.
Demolished in 1968. Nickel discovered and
photographed the building and salvaged
ornament.

E. L. BRAND STORE
Jackson Boulevard between State Street and
Plymouth Court
Demolished before 1950.

1885
ZION TEMPLE
Southeast corner of Ogden Avenue and
Washington Boulevard
Demolished during the early 1950s.

MARCUS C. STEARNS RESIDENCE
Southwest corner of 35th Street and Lake Park
Avenue
Demolished before 1950.

HENRY STERN RESIDENCE
2915 South Prairie Avenue
Demolished in 1959. Nickel photographed the
building and salvaged ornament.

SAMUEL STERN RESIDENCE
2963 South Prairie Avenue
Demolished in 1959. Nickel photographed the
building and salvaged ornament.

BENJAMIN LINDAUER RESIDENCE
3312 South Wabash Avenue
Demolished in 1958. Nickel photographed the
building and salvaged ornament.

ABRAHAM KUH RESIDENCE
3141 South Michigan Avenue
Demolished before 1950. Nickel photographed
the remaining outline of the building.

KOHN-ADLER-FELSENTHAL ROW
HOUSES
3541-45 South Ellis Avenue
Demolished in sections between 1958 and
1961. Nickel photographed the houses and salvaged ornament.

1886
HUGO GOODMAN RESIDENCE
3333 South Wabash Avenue
Demolished before 1950.

MRS. HENRY HORNER RESIDENCE
1705 South Michigan Avenue
Demolished before 1950.

WALTER AND CLARENCE PECK
WAREHOUSE
Southeast corner of North LaSalle Street and
West Wacker Drive
Demolished around 1928.

WEST CHICAGO CLUBHOUSE
119 South Throop Street
Demolished around 1953.

MARTIN RYERSON CHARITIES TRUST
BUILDING
316 West Adams Street
Demolished around 1929.

WORLD'S PASTIME EXPOSITION
BUILDINGS AT CHELTENHAM BEACH
79th Street at Lake Michigan
Demolished around 1900. Nickel discovered
renderings of the buildings.

SUBURBAN ILLINOIS CENTRAL
RAILROAD STATION
39th Street
Demolished before 1950.

SUBURBAN ILLINOIS CENTRAL
RAILROAD STATION
43rd Street
Demolished before 1950.

JOSEPH DEIMEL RESIDENCE
3141 South Calumet Avenue
Still standing. Nickel discovered and
photographed the building.

EDWARD G. PAULING FLATS
Northeast corner of Scott and Astor streets
Demolished around 1913. Nickel discovered
old photographs of the building.

LEVI A. ELIEL RESIDENCE
3538 South Ellis Avenue
Demolished in 1961. Nickel photographed the
building and salvaged ornament.

GUSTAV ELIEL RESIDENCE
4122 South Ellis Avenue
Still standing. Nickel photographed the
building.

SELZ, SCHWAB & COMPANY FACTORY
Northeast corner of Larabee and Superior
streets
Demolished around 1939.

1887
WIRT DEXTER BUILDING
630 South Wabash Avenue
Still standing. Nickel photographed the
building.

SPRINGER BUILDING (remodeling and
addition)
134-146 North State Street
Demolished in 1990. Nickel photographed the
building.

1888
GEORGE M. HARVEY RESIDENCE
600 Stratford Place
Still standing. Nickel photographed the building.

STANDARD CLUBHOUSE
Southwest corner of Michigan Avenue and
24th Street
Demolished in 1931.

WALKER WAREHOUSE BUILDING
Southwest corner of Adams Street and Wacker
Drive
Demolished in 1953. Nickel photographed the
building.

VICTOR A. FALKENAU ROW HOUSES
3420-24 South Wabash Avenue
Demolished in 1958. Nickel photographed the
building and salvaged ornament.

1889
AUDITORIUM BUILDING
430 North Michigan Avenue
Still standing. Nickel photographed the building and salvaged ornament during remodelings.

ELI B. FELSENTHAL FACTORY
63-71 North Canal Street
Demolished around 1908.

MARTIN RYERSON TOMB
Graceland Cemetery, 4001 North Clark Street
Still standing. Nickel photographed the
structure.

HEBREW MANUAL TRAINING SCHOOL
554 West 12th Place
Demolished by fire about 1953.

1890
LOUIS H. SULLIVAN AND JAMES
CHARNLEY COTTAGES
East Beach in Ocean Springs, Mississippi
Still standing. Nickel photographed the
buildings.

CARNEGIE MUSIC HALL
Southeast corner of 57th Street and Seventh
Avenue in New York City
Adler and Sullivan served as associated archi-
tects. Still standing. Nickel photographed the
building.

OPERA HOUSE BLOCK
Pueblo, Colorado
Destroyed by fire in 1922. Nickel pho-
tographed remaining brick walls.

KEHILATH ANSHE MA'ARIV
SYNAGOGUE
Southeast corner of 33rd Street and Indiana
Avenue
Still standing as Pilgrim Baptist Church. Nickel
photographed the building.

1891

CHICAGO COLD STORAGE WAREHOUSE
Between Lake and Randolph streets on south
branch of the Chicago River
Demolished in 1902.

GRAND OPERA HOUSE (remodeling)
144 East Wells Street in Milwaukee, Wisconsin
Adler and Sullivan served as associated architects. Still standing as Pabst Theater. Nickel
photographed the building.

HOTEL ONTARIO (never completed)
Northwest corner of West Temple and Second
South streets, Salt Lake City, Utah
Nickel photographed the foundation of the
building.

GETTY TOMB
Graceland Cemetery, 4001 North Clark Street
Still standing. Nickel photographed the
structure.

DOOLY BLOCK
111 West Second South Street, Salt Lake City,
Utah
Demolished in 1965. Nickel photographed the
building.

WAINWRIGHT BUILDING
Northwest corner of Seventh and Chestnut
streets in St. Louis, Missouri
Still standing. Nickel photographed and
salvaged ornament during remodeling.

GARRICK THEATER BUILDING
64 West Randolph Street
Demolished in 1961. Nickel fought to save the
building. He photographed it and salvaged
ornament.

JAMES CHARNLEY RESIDENCE
1365 North Astor Street
Still standing. Nickel photographed the
building.

STANDARD ELEVATOR COMPANY
FACTORY
1515 West 15th Street
Still standing. Nickel discovered and
photographed the building.

ADOLPH AND WILLIAM LOEB
APARTMENT BUILDING
157-159 North Elizabeth Street
It was mostly razed in 1972. Nickel discovered
and photographed the building.

ALBERT W. SULLIVAN RESIDENCE
4575 South Lake Park Avenue
Demolished in 1970. Nickel photographed the
building and salvaged ornament.

J. W. OAKLEY WAREHOUSE
Southwest corner of LaSalle and Hubbard
streets
Demolished around 1976. Nickel discovered
and photographed the building.

NEW ORLEANS PASSENGER STATION
FOR ILLINOIS CENTRAL RAILROAD
1001 South Rampart Street in New Orleans,
Louisiana
Demolished around 1954. Nickel traveled to
see the station, but it no longer existed.

TRANSPORTATION BUILDING AT
WORLD'S COLUMBIAN EXPOSITION
Jackson Park
Demolished after the fair.

WAINWRIGHT MEMORIAL TOMB
Bellefontaine Cemetery, 4947 West Florissant
Avenue in St. Louis, Missouri
Still standing. Nickel photographed the struc-
ture.

1892

UNION TRUST BUILDING
Northwest corner of Seventh and Olive streets
in St. Louis, Missouri
Still standing. Nickel photographed the
building.

VICTORIA HOTEL
Northwest corner of Illinois and Halsted streets
in Chicago Heights
Demolished by fire in 1961. Nickel photographed the building and salvaged ornament.

ST. NICHOLAS HOTEL
Northwest corner of Eighth and Locust streets
in St. Louis, Missouri
Demolished in 1973. Nickel photographed
the building.

ILLINOIS LEATHER COMPANY FACTORY
Southwest corner of Halsted and Hooker
streets
Nickel discovered and photographed the
building. Demolished about 1973.

ILLINOIS EYE AND EAR INFIRMARY
(addition)
904 West Adams Street
Demolished about 1990. Nickel discovered and photographed the building.

1893
STOCK EXCHANGE BUILDING
30 North LaSalle Street
Demolished in 1971–72. Nickel photographed the building and salvaged ornament. He was killed during demolition.

1895
GUARANTY BUILDING
Southwest corner of Church and Pearl streets in Buffalo, New York
Still standing. Nickel photographed the building and salvaged ornament.

Major buildings by Louis Sullivan

1897
COLISEUM
South side of St. Charles Street between 13th and 14th streets in St. Louis, Missouri
Demolished in 1907.

BAYARD BUILDING
65-69 Bleecker Street in New York City
Still standing. Nickel photographed the building.

1898
GAGE BUILDING FACADE
18 South Michigan Avenue
First-floor facade modernized around 1953. Nickel photographed the building.

CYRUS H. MCCORMICK RESIDENCE
(remodeling)
675 North Rush Street
Demolished in 1954. Nickel photographed the building.

1899
CARSON PIRIE SCOTT STORE
Southeast corner of State and Madison streets
Still standing. Nickel photographed the building and salvaged ornament during remodelings.

EUSTON & COMPANY LINSEED OIL AND LINOLEUM PLANT
West side of Kingsbury Street between Blackhawk and Eastman streets
Still standing. Nickel discovered and photographed the building.

1901
VIRGINIA HALL
Girl's dormitory at Tusculum College in Greenville, Tennessee
Still standing. Nickel discovered and photographed the building.

1902
HOLY TRINITY ORTHODOX CHURCH AND RECTORY
1121 North Leavitt Street
Still standing. Nickel photographed the building.

1906
ELI B. FELSENTHAL STORE
701-703 East 47th Street
Demolished in 1982. Nickel photographed the building.

1908
NATIONAL FARMERS' BANK
Northwest corner of Broadway and Cedar streets in Owatonna, Minnesota
Still standing. Nickel photographed the building and salvaged ornament.

1909
HENRY BABSON RESIDENCE
230 North Longcommon Road in Riverside, Illinois
Demolished in 1960. Nickel photographed the building and salvaged ornament.

JOSEPHINE CRANE BRADLEY RESIDENCE
106 North Prospect Street in Madison, Wisconsin
Still standing as a fraternity house. Nickel photographed the building.

1911
PEOPLE'S SAVINGS BANK
Southwest corner of Third Avenue and First Street in Cedar Rapids, Iowa
Still standing. Nickel photographed the building and salvaged ornament.

1912
ST. PAUL'S METHODIST EPISCOPAL CHURCH
Northeast corner of Third Avenue and 14th Street Southeast, Cedar Rapids, Iowa
Design executed by other architects. Still standing. Nickel photographed the building.

1913
JOHN D. VAN ALLEN & SONS DRY GOODS STORE
Northwest corner of Fifth Avenue South at Second Street in Clinton, Iowa
Still standing. Nickel photographed the building.

HENRY C. ADAMS BUILDING
Northwest corner of Moore and State streets in Algona, Iowa
Still standing. Nickel photographed the building.

1914
MERCHANTS NATIONAL BANK
Northwest corner of Fourth Avenue and Broad Street in Grinnell, Iowa
Still standing. Nickel photographed the building.

HOME BUILDING ASSOCIATION BANK
Northwest corner of West Main and North Third streets in Newark, Ohio
Still standing. Nickel photographed the building.

PURDUE STATE BANK
Corner of State and South streets in West Lafayette, Indiana
Still standing. Nickel photographed the building.

1918
PEOPLE'S SAVINGS AND LOAN ASSOCIATION BANK
Southeast corner of Court Street and Ohio Avenue in Sidney, Ohio
Still standing. Nickel photographed the building.

1919
FARMERS' AND MERCHANTS' UNION BANK
Southeast corner of James Street and Broadway Avenue in Columbus, Wisconsin
Still standing. Nickel photographed the building.

1922
KRAUSE MUSIC STORE FACADE
4611 North Lincoln Avenue
Still standing. Nickel photographed the building.

Page numbers in *italics* indicate photographs and captions. Images included in the special section of photographs are indicated with the word "gallery." References to buildings or other entities given personal names include the surname first, followed by the first name in parentheses.

Wright, Frank Lloyd, *74*
    Carson Pirie Scott store, 176
    meeting Nickel, 76, 83
    Midway Gardens, 200
    "Prairie Skyscraper" (Bartlesville, Okla.),
        72, 75
    Robie House, 101–02, 106
    Steffens (Oscar) House, 136
    work with Adler and Sullivan, 60, 62, 65
    writing about Chicago and architecture,
        57, 67, 123, 154
Wright, Olgivanna, 105
Wright (Frank Lloyd) Foundation, 132
Wright Junior College, 69, 147

Y

Yale University, 132, 180
Yellowstone, Wyoming, 164
Yosemite Valley, 154